Solicitors' Code of Conduct 2007

JUNE 2009 EDITION

Solicitors' Code of Conduct 2007

Including SRA Recognised Bodies
Regulations 2009

JUNE 2009 EDITION

© The Law Society 2009

ISBN-13: 978-1-85328-813-5

First published in 2007

This edition published in 2009 by the Law Society
113 Chancery Lane, London WC2A 1PL

Reprinted in 2010

Typeset by Columns Design Ltd, Reading
Printed by TJ International Ltd, Padstow, Cornwall

FSC

Mixed Sources
Product group from well-managed
forests and other controlled sources

Cert no. SGS-COC-2482
www.fsc.org
© 1996 Forest Stewardship Council

The paper used for the text of this book is FSC certified. FSC (The Forest Stewardship Council) is an international network to promote responsible management of the world's forests.

Contents

CONTENTS

Foreword to the 2009 edition

It gives me great pleasure as Chair of the Board of the Solicitors Regulation Authority (SRA) to introduce to you the 2009 edition of the Solicitors' Code of Conduct.

The shape and structure of both legal regulation and legal practice are undergoing radical transformation. The introduction of legal disciplinary practices (LDPs) and firm based regulation in March 2009, and the prospect of greater competition through alternative business structures in two years' time, create challenges and opportunities for legal professionals and their colleagues – as do the economic pressures faced by the whole sector.

Amid all this, we must keep our sights firmly set on the public interest and the interests of clients. Consumers are right to have high expectations of both the standard of service and the manner in which lawyers serve their needs.

Professional ethics form the very bedrock of the delivery of legal services. The "core duties" set out in rule 1 of the Code define the values to be displayed in everything lawyers and their colleagues do. Integrity and independence – together with fairness and the values of equality and diversity – must remain constants, whatever the structures in which we work.

This new edition enables our core values to be applied in the new circumstances of LDPs. I urge all those involved in legal practices regulated by the SRA to familiarise themselves with the new provisions.

I would like to take this opportunity to thank those who responded so thoughtfully to our consultations, including our colleagues in the representative Law Society. I am also grateful to our Board and Committee members, and to the staff involved in this project (particularly Alison Crawley, Chris Bramall and Penny Butler), for their hard work and commitment.

Peter Williamson
Chair
Board of the Solicitors Regulation Authority
June 2009

Introduction to the 2009 edition

The 2007 edition of the Solicitors' Code of Conduct (the Code) marked a significant change in the historical approach to setting standards for solicitors. This 2009 edition comes barely two years later, reflecting the fast pace of change in the legal services sector. Brief details of what has changed are set out below.

Core duties

The Code is built around a set of core duties laying out the primary obligations for those we regulate, including integrity, independence and the best interests of clients. We have not significantly changed the core duties in this edition.

The core duties perform a number of functions:

- They define ethical behaviour.

- They form a framework for the rest of the rules.

- They provide a reference point to help you navigate through situations not covered by the other rules.

- They are mandatory obligations.

The core duties pervade all of the other rules, and we therefore place them at the forefront of the SRA's regulatory activity.

Rules and guidance

We have written the rules which form the Code in plain English for the benefit both of those who have to comply with them, and of clients and others who need to know the standards which they can expect.

The SRA believes that the regulation of legal services must target risks to clients and the public, and should maintain public confidence in the legal profession and the organisations in which they work. The Code contains provisions covering key areas of professional conduct. For instance, the risks to clients and the public are greater where a firm is badly managed, and so the Code contains requirements for management and supervision to ensure that these risks are minimised. The Code incorporates other key obligations such as the rules on conflict of interests, confidentiality and referrals of business.

The rules in the Code are backed by guidance notes to aid understanding and compliance. Although this guidance is not mandatory, it may have evidential force in deciding whether there has been compliance with a rule. Solicitors (and others who are subject to the rules) who do not follow the guidance may be required to demonstrate how they have nevertheless complied with the rule.

In addition to the guidance notes in the Code, we publish "free standing" guidance from time to time to alert practitioners to new issues of public interest. We recommend that you visit our website regularly and subscribe to our e-alerts – see **www.sra.org.uk**.

What has changed?

LDPs and firm based regulation

As a consequence of the changes made by the Legal Services Act 2007 (LSA) the Code now reflects the introduction on 31 March 2009 of legal disciplinary practices (LDPs) and firm based regulation. It is not possible to provide here full details of these changes. You can, however, find fuller details of the changes to the Code (including a version in "track changes" mode), and proposals for future regulatory changes, on our website. Key points to note are:

- The LSA allows us to regulate not only individuals but also firms. An important change is that all firms regulated by the SRA must be recognised bodies or recognised sole practitioners.

- For the first time solicitors are able to practise through LDPs – firms that can be owned and managed by a combination of different types of lawyer, and up to 25 per cent approved non-lawyers. Note, however, that there can be no external ownership of an LDP.

- LDPs can be firms that are regulated by the SRA or by one of the other approved regulators.

- These developments have meant extensive changes to the "structure rules" in the Code, particularly:

  – rule 12 – Framework of practice;

  – rule 14 – Recognised bodies (formerly "Incorporated practice");

  – rule 20 – Rights and obligations of practice;

  – rule 23 – Application of these rules.

- There are new SRA Recognised Bodies Regulations 2009 published with the Code, and new SRA Practising Regulations 2009 to be published on our website as soon as they are available.

- A significant change throughout the Code is the introduction of the term "manager" to refer to a partner in a partnership, a member of an LLP or a director of a company. We have made this change to reflect the terminology in the LSA.

- The rules now apply to all employees in firms, but the impact will vary depending on the nature of the work and the responsibility of the employee concerned.

Other key changes

As well as the changes to the Code arising from the LSA, we have made a number of other amendments. Some key points are:

- We have updated rule 7.03 (Unsolicited approaches in person or by telephone) to make clear that the ban relates to unsolicited approaches generally, and not simply to knocking on front doors.

- In the interests of transparency, we have broadened the requirements of rule 7.07 concerning the information which firms must display on their letterhead, websites and e-mails.

- The Home Information Pack Regulations (made under the Housing Act 2004) are applied to firms by changes to rule 18 (Property selling).

Some other key rules and regulations

You can find other regulatory material on our website, including:

- Solicitors' Accounts Rules (**www.sra.org.uk/accounts-rules**);

- Solicitors' Indemnity Insurance Rules and Solicitors' Indemnity Rules (**www.sra.org.uk/indemnity**);

- Solicitors' Financial Services (Scope) Rules and Solicitors' Financial Services (Conduct of Business) Rules (**www.sra.org.uk/financial-services**);

- SRA Practising Regulations (**www.sra.org.uk/framework**).

Looking towards the future

Regulation of legal services is going through a period of dynamic development with the advent of alternative business structures (ABSs) on the horizon. This will necessitate further changes to our rules and the way in which we regulate. We look forward to working with you in designing a regulatory structure to support these exciting opportunities, while keeping the public interest and the interests of clients firmly at the centre of all we do.

In the shorter term we expect to conduct a major review of the Solicitors' Accounts Rules. We are also working on possible amendments to a number of rules in the Code including rule 2 (Client relations), rule 3 (Conflict of interests) and rule 11 (Litigation and advocacy).

We value your views. Keep an eye on our website for details of current consultations and other news.

Help is available

You can access the Code and other rules and guidance via our website which shows the most up-to-date versions – see **www.sra.org.uk**.

You can also seek guidance on professional conduct from our Professional Ethics Guidance Team (tel. 0870 606 2577 or e-mail **professional.ethics @sra.org.uk**).

June 2009

The Solicitors' Code of Conduct 2007

Preamble

Rules dated 10 March 2007 commencing 1 July 2007 made under Part II of the Solicitors Act 1974 and sections 9 and 9A of the Administration of Justice Act 1985 with the concurrence of the Master of the Rolls under sections 32 and 33A of the Solicitors Act 1974, section 9 of the Administration of Justice Act 1985 and paragraph 16 of Schedule 22 to the Legal Services Act 2007, the concurrence of the Lord Chancellor under paragraph 16 of Schedule 22 to the Legal Services Act 2007 and the approval of the Secretary of State under Schedule 4 to the Courts and Legal Services Act 1990, regulating the conduct of solicitors and their employees, registered European lawyers and their employees, registered foreign lawyers, and recognised bodies and their managers and employees.

The guidance and explanatory introductions issued with these rules are not mandatory and do not form part of the Solicitors' Code of Conduct. However, solicitors, and others subject to the rules, who do not follow the guidance may be required to demonstrate how they have nevertheless complied with the rule.

Rule 1   Core duties

1.01   Justice and the rule of law

You must uphold the rule of law and the proper administration of justice.

1.02   Integrity

You must act with integrity.

1.03   Independence

You must not allow your independence to be compromised.

1.04   Best interests of clients

You must act in the best interests of each client.

1.05   Standard of service

You must provide a good standard of service to your clients.

1.06   Public confidence

You must not behave in a way that is likely to diminish the trust the public places in you or the legal profession.

Guidance to rule 1 – Core duties

General

1. A modern just society needs a legal profession which adopts high standards of integrity and professionalism. Lawyers, law firms and those who work in them serve both clients and society. In serving society, you uphold the rule of law and the proper administration of justice. In serving clients, you work in partnership with the client making the client's business your first concern. The core duties contained in rule 1 set the standards which will meet the needs of both clients and society. The core duties apply to solicitors, registered European lawyers (RELs), registered foreign lawyers (RFLs), recognised bodies, managers and employees of recognised bodies, and employees of recognised sole practitioners.

2. The core duties perform a number of functions:

    (a) They define the values which should shape your professional character and be displayed in your professional behaviour.

    (b) They form an overarching framework within which the more detailed and context-specific rules in the rest of the Code can be understood, thus illuminating the nature of those obligations and helping you to comply.

    (c) The core duties can help you to navigate your way through those situations not covered in the detailed rules, as no code can foresee or address every ethical dilemma which may arise in legal practice.

    (d) The core duties are fundamental rules. A breach may result in the imposition of sanctions.

3. Where two or more core duties come into conflict, the factor determining precedence must be the public interest, and especially the public interest in the administration of justice. Compliance with the core duties, as with all the rules, is subject to any overriding legal obligations.

4. It will be a breach of rule 1 if you permit another person to do anything on your behalf which would compromise or impair your ability to comply with any of the core duties.

Justice and the rule of law – 1.01

5. You have obligations not only to clients but also to the court and to third parties with whom you have dealings on your clients' behalf – see in particular rule 10 (Relations with third parties) and rule 11 (Litigation and advocacy).

Integrity – 1.02

6. Personal integrity is central to your role as the client's trusted adviser and must characterise all your professional dealings – with clients, the court, other lawyers and the public.

Independence – 1.03

7. "Independence" means your own and your firm's independence, and not merely your ability to give independent advice to a client. Examples of situations which might put your independence at risk include:

    (a) finance agreements/loans to your firm with particular strings attached;

    (b) finance arrangements which suggest dependency upon an outside body, such as could, at that body's discretion, effectively put your firm out of business;

    (c) contractual conditions in agreements with referrers of business or funders which effectively cede control of your firm to the outside body;

    (d) granting options to purchase your interest in your firm for nominal value;

    (e) allowing a third party access to confidential information concerning your clients;

    (f) a relationship with an outside body which is not at arm's length, and/or which suggests that your firm is more akin to a part of or subsidiary of that body, rather than an independent law firm;

    (g) fee sharing arrangements which go beyond what is allowed under rule 8.02;

    (h) any arrangement for a third party to fund legal actions which lays constraints on the conduct of the matter which go beyond the legitimate interests of a funder.

    See also rule 3 (Conflict of interests) and rule 9 (Referrals of business).

Best interests of clients – 1.04

8. You must always act in good faith and do your best for each of your clients. Most importantly, you must observe:

(a) your duty of confidentiality to the client – see rule 4 (Confidentiality and disclosure);

(b) your obligations with regard to conflicts of interests – see rule 3 (Conflict of interests); and

(c) your obligation not to use your position to take unfair advantage of the client – see 10.01 (Not taking unfair advantage).

Standard of service – 1.05

9. You must provide a good standard of client care and of work, including the exercise of competence, skill and diligence. Disciplinary action will not always follow where breaches of this duty are minor and isolated.

Public confidence – 1.06

10. Members of the public must be able to place their trust in you. Any behaviour within or outside your professional practice which undermines this trust damages not only you but the ability of the legal profession as a whole to serve society.

Rule 2 Client relations

Introduction

Rule 2 is designed to help both you and your clients understand each other's expectations and responsibilities. In particular, the purpose of 2.02 (Client care) and 2.03 (Information about the cost) is to ensure that clients are given the information necessary to enable them to make appropriate decisions about if and how their matter should proceed. Under rule 5 (Business management) a recognised body, a manager of a recognised body and a recognised sole practitioner must effect supervision and put in place management arrangements to provide for compliance with rule 2. The rule does not apply to your overseas practice but you must comply with 15.02.

Rule 2 – Client relations

2.01 Taking on clients

(1) You are generally free to decide whether or not to take on a particular client. However, you must refuse to act or cease acting for a client in the following circumstances:

    (a) when to act would involve you in a breach of the law or a breach of the rules of professional conduct;

    (b) where you have insufficient resources or lack the competence to deal with the matter;

    (c) where instructions are given by someone other than the client, or by only one client on behalf of others in a joint matter, you must not proceed without checking that all clients agree with the instructions given; or

    (d) where you know or have reasonable grounds for believing that the instructions are affected by duress or undue influence, you must not act on those instructions until you have satisfied yourself that they represent the client's wishes.

(2) You must not cease acting for a client except for good reason and on reasonable notice.

2.02 Client care

(1) You must:

    (a) identify clearly the client's objectives in relation to the work to be done for the client;

(b)   give the client a clear explanation of the issues involved and the options available to the client;

(c)   agree with the client the next steps to be taken; and

(d)   keep the client informed of progress, unless otherwise agreed.

(2) You must, both at the outset and, as necessary, during the course of the matter:

(a)   agree an appropriate level of service;

(b)   explain your responsibilities;

(c)   explain the client's responsibilities;

(d)   ensure that the client is given, in writing, the name and status of the person dealing with the matter and the name of the person responsible for its overall supervision; and

(e)   explain any limitations or conditions resulting from your relationship with a third party (for example a funder, fee sharer or introducer) which affect the steps you can take on the client's behalf.

(3) If you can demonstrate that it was inappropriate in the circumstances to meet some or all of these requirements, you will not breach 2.02.

2.03   Information about the cost

(1) You must give your client the best information possible about the likely overall cost of a matter both at the outset and, when appropriate, as the matter progresses. In particular you must:

(a)   advise the client of the basis and terms of your charges;

(b)   advise the client if charging rates are to be increased;

(c)   advise the client of likely payments which you or your client may need to make to others;

(d)   discuss with the client how the client will pay, in particular:

(i)   whether the client may be eligible and should apply for public funding; and

(ii)   whether the client's own costs are covered by insurance or may be paid by someone else such as an employer or trade union;

(e)   advise the client that there are circumstances where you may be entitled to exercise a lien for unpaid costs;

(f)   advise the client of their potential liability for any other party's costs; and

(g)   discuss with the client whether their liability for another party's costs may be covered by existing insurance or whether specially purchased insurance may be obtained.

(2)   Where you are acting for the client under a conditional fee agreement, (including a collective conditional fee agreement) in addition to complying with 2.03(1) above and 2.03(5) and (6) below, you must explain the following, both at the outset and, when appropriate, as the matter progresses:

(a)   the circumstances in which your client may be liable for your costs and whether you will seek payment of these from the client, if entitled to do so;

(b)   if you intend to seek payment of any or all of your costs from your client, you must advise your client of their right to an assessment of those costs; and

(c)   where applicable, the fact that you are obliged under a fee sharing agreement to pay to a charity any fees which you receive by way of costs from the client's opponent or other third party.

(3)   Where you are acting for a publicly funded client, in addition to complying with 2.03(1) above and 2.03(5) and (6) below, you must explain the following at the outset:

(a)   the circumstances in which they may be liable for your costs;

(b)   the effect of the statutory charge;

(c)   the client's duty to pay any fixed or periodic contribution assessed and the consequence of failing to do so; and

(d)   that even if your client is successful, the other party may not be ordered to pay costs or may not be in a position to pay them.

(4)   Where you agree to share your fees with a charity in accordance with 8.01(h) you must disclose to the client at the outset the name of the charity.

(5)   Any information about the cost must be clear and confirmed in writing.

(6)   You must discuss with your client whether the potential outcomes of any legal case will justify the expense or risk involved including, if relevant, the risk of having to pay an opponent's costs.

(7)   If you can demonstrate that it was inappropriate in the circumstances to meet some or all of the requirements in 2.03(1) and (5) above, you will not breach 2.03.

2.04   Contingency fees

(1)   You must not enter into an arrangement to receive a contingency fee for work done in prosecuting or defending any contentious proceedings before a court of England and Wales, a British court martial or an arbitrator where the seat of the arbitration is in England and Wales, except as permitted by statute or the common law.

(2)   You must not enter into an arrangement to receive a contingency fee for work done in prosecuting or defending any contentious proceedings before a court of an overseas jurisdiction or an arbitrator where the seat of the

arbitration is overseas except to the extent that a lawyer of that jurisdiction would be permitted to do so.

2.05   Complaints handling *Amendment*

(1) If you are a recognised body, a manager of a recognised body or a recognised sole practitioner, you must ensure:

    (a) that the firm has a written complaints procedure and that complaints are handled promptly, fairly and effectively in accordance with it;

    (b) that the client is told, in writing, at the outset:

        (i)   that, in the event of a problem, the client is entitled to complain; and

        (ii)   to whom the client should complain;

    (c) that the client is given a copy of the complaints procedure on request; and

    (d) that once a complaint has been made, the person complaining is told in writing:

        (i)   how the complaint will be handled; and

        (ii)   within what timescales they will be given an initial and/or substantive response.

(2) If you can demonstrate that it was inappropriate in the circumstances to meet some or all of these requirements, you will not breach 2.05.

(3) You must not charge your client for the cost of handling a complaint.

2.06   Commissions

If you are a recognised body, a manager of a recognised body or a recognised sole practitioner, you must ensure that your firm pays to your client commission received over £20 unless the client, having been told the amount, or if the precise amount is not known, an approximate amount or how the amount is to be calculated, has agreed that your firm may keep it.

2.07   Limitation of civil liability by contract

If you are a recognised body or a recognised sole practitioner, you must not exclude or attempt to exclude by contract all liability to your clients. However, you may limit your liability, provided that such limitation:

    (a) is not below the minimum level of cover required by the Solicitors' Indemnity Insurance Rules for a policy of qualifying insurance;

    (b) is brought to the client's attention; and

    (c) is in writing.

Guidance to rule 2 – Client relations

2

General

1. The requirements of rule 2 do not exhaust your obligations to clients. As your client's trusted adviser, you must act in the client's best interests (see 1.04) and you must not abuse or exploit the relationship by taking advantage of a client's age, inexperience, ill health, lack of education or business experience, or emotional or other vulnerability.

2. It is not envisaged or intended that a breach of 2.02, 2.03 or 2.05 should invariably render a retainer unenforceable. As noted in the introduction to this rule, the purpose of 2.02 and 2.03 is to ensure that clients are given the information necessary to enable them to make appropriate decisions about if and how their matter should proceed. These parts of the rule together with 2.05 require you to provide certain information to your client. Rules 2.02(3), 2.03(7) and 2.05(2) recognise that it is not always necessary to provide all this information to comply with the underlying purpose of the rule. Similarly, the information you are required to give to your client varies in importance both inherently and in relation to the individual client and the retainer. Consequently, the rule will be enforced in a manner which is proportionate to the seriousness of the breach. For example, if you were to fail to tell your client that they would be liable to pay another party's costs in breach of 2.03(1)(f), this is likely to be treated as a more serious breach than your failure to advise your client about your right to exercise a lien for unpaid costs in breach of 2.03(1)(e).

    You should note that a breach of rule 2 may provide evidence against a solicitor, an REL or a recognised body of inadequate professional services under section 37A of the Solicitors Act 1974. The powers of the Legal Complaints Service on a finding of an inadequate professional service include disallowing all or part of the solicitor's or REL's costs and directing the solicitor or REL to pay compensation to the client. Section 37A does not apply directly to an RFL, but solicitor and REL partners in a multi-national partnership (MNP) are subject to section 37A in respect of services provided by the MNP, and the MNP itself (and, therefore, all the partners) will be subject to section 37A as a recognised body.

Taking on clients – 2.01

3. Rule 2.01 identifies some situations where you must refuse to act for a client or, if already acting, must stop doing so.

    The retainer is a contractual relationship and subject to legal considerations. You should be sure of your legal position as to who is your client if you contract to provide services to a third party. For example, if you agree to provide all or part of a Home Information Pack to an estate agent or Home Information Pack provider for the benefit of a seller, you should ensure there is an agreed understanding as to whether the estate agent/pack provider or the seller is your client.

4. Your right to decide not to accept instructions is subject to restrictions, including the following:

(a) You must not refuse for a reason that would breach rule 6 (Equality and diversity).

(b) Rule 11 (Litigation and advocacy), governing a solicitor or REL acting as an advocate, contains restrictions on when the solicitor or REL may refuse instructions.

(c) Be aware of restrictions on when you can refuse to act or cease acting for a publicly funded client in a criminal matter.

5. If you are an in-house solicitor or in-house REL you are already in a contractual relationship with your employer who is, for the purpose of these rules, your client. You are not therefore usually as free as a solicitor or REL in a firm to refuse instructions, and will need to use your professional judgement in applying 2.01.

6. Rule 2.01 sets out situations in which you must refuse instructions or, where appropriate, cease acting. These might include the following:

(a) **Breach of the law or rules**

(i) where there is a conflict of interests between you and your client or between two or more clients – see rule 3 (Conflict of interests);

(ii) where money laundering is suspected, your freedom to cease acting is curtailed (see the Proceeds of Crime Act 2002, the Money Laundering Regulations 2007, other relevant law and directives, and guidance issued by the SRA Board on this subject); and

(iii) where you may be dealing with a client who does not have mental capacity as defined in the Mental Capacity Act 2005 or where the client is a child special circumstances apply. You need to bear in mind that the question of capacity relates to the particular decision that needs to be made, and it is, for instance, entirely possible for someone to lack capacity to make certain decisions but have the capacity to instruct a solicitor on other matters. To ensure that you comply with the law you need to have regard to the provisions of that Act and its accompanying Code.

2

(b) **Insufficient resources**

Before taking on a new matter, you must consider whether your firm has the resources – including knowledge, qualifications, expertise, time, sufficient support staff and, where appropriate, access to external expertise such as agents and counsel – to provide the support required to represent the client properly. The obligation is a continuing one, and you must ensure that an appropriate or agreed level of service can be delivered even if circumstances change.

(c) **Duress or undue influence**

It is important to be satisfied that clients give their instructions freely. Some clients, such as the elderly, those with language or learning difficulties and those with disabilities are particularly vulnerable to pressure from others. If you suspect that a client's instructions are the result of undue influence you need to exercise your judgement as to whether you can proceed on the client's behalf. For example, if you suspect that a friend or relative who accompanies the client is exerting undue influence, you should arrange to see the client alone or if appropriate with an independent third party or interpreter. Where there is no actual evidence of undue influence but the client appears to want to act against their best interests, it may be sufficient simply to explain the consequences of the instructions the client has given and confirm that the client wishes to proceed. For evidential purposes, it would be sensible to get this confirmation in writing.

7. As a matter of good practice you should not act for a client who has instructed another firm in the same matter unless the other firm agrees. If you are asked to provide a second opinion, you may do so but you should satisfy yourself that you have sufficient information to handle the matter properly.

Ceasing to act

8. A client can end the retainer with you at any time and for any reason. You may only end the relationship with the client if there is a good reason and after giving reasonable notice. Examples of good reasons include where there is a breakdown in confidence between you and the client, and where you are unable to obtain proper instructions.

9. If there is good reason to cease acting, you must give reasonable notice to the client. What amounts to reasonable notice will depend on the circumstances. For example, it would normally be unreasonable to stop acting for a client immediately before a court hearing where it is impossible for the client to find alternative representation. In such a case, if there is no alternative but to cease acting immediately, you should attend and explain

the circumstances to the court – see rule 11 (Litigation and advocacy). There may be circumstances where it is reasonable to give no notice.

10. The relationship between you and your client can also be ended automatically by law, for example by the client's bankruptcy or mental incapacity (see note 6(a)(iii) above).

11. When you cease acting for a client, you will need to consider what should be done with the paperwork. You must hand over the client's files promptly on request subject to your right to exercise a lien in respect of outstanding costs. You should try to ensure the client's position is not prejudiced, and should also bear in mind his or her rights under the Data Protection Act 1998. Undertakings to secure the costs should be used as an alternative to the exercise of a lien if possible. There may be circumstances where it is unreasonable to exercise a lien, for example, where the amount of the outstanding costs is small and the value or importance of the matter is very great. In any dispute over the ownership of documents you should refer to the law. Further advice about the law of lien or the ownership of documents can be found in *Cordery on Solicitors* or other reference books on the subject.

Client care – 2.02

12. The purpose of 2.02 is to set out the type of information that must normally be given to a client. This information must be provided in a clear and readily accessible form.

13. Rule 2.02 is flexible about the extent of the information to be given in each individual case. Over-complex or lengthy terms of business letters may not be helpful.

14. The "level of service" to be provided should be agreed at the outset. For example, the client may want regular written reports. Alternatively, the client may want to provide initial instructions then to hear no more until an agreed point has been reached. This will affect the projected costs of the matter.

15. When considering the options available to the client (2.02(1)(b)), if the matter relates to a dispute between your client and a third party, you should discuss whether mediation or some other alternative dispute resolution (ADR) procedure may be more appropriate than litigation, arbitration or other formal processes. There may be costs sanctions if a party refuses ADR – see *Halsey v Milton Keynes NHS Trust and Steel and Joy* [2004] EWCA (Civ) 576. More information may be obtained from the Law Society's Practice Advice Service.

16. Rule 2.02(2)(e) requires you to explain limitations or conditions on your acting arising from your relationship with a third party. Where such a relationship involves sharing any client information with a third party, you

2

must inform the client and obtain their consent. Failure to do so would be a breach of client confidentiality (see rule 4 (Confidentiality and disclosure)) and possibly also a breach of the Data Protection Act 1998. Some arrangements with third parties, such as introducers under rule 9 (Referrals of business) or fee sharers under rule 8 (Fee sharing), may constrain the way in which you handle clients' matters.

17. The constraints that such arrangements impose may fall into one of the following categories:

    (a) Constraints which are proper and do not require disclosure to the client. These normally relate to service standards such as dealing with client enquiries within a specified time, the use of specified computer software, telecommunications systems, a particular advertising medium, or particular training provision.

    (b) Constraints which are proper but require disclosure to the client. Some third parties may have a legitimate interest in the progress of the client's matter and the way it is dealt with – for instance, third parties who fund a client's matter, and insurers. Constraints that they impose, e.g. that you will not issue proceedings without the authority of the funder are proper provided they do not operate against the client's best interests, but should be disclosed to the client.

    (c) Constraints which are improper cannot be remedied by disclosing them to the client. These are constraints which impair your independence and ability to act in the client's best interests. You cannot accept an arrangement which involves such constraints. They might include, for instance, requirements that you do not disclose information to the client to which the client is entitled, or give advice to the client which you know is contrary to the client's best interests, or with which you disagree, or that you act towards the court in a deceitful manner or lie to a third party.

18. You must give the required information to the client as soon as possible after you have agreed to act. You must then keep the client up to date with the progress of the matter and any changes affecting the original agreement.

19. The status of the person dealing with your client must be made absolutely clear, for legal and ethical reasons. For example, a person who is not a solicitor must not be described as one, either expressly or by implication. All staff having contact with clients, including reception, switchboard and secretarial staff, should be advised accordingly.

20. All clients affected by a material alteration to the composition of the firm must be informed personally. Where the person having conduct of a matter leaves a firm, the client in question must be informed, preferably in advance, and told the name and status of the person who is to take over their matter.

21. Rule 2.02(2)(d) refers to the person responsible for the overall supervision of a matter. Supervision requirements are dealt with in rule 5 (Business management) and guidance about who can supervise matters may be found there.

22. There may be circumstances when it would be inappropriate to provide any or all of the information required by 2.02. It will be for you to justify why compliance was not appropriate in an individual matter. For example, where you are asked for one-off advice, or where you have a long-standing client who is familiar with your firm's terms of business and knows the status of the person dealing with the matter, this information may not need to be repeated. However, other aspects of 2.02 must be complied with and the client must be kept up to date and informed of changes.

23. If you are an in-house solicitor or in-house REL much of 2.02 will be inappropriate when you are acting for your employer. However, it may be necessary for you to comply with aspects of 2.02 when you are acting for someone other than your employer in accordance with rule 13 (In-house practice).

24. If you receive instructions from someone other than your client, you must still give the client the information required under 2.02. There are, however, exceptions to this. For example, where your client has an attorney appointed by an enduring power of attorney which has been registered with the Court of Protection, or a donee of a lasting power of attorney which has similarly been registered, or a deputy for financial affairs, the information required by 2.02 should be given to the attorney, donee or deputy. However, because the question of capacity relates to the particular decision that needs to be made (that is, just because a person lacks capacity as defined in the Mental Capacity Act 2005 to make certain decisions they do not necessarily lack the capacity to instruct a solicitor in other matters), you need to have regard to the provisions of that Act and its accompanying Code and must not assume that a person subject to the provisions of that Act lacks the capacity to instruct you in an area not covered by the power of attorney or the scope of the deputy's appointment.

25. In order to provide evidence of compliance with 2.02, you should consider giving the information in writing even though this is not a requirement.

26. Where you are, in effect, your firm's client – for example, as an executor administering a deceased's estate or a trustee of a trust – you should consider what information, if any, should be given to interested parties. There is no requirement, for example, that beneficiaries under a will or trust should be treated as though they were clients. It may, however, be good practice to provide some information – for example, about the type of work to be carried out and approximate timescales.

2

Information about the cost – 2.03

27. The purpose of 2.03 is to ensure that the client is given relevant costs information and that this is clearly expressed. Information about costs must be worded in a way that is appropriate for the client. All costs information must be given in writing and regularly updated.

28. Rule 2.03 recognises that there may be circumstances where it would be inappropriate to provide any or all of the information required. It will be for you to justify why compliance was not appropriate in an individual matter. For example, your firm may regularly do repeat work for the client on agreed terms and the client might not need the costs information repeated. However, the client should be informed, for example, of any changes in a firm's charging rates.

29. If you are an in-house solicitor or REL, much of 2.03 will be inappropriate if you are acting for your employer.

30. This guidance does not deal with the form a bill can take, final and interim bills, when they can be delivered and when and how a firm can sue on a bill. All these matters are governed by complex legal provisions, and there are many publications that provide help to firms and clients. Advice on some aspects of costs is available from the Law Society's Practice Advice Service.

31. You will usually be free to negotiate the cost and the method of payment with your clients. It will not normally be necessary for the client to be separately advised on the cost agreement. Different cost options may have different implications for the client – for example, where the choice is between a conditional fee agreement and an application for public funding. In those circumstances clients should be made aware of the implications of each option.

32. The rule requires you to advise the client of the circumstances in which you may be entitled to exercise a lien for unpaid costs. For more information see note 11 above.

33. Clients may be referred to you at a stage when they have already signed a contract for a funding arrangement – see also rule 9 (Referrals of business). You should explain the implications of any such arrangement fully including the extent to which the charges associated with such an arrangement may be recovered from another party to the proceedings.

34. There may be some unusual arrangements, however, where it should be suggested that the client considers separate advice on what is being proposed – for example, where you are to receive shares in a new company instead of costs. See also rule 3 (Conflict of interests) and 9.02(g) for details about your obligations to clients who have been referred to you.

35. Rule 2.03 does not cover all the different charging arrangements possible or the law governing them. However, it does require that the chosen option is explained as fully as possible to the client. It also requires that if you have agreed to pay all, or part, of your fees to a charity in accordance with rule 8 (Fee sharing) the client must be informed at the outset of the name of that charity.

36. It is often impossible to tell at the outset what the overall cost will be. Rule 2.03 allows for this and requires that you provide the client with as much information as possible at the start and that you keep the client updated. If a precise figure cannot be given at the outset, you should explain the reason to the client and agree a ceiling figure or review dates.

37. Particular information will be of relevance at particular stages of a client's matter. You should, for example, ensure that clients understand the costs implications of any offers of settlement. Where offers of settlement are made, clients must be fully informed of the amount to be deducted in respect of costs and how this figure is calculated. You should advise clients of their rights to assessment of your costs in such circumstances.

38. When a potential client contacts you with a view to giving you instructions you should always, when asked, try to be helpful in providing information on the likely costs of their matter.

Work under a conditional fee agreement or for a publicly funded client

39. Rules 2.03(2) and 2.03(3) set out additional information which must be explained to the client when work is done under a conditional fee agreement or on a publicly funded basis. Conditional fee agreements are subject to statutory requirements and all agreements must conform to these. Where you are acting under a conditional fee agreement and you are obliged under a fee sharing agreement to pay to a charity any fees which you receive by way of costs from the client's opponent or other third party, the client must be informed at the outset of the name of that charity.

Payments to others

40. You must explain at the outset to your client any likely payments they will have to make. These could include court fees, search fees, experts' fees and counsel's fees. Where possible, you should give details of the probable cost and if this is not possible you should agree with the client to review these expenses and the need for them nearer the time they are likely to be incurred.

2

Contingency fees – 2.04

41. A "contingency fee" is defined in rule 24 (Interpretation) as any sum (whether fixed, or calculated either as a percentage of the proceeds or otherwise) payable only in the event of success.

42. If you enter into an arrangement for a lawful contingency fee with a client, what amounts to "success" should be agreed between you and your client prior to entering into the arrangement.

43. Under rule 24 (Interpretation), "contentious proceedings" is to be construed in accordance with the definition of "contentious business" in section 87 of the Solicitors Act 1974.

44. Conditional fees are a form of contingency fees. In England and Wales a conditional fee agreement for certain types of litigation is permitted by statute. See section 58 of the Courts and Legal Services Act 1990 (as amended by section 27 of the Access to Justice Act 1999) and 2.03(2) above for more information.

45. It is acceptable to enter into a contingency fee arrangement for non-contentious matters (see section 87 of the Solicitors Act 1974 for the definition of "non-contentious business") but you should note that to be enforceable the arrangement must be contained in a non-contentious business agreement.

46. An otherwise contentious matter remains non-contentious up to the commencement of proceedings. Consequently, you may enter into a contingency fee arrangement for, for example, the receipt of commission for the successful collection of debts owed to a client, provided legal proceedings are not started.

Complaints handling – 2.05

47. The purpose of 2.05 is to encourage complaints to be properly and openly dealt with. There are huge benefits in terms of time, money and client satisfaction if complaints can be dealt with effectively at firm level.

48. The content of your firm's complaints handling procedure is a matter for the firm, but the procedure must be in writing, clear and unambiguous. If a complaint is made to the Legal Complaints Service (LCS) or the Solicitors Regulation Authority the firm will need to be able to demonstrate compliance. Everyone in the firm will need to know about this obligation to ensure that clients know who to contact if they have a problem, the information to give the client when a complaint is made, and the importance of recording the stages of the complaint and the final outcome. When you acknowledge the complaint, your letter should contain details of the LCS, with the post and web addresses of that organisation. You should also explain that the client(s) can ask the LCS to become involved at the

end of the firm's own complaints procedure if they are unhappy with the outcome. It is important to advise of the time limit, which is generally 6 months from the end of the firm's procedure, and can be checked by looking at the LCS website or by telephoning the LCS.

49. Your firm's arrangements for dealing with complaints must be fair and effective. Any investigation must be handled within an agreed timescale. Any arrangements must also comply with rule 6 (Equality and diversity).

50. Rule 2.05(3) prevents you charging your client for the cost of handling a complaint. Dealing properly with complaints is an integral part of any professional business. The associated costs are part of the firm's overheads, and complainants must not be charged separately.

51. Rule 2.05(2) allows for situations where it may be inappropriate to give all the information required.

Commissions – 2.06

52. Rule 2.06 reflects the legal position, preventing a solicitor making a secret profit arising from the solicitor–client relationship.

53. A commission:

   (a) is a financial benefit you receive by reason of and in the course of the relationship of solicitor and client; and

   (b) arises in the context that you have put a third party and the client in touch with one another. (See *The Law Society v Mark Hedley Adcock and Neil Kenneth Mocroft* [2006] EWHC 3212 (Admin).)

54. Examples of what amounts to a commission include payments received from a stockbroker on the purchase of stocks and shares, from an insurance company or an intermediary on the purchase or renewal of an insurance policy, and from a bank or building society on the opening of a bank account. Also, a payment made to you for introducing a client to a third party (unless the introduction was unconnected with any particular matter which you were currently or had been handling for the client) amounts to a commission.

55. On the other hand, a discount on a product or a rebate on, for example, a search fee would not amount to a commission because it does not arise in the context of referring your client to a third party. Such payments are disbursements and the client must get the benefit of any discount or rebate.

56. A client can give informed consent only if you:

   (a) provide details concerning the amount; and

   (b) make it clear that they can withhold their consent and, if so, the commission will belong to them when it is received by you.

57. Commission received may be retained only if the conditions within 2.06 are complied with and the arrangement is in your client's best interests – either:

   (a) it is used to offset a bill of costs; or

   (b) you must be able to justify its retention – for example, the commission is retained in lieu of costs which you could have billed for work done in placing the business, but were not so billed.

58. It cannot be in the best interests of the client for you to receive the commission as a gift. There must be proper and fair legal consideration, such as your agreement to undertake legal work. In consequence, except where the commission is to be offset against a bill of costs:

   (a) it is important that consent is obtained prior to the receipt of the commission (and preferably before you undertake the work leading to the paying of the commission);

   (b) for the purposes of complying with 2.06 you may not obtain your client's consent to retain the commission after you have received it. If consent is not given beforehand, there can be no legal consideration and so the money belongs to the client; and

   (c) if you have obtained consent but the amount actually received is materially in excess of the estimate given to your client, you cannot retrospectively obtain consent to retain the excess. The excess belongs to your client and should be handled accordingly.

59. In order to minimise possible confusion and misunderstanding, and to protect both you and your client, it is recommended that the agreement containing the details about the commission be in writing.

60. If it is your intention from the outset to use the commission to offset a bill of costs, it should be (subject to there being no specific instructions concerning the use of the commission):

   (a) paid into client account as money on account of costs, if received before the bill has been submitted; or

   (b) paid straight into office account if the bill has already been submitted.

61. Where you intend to retain the commission in lieu of costs and your client has provided their consent in accordance with 2.06, the money may be paid into office account as soon as it is received. Where you have requested your client's consent and it has been refused, the commission will belong to the client on receipt and must be paid into client account. It may then be paid to the client or used to offset a bill subject to note 60 above. See the Solicitors' Accounts Rules 1998 for more information.

62. Where you are a sole trustee or attorney or a joint trustee or attorney only with other solicitors, you cannot give proper consent to your retaining

commission by purporting to switch capacities. Furthermore, you are very likely to be acting contrary to your fiduciary obligations at law.

63. For further information about dealing with commission see the Solicitors' Financial Services (Scope) Rules 2001.

Limitation of civil liability by contract – 2.07

64. For the qualifying insurance cover currently required see the Solicitors' Indemnity Insurance Rules.

65. The details of any limitation must be in writing and brought to the attention of the client. Because such a limitation goes to the heart of the agreement between you and your client, you should ensure that your client knows about the limitation and, in your opinion, understands its effect. Consequently, it would not be appropriate to include the limitation within a "terms of business" letter without specifically drawing your client's attention to it.

66. Where you are preparing a trust instrument for a client and that instrument includes a term or terms which has or have the effect of excluding or limiting liability in negligence for a prospective trustee, you should take reasonable steps before the trust is created to ensure that your client is aware of the meaning and effect of the clause. Extra care will be needed if you are, or anyone in or associated with your firm is, or is likely later to become, a paid trustee of the trust.

67. Where you or another person in, or associated with, your firm is considering acting as a paid trustee you should not cause to be included a clause in a trust instrument which has the effect of excluding or limiting liability for negligence without taking reasonable steps before the trust is created to ensure that the settlor is aware of the meaning and effect of the clause.

It would be prudent to ensure both that:

(a)   there is evidence that you have taken the appropriate steps; and

(b)   that evidence is retained for as long as the trust exists and for a suitable period afterwards.

68. Rule 2.07 is subject to the position in law. The points which follow should be noted. The Solicitors Regulation Authority is entitled to expect you to undertake your own research and/or take appropriate advice as to the general law in this area. Relying upon this guidance alone may not be sufficient to ensure compliance with the law.

(a)   Liability for fraud or reckless disregard of professional obligations cannot be limited.

2

(b) Existing legal restraints cannot be overridden. In particular, the courts will not enforce in your favour an unfair agreement with your client.

(c) Under section 60(5) of the Solicitors Act 1974 and paragraph 24 of Schedule 2 to the Administration of Justice Act 1985, a provision in a contentious business agreement that a firm shall not be liable for negligence, or shall be relieved from any responsibility which would otherwise apply is void.

(d) By section 2(2) of the Unfair Contract Terms Act 1977, a contract term which seeks to exclude liability for negligence is of no effect except insofar as it satisfies the requirement of reasonableness set out in section 11 of that Act. Section 11 specifies that the contract term must be fair and reasonable having regard to the circumstances which were or ought reasonably to have been known to, or in the contemplation of, the parties when the contract was made. Schedule 2 to the Act sets out guidelines as to the factors to be taken into account in considering whether the contract term meets the test of reasonableness.

(e) Section 11(4) of the Unfair Contract Terms Act 1977 provides that where a contractual term seeks to restrict liability to a specified sum of money, the question of whether the requirement of reasonableness has been satisfied must also take into account the resources available to you for the purpose of meeting the liability, and the extent to which insurance is available.

(f) The Unfair Terms in Consumer Contracts Regulations 1999 (SI 1999/2083) have a comparable effect to the Unfair Contract Terms Act 1977 as to limitation or exclusion of liability, where your client is a consumer and the term in question has not been individually negotiated. Regulation 3(1) of the 1999 Regulations defines a consumer as any natural person who, in contracts covered by those Regulations, is acting for purposes which are outside their trade, business or profession. Regulation 5(2) states that a term shall always be regarded as not having been individually negotiated where it has been drafted in advance and the consumer has therefore not been able to influence the substance of the term. Regulation 5(1) provides that a term is unfair if, contrary to the requirements of good faith, it causes a significant imbalance in the parties' rights and obligations. Schedule 2 to the Regulations contains an indicative, non-exhaustive list of contract terms which may be regarded as unfair. The test of fairness under these Regulations is not identical to the test of reasonableness under the Unfair Contract Terms Act 1977.

(g) When the retainer may be affected by foreign law, such matters may need to be considered according to the law applicable to the contract.

69. You should also note that if you want to limit your firm's liability to a figure above the minimum level for qualifying insurance but within your firm's top-up insurance cover, you will need to consider whether the top-up insurance will adequately cover a claim arising from the matter in question. For example:

   (a) If your firm agrees with a client that its liability will not exceed £4 million, and the top-up insurance is calculated on an aggregate yearly basis, there is no guarantee that the amount of the top-up cover would be sufficient where there have been multiple claims already.

   (b) Because insurance cover available to meet any particular claim is usually ascertained by reference to the year in which the claim itself is first made, or notice of circumstances which may give rise to a claim is first brought to the attention of insurers, the top-up cover when the claim is brought (or notice of circumstances given) may not be the same as it was when the contract was made.

70. You will not breach 2.07 by agreeing with your client that liability will rest with your firm and not with any employee, director, member or shareowner who might otherwise be liable. However, any such agreement is subject to section 60(5) of the Solicitors Act 1974, the Unfair Contract Terms Act 1977 and the Unfair Terms in Consumer Contracts Regulations 1999.

71. Rule 2.07 does not apply in relation to your overseas practice. However, if you are a principal or a recognised body 15.02(3) prohibits you from seeking to limit your civil liability below the minimum level of cover you would need in order to comply with 15.26 (Professional indemnity).

72. You will not breach 2.07 by a term limiting or excluding any liability to persons who are not your client under the principle in *Hedley Byrne & Co Ltd v Heller & Partners Ltd* [1964] AC 465. However, any such term will be subject to section 60(5) of the Solicitors Act 1974, the Unfair Contract Terms Act 1977 and the Unfair Terms in Consumer Contracts Regulations 1999, where appropriate.

Rule 3   Conflict of interests

Introduction

Rule 3 sets out provisions for dealing with conflicts of interests. Conflicts between the duty of confidentiality and duty of disclosure owed by an individual or a firm to two or more clients are dealt with in rule 4 (Confidentiality and disclosure).

Rules 3.01 to 3.03 deal with conflicts generally.

Rules 3.04 to 3.06 deal with conflicts in particular high risk situations – gifts from clients, public offices and appointments leading to conflict, and alternative dispute resolution (ADR).

Rules 3.07 to 3.22 deal with conflicts in conveyancing. Note the special meaning of "you" in 3.07 to 3.15 (acting for seller and buyer) and 3.16 to 3.22 (acting for lender and borrower). See also 18.03 which sets out additional requirements which apply to the provision of property selling services.

Rule 3.23 sets out that there is no power to waive 3.01 to 3.05.

Rules 3.07 to 3.22 do not apply to your overseas practice unless the land conveyed is situated in England and Wales.

Rule 3 – Conflict of interests

3.01   Duty not to act

(1)   You **must** not act if there is a conflict of interests (except in the limited circumstances dealt with in 3.02).

(2)   There is a conflict of interests if:

    (a)   you owe, or your firm owes, separate duties to act in the best interests of two or more clients in relation to the same or related matters, and those duties conflict, or there is a significant risk that those duties may conflict; or

    (b)   your duty to act in the best interests of any client in relation to a matter conflicts, or there is a significant risk that it may conflict, with your own interests in relation to that or a related matter.

(3)   For the purpose of 3.01(2), a related matter will always include any other matter which involves the same asset or liability.

3.02   Exceptions to duty not to act

common interest (1) You or your firm may act for two or more clients in relation to a matter in situations of conflict or possible conflict if:

(a)   the different clients have a substantially common interest in relation to that matter or a particular aspect of it; and

(b)   all the clients have given in writing their informed consent to you or your firm acting.

commercial interest (2) Your firm may act for two or more clients in relation to a matter in situations of conflict or possible conflict if:

(a)   the clients are competing for the same asset which, if attained by one client, will make that asset unattainable to the other client(s);

(b)   there is no other conflict, or significant risk of conflict, between the interests of any of the clients in relation to that matter;

(c)   the clients have confirmed in writing that they want your firm to act in the knowledge that your firm acts, or may act, for one or more other clients who are competing for the same asset; and

(d)   unless the clients specifically agree, no individual acts for, or is responsible for the supervision of, more than one of those clients.

(3)   When acting in accordance with 3.02(1) or (2) it must be reasonable in all the circumstances for you or your firm to act for all those clients.

(4)   If you are relying on the exceptions in 3.02(1) or (2), you must:

(a)   draw all the relevant issues to the attention of the clients before agreeing to act or, where already acting, when the conflict arises or as soon as is reasonably practicable, and in such a way that the clients concerned can understand the issues and the risks involved;

(b)   have a reasonable belief that the clients understand the relevant issues; and

(c)   be reasonably satisfied that those clients are of full capacity.

3.03   Conflict when already acting

If you act, or your firm acts, for more than one client in a matter and, during the course of the conduct of that matter, a conflict arises between the interests of two or more of those clients, you, or your firm, may only continue to act for one of the clients (or a group of clients between whom there is no conflict) provided that the duty of confidentiality to the other client(s) is not put at risk.

3.04   Accepting gifts from clients

Where a client proposes to make a lifetime gift or a gift on death to, or for the benefit of:

(a) you;

(b) any manager, owner or employee of your firm;

(c) a family member of any of the above,

and the gift is of a significant amount, either in itself or having regard to the size of the client's estate and the reasonable expectations of the prospective beneficiaries, you must advise the client to take independent advice about the gift, unless the client is a member of the beneficiary's family. If the client refuses, you must stop acting for the client in relation to the gift.

3

3.05 Public office or appointment leading to conflict

You must decline to act where you, a member of your family, or a manager, owner or employee of your firm holds some public office or appointment as a result of which:

(a) a conflict of interests, or a significant risk of a conflict, arises;

(b) the public might reasonably conclude that you, or your firm, had been able to make use of the office or appointment for the advantage of the client; or

(c) your ability to advise the client properly and impartially is inhibited.

3.06 Alternative dispute resolution (ADR)

If you provide ADR services you must not:

(a) advise or act for any party in respect of a dispute in which you or any person within your firm is acting, or has acted, as mediator;

(b) provide ADR services in connection with a matter in which you or any person within your firm has acted for any party; or

(c) provide ADR services where you or any person within your firm has acted for any of the parties in issues not relating to the mediation, unless that has been disclosed to the parties and they consent to your acting.

3.07 Acting for seller and buyer in conveyancing, property selling and mortgage related services

(1) Rules 3.07 to 3.15 apply to the transfer of land for value, and the grant or assignment of a lease or some other interest in land for value. Both commercial and residential conveyancing transactions are covered. The terms "seller" and "buyer" include a lessor and lessee. "You" is defined in 23.01, but is to be construed in 3.07 to 3.15 as including an associated firm (see rule 24 (Interpretation) for the meaning of "associated firms").

(2) You must not act for more than one party in conveyancing, property selling or mortgage related services other than as permitted by, and in accordance with,

3.08 to 3.15. "Property selling" means negotiating the sale for the seller. "Mortgage related services" means advising on or arranging a mortgage, or providing mortgage related financial services, for a buyer. "Mortgage" includes a remortgage.

3.08   Conveyancing transactions *personal* not at arm's length

Subject to the prohibition in 10.06(3) and 10.06(4), you may act for seller and buyer when the transaction between the parties is not at arm's length, provided there is no conflict or significant risk of conflict.

3.09   Conveyancing transactions at arm's length *(between two independent, unaffiliated parties)*

Subject to the prohibition in 10.06(3) and (4), you may act for seller and buyer if the conditions set out in 3.10 below are satisfied and one of the following applies:

(a)   both parties are established clients;

(b)   the consideration is £10,000 or less and the transaction is not the grant of a lease; or

(c)   seller and buyer are represented by two separate offices in different localities.

3.10   Conditions for acting under 3.09

In order to act for seller and buyer under 3.09 above, the following conditions must be met:

(a)   the written consent of both parties must be obtained;

(b)   no conflict of interests must exist or arise;

(c)   the seller must not be selling or leasing as a builder or developer; and

(d)   when the seller and buyer are represented by two separate offices in different localities:

(i)   different individuals authorised to do the work, who normally work at each office, conduct or supervise the transaction for seller and buyer; and

(ii)   no office of the firm (or an associated firm) referred either client to the office conducting the transactions.

3.11   Property selling and mortgage related services

Subject to the prohibition in 10.06(3) and (4), you may act for seller and buyer if the conditions set out in 3.13 below are satisfied and one of the following applies:

(a)   the only way in which you are acting for the buyer is in providing mortgage related services; or

(b) the only way in which you are acting for the seller is in providing property selling services through a Solicitors' Estate Agency Limited (SEAL).

3.12 SEALs and participating firms

A SEAL means a recognised body which:

(a) is a company;

(b) does not undertake conveyancing;

(c) is owned jointly by at least four participating firms which are not associated firms;

(d) has no participating firm with majority control;

(e) has at least one participating firm which is a recognised body or recognised sole practitioner; and

(f) is conducted from accommodation physically divided from, and clearly differentiated from that of any participating firm.

A "participating firm" means a recognised sole practitioner, recognised body or authorised non-SRA firm which is a manager or owner of the SEAL, or one or more of whose managers or owners is a manager or owner of the SEAL.

3.13 Conditions for acting under 3.11

In order to act for seller and buyer under 3.11 above, the following conditions must be met:

(a) the written consent of both parties must be obtained;

(b) no conflict of interests must exist or arise;

(c) the seller must not be selling or leasing as a builder or developer;

(d) different individuals must conduct the work for the seller and the work for the buyer and, if these individuals need supervision, they must be supervised by different individuals who are authorised to do the work;

(e) you must inform the seller in writing, before accepting instructions to deal with the property selling, of any services which might be offered to a buyer, whether through the same firm or any associated firm; and

(f) you must explain to the buyer, before the buyer gives consent to the arrangement:

(i) the implications of a conflict of interests arising;

(ii) your financial interest in the sale going through; and

(iii) if you propose to provide mortgage related services to the buyer through a SEAL which is also acting for the seller, that you cannot advise the buyer on the merits of the purchase.

3.14   Special circumstances in property selling and conveyancing

If any of the circumstances set out in 3.09 apply (established clients; consideration of £10,000 or less; representation by two separate offices), you may sell the property, provide mortgage related services, and act for seller and buyer in the conveyancing, subject to the prohibition in 10.06(3) and (4) and compliance with the conditions set out in 3.10 and 3.13 as appropriate.

3.15   Conflict arising when acting for seller and buyer

If a conflict arises during the course of a transaction in which you are acting for more than one party, you may continue to act for one of the parties only if the duty of confidentiality to the other party is not at risk.

3.16   Acting for lender and borrower in conveyancing transactions

(1) Rules 3.16 to 3.22 cover the grant of a mortgage of land and are intended to avoid conflicts of interests. "Mortgage" includes a remortgage. Both commercial and residential conveyancing transactions are covered. "You" is defined in 23.01, but is to be construed in 3.16 to 3.22 as including an associated firm (see rule 24 (Interpretation) for the meaning of "associated firms").

(2) You must not act for both lender and borrower on the grant of a mortgage of land:

(a) if a conflict of interests exists or arises;

(b) on the grant of an individual mortgage of land at arm's length;

(c) if, in the case of a standard mortgage of property to be used as the borrower's private residence only, the lender's mortgage instructions extend beyond the limitations contained in 3.19 and 3.21, or do not permit the use of the certificate of title required by 3.20; or

(d) if, in the case of any other standard mortgage, the lender's mortgage instructions extend beyond the limitations contained in 3.19 and 3.21.

3.17   Standard and individual mortgages

(1) A mortgage is a "standard mortgage" where:

(a) it is provided in the normal course of the lender's activities;

(b) a significant part of the lender's activities consists of lending; and

(c) the mortgage is on standard terms.

An "individual mortgage" is any other mortgage.

(2) A mortgage will not be on standard terms if material terms in any of the documents relating to the mortgage transaction are negotiated between the lender's and borrower's lawyers contemporaneously with effecting the mortgage. In commercial transactions, the element of negotiation will often relate to the facility letter or facility agreement rather than the mortgage deed itself.

(3) Provided there has been no contemporaneous negotiation of material terms between the parties' lawyers, a mortgage will be on standard terms where the lender uses a prescribed form of mortgage deed. Minor variations, such as the usual clause limiting the liability of trustee mortgagors, are not regarded as material and do not alter the nature of these terms as standard.

(4) In addition to its normal standard terms, a lender may have a different set or sets of standard terms applicable to specialised types of borrower, such as registered social landlords. Provided these terms are applied by the lender to all equivalent specialist borrowers or have been agreed between the lender and a specialist borrower as applicable to all transactions between them, they will constitute standard terms for the purposes of 3.16 to 3.22.

(5) The lender and the borrower must be separately represented on the grant of an individual mortgage at arm's length (see 3.16(2)(b)). Rules 3.16 to 3.22 are not then applicable.

(6) You may act for both lender and borrower in a standard mortgage (see 3.16(2)(c) to (d)), provided:

(a) there is no conflict of interests;

(b) the mortgage instructions do not go beyond the limits set out in 3.19; and

(c) in the case of a property to be used solely as the borrower's private residence, the approved certificate of title set out in the annex to rule 3 is used.

(7) The limitations of 3.19 also apply to a standard mortgage where the lender and the borrower are separately represented (see 3.22(1) which includes certificates of title). However, 3.22(2) allows the borrower's lawyer, in a transaction where the property is not to be used solely as the borrower's private residence, to give a certificate of title in any form recognised by the Solicitors Regulation Authority Board. You also remain free to give any other form of certificate which complies with this rule.

(8) There may be cases where the lapse of time between the mortgage offer and completion (for example, when new properties are added) results in use of an earlier edition of a recognised certificate. That is acceptable.

3.18 Notification of certain circumstances to lender

(1) If you wish to act for both lender and borrower on the grant of a standard mortgage of land, you must first inform the lender in writing of the circumstances if:

(a)   the prospective borrower is:

   (i)   the firm or any of its managers or owners, or a member of their immediate family;

   (ii)   an associated firm, any of its managers or owners, or a member of their immediate family; and/or

   (iii) the individual conducting or supervising the transaction, or a member of their immediate family; or

(b)   you propose to act for seller, buyer and lender in the same transaction.

(2) "Immediate family" means spouse, children, parents, brothers and sisters.

3.19   Types of instruction which may be accepted

If acting for both lender and borrower in a standard mortgage, you and the individual conducting or supervising the transaction may only accept or act upon instructions from the lender which are limited to the following matters:

(a)   (i)   taking reasonable steps to check the identity of the borrower (and anyone else required to sign the mortgage deed or other document connected with the mortgage) by reference to a document or documents, such as a passport, precisely specified in writing by the lender;

   (ii)   following the guidance given by the Law Society or the Solicitors Regulation Authority on property fraud and on money laundering;

   (iii) checking that the seller's conveyancers (if unknown to you) appear in a current legal directory or hold practising certificates issued by their professional body; and

   (iv)   in the case of a lender with no branch office within reasonable proximity of the borrower, carrying out the money laundering checks precisely specified in writing by the lender;

(b)   making appropriate searches relating to the property in public registers (for example, local searches, commons registration searches, mining searches), and reporting any results specified by the lender or which you consider may adversely affect the lender; or effecting search insurance;

(c)   making enquiries on legal matters relating to the property reasonably specified by the lender, and reporting the replies;

(d)   reporting the purchase price stated in the transfer and on how the borrower says that the purchase money (other than the mortgage advance) is to be provided; and reporting if you will not have control over the payment of all the purchase money (other than a deposit paid to an estate agent or a reservation fee paid to a builder or developer);

(e)   reporting if the seller or the borrower (if the property is already owned by the borrower) has not owned or been the registered owner of the property for at least six months;

(f) if the lender does not arrange insurance, confirming receipt of satisfactory evidence that the buildings insurance is in place for at least the sum required by the lender and covers the risks specified by the lender; giving notice to the insurer of the lender's interest and requesting confirmation that the insurer will notify the lender if the policy is not renewed or is cancelled; and supplying particulars of the insurance and the last premium receipt to the lender;

3

(g) investigating title to the property and appurtenant rights; reporting any defects revealed, advising on the need for any consequential statutory declarations or indemnity insurance, and approving and effecting indemnity cover if required by the lender; and reporting if you are aware of any rights needed for the use or enjoyment of the property over other land;

(h) reporting on any financial charges (for example, improvement or repair grants or Housing Act discounts) secured on the property revealed by your searches and enquiries which will affect the property after completion of the mortgage;

(i) in the case of a leasehold property:

    (i) confirming that the lease contains the terms stipulated by the lender and does not include any terms specified by the lender as unacceptable;

    (ii) obtaining a suitable deed of variation or indemnity insurance if the terms of the lease are unsatisfactory;

    (iii) enquiring of the seller or the borrower (if the property is already owned by the borrower) as to any known breaches of covenant by the landlord or any superior landlord and reporting any such breaches to the lender;

    (iv) reporting if you become aware of the landlord's absence or insolvency;

    (v) making a company search and checking the last three years' published accounts of any management company with responsibilities under the lease;

    (vi) if the borrower is required to be a shareholder in the management company, obtaining the share certificate, a blank stock transfer form signed by the borrower and a copy of the memorandum and articles of association;

    (vii) obtaining any necessary consent to or prior approval of the assignment and mortgage;

    (viii) obtaining a clear receipt for the last payment of rent and service charge; and

    (ix) serving notice of the assignment and mortgage on the landlord;

(j) in the case of a commonhold unit:

(i)   confirming receipt of satisfactory evidence that common parts insurance is in place for at least the sum required by the lender and covers the risks specified by the lender;

(ii)   confirming that the commonhold community statement contains the terms specified by the lender and does not include any restrictions on occupation or use specified by the lender as unacceptable;

(iii)   enquiring of the seller (or the borrower if the property is already owned by the borrower) and the commonhold association as to any known breaches of the commonhold community statement by the commonhold association or any unit-holder, and reporting any such breaches to the lender;

(iv)   making a company search to verify that the commonhold association is in existence and remains registered, and that there is no registered indication that it is to be wound up;

(v)   obtaining the last three years' published accounts of the commonhold association and reporting any apparent problems with the association to the lender;

(vi)   obtaining a commonhold unit information certificate; and

(vii)   serving notice of the transfer and mortgage of the commonhold unit on the commonhold association;

(k) if the property is subject to a letting, checking that the type of letting and its terms comply with the lender's requirements;

(l) making appropriate pre-completion searches, including a bankruptcy search against the borrower, any other person in whom the legal estate is vested and any guarantor;

(m) receiving, releasing and transmitting the mortgage advance, including asking for any final inspection needed and dealing with any retentions and cashbacks;

(n) procuring execution of the mortgage deed and form of guarantee as appropriate by the persons whose identities have been checked in accordance with any requirements of the lender under (a) above as those of the borrower, any other person in whom the legal estate is vested and any guarantor; obtaining their signatures to the forms of undertaking required by the lender in relation to the use, occupation or physical state of the property; and complying with the lender's requirements if any document is to be executed under a power of attorney;

(o) asking the borrower for confirmation that the information about occupants given in the mortgage instructions or offer is correct; obtaining consents in the form required by the lender from existing or prospective occupiers of the property aged 17 or over specified by the lender, or of whom you are aware;

(p)   advising the borrower on the terms of any document required by the lender to be signed by the borrower;

(q)   advising any other person required to sign any document on the terms of that document or, if there is a conflict of interests between that person and the borrower or the lender, advising that person on the need for separate legal advice and arranging for them to see an independent conveyancer;

(r)   obtaining the legal transfer of the property to the mortgagor;

(s)   procuring the redemption of:

    (i)   existing mortgages on property the subject of any associated sale of which you are aware; and

    (ii) any other mortgages secured against a property located in England or Wales made by an identified lender where an identified account number or numbers or a property address has been given by the lender;

(t)   ensuring the redemption or postponement of existing mortgages on the property, and registering the mortgage with the priority required by the lender;

(u)   making administrative arrangements in relation to any collateral security, such as an endowment policy, or in relation to any collateral warranty or guarantee relating to the physical condition of the property, such as NHBC documentation;

(v)   registering the transfer and mortgage;

(w)   giving legal advice on any matters reported on under 3.19, suggesting courses of action open to the lender, and complying with the lender's instructions on the action to be taken;

(x)   disclosing any relationship specified by the lender between you and the borrower;

(y)   storing safely the title deeds and documents pending registration and delivery to or as directed by the lender; and

(z)   retaining the information contained in your conveyancing file for at least six years from the date of the mortgage.

3.20   Using the approved certificate of title

In addition, if acting for both lender and borrower in a standard mortgage of property to be used as the borrower's private residence only:

(a)   you must use the certificate of title set out in the annex to rule 3 (below) ("the approved certificate"); and

(b)   unless the lender has certified that its mortgage instructions are subject to the limitations contained in 3.19 above and 3.21 below, you must notify the lender on receipt of instructions that the approved certificate will be used, and that your duties to the lender are limited to the matters contained in the approved certificate.

3.21   Terms of rule to prevail

The terms of 3.16 to 3.20 above will prevail in the event of any ambiguity in the lender's instructions, or discrepancy between the instructions and 3.19 above or the approved certificate.

3.22   Anti-avoidance

(1) Subject to (2) below, if acting only for the borrower in a standard mortgage of property you must not accept or act upon any requirements by way of undertaking, warranty, guarantee or otherwise of the lender, the lender's lawyer or other agent which extend beyond the limitations contained in 3.19.

(2) Provided the property is not to be used solely as the borrower's private residence, (1) above does not prevent you from giving any form of certificate of title recognised from time to time by the Solicitors Regulation Authority Board (a "recognised certificate"). Additions or amendments which arise from the individual transaction may be made to the text of a recognised certificate but, to the extent to which they create an increased or additional obligation, must not extend beyond the limitations contained in 3.19.

3.23   Waivers

In spite of 22.01(1) (Waivers), the Solicitors Regulation Authority Board shall not have power to waive any of the provisions of 3.01 to 3.05.

ANNEX

Certificate of title

Details box

TO: (Lender)
Lender's Reference or Account No:
The Borrower:
Property:
Title Number:
Mortgage Advance:
Price stated in transfer:
Completion Date:

| Conveyancer's Name & Address: |
| Conveyancer's Reference: |
| Conveyancer's bank, sort code and account number: |
| Date of instructions: |

WE THE CONVEYANCERS NAMED ABOVE CERTIFY as follows:

(1) If so instructed, we have checked the identity of the Borrower (and anyone else required to sign the mortgage deed or other document connected with the mortgage) by reference to the document or documents precisely specified in writing by you.

(2) Except as otherwise disclosed to you in writing:

(i) we have investigated the title to the Property, we are not aware of any other financial charges secured on the Property which will affect the Property after completion of the mortgage and, upon completion of the mortgage, both you and the mortgagor (whose identity has been checked in accordance with paragraph (1) above) will have a good and marketable title to the Property and to appurtenant rights free from prior mortgages or charges and from onerous encumbrances which title will be registered with absolute title;

(ii) we have compared the extent of the Property shown on any plan provided by you against relevant plans in the title deeds and/or the description of the Property in any valuation which you have supplied to us, and in our opinion there are no material discrepancies;

(iii) the assumptions stated by the valuer about the title (its tenure, easements, boundaries and restrictions on use) in any valuation which you have supplied to us are correct;

(iv) if the Property is leasehold the terms of the lease accord with your instructions, including any requirements you have for covenants by the Landlord and/or a management company and/or by a deed of mutual covenant for the insurance, repair and maintenance of the structure, exterior and common parts of any building of which the Property forms part, and we have or will obtain on or before completion a clear receipt for the last payment of rent and service charge;

(v) if the Property is a commonhold unit, the commonhold community statement contains the terms specified by you and does not include any restrictions on occupation or use specified by you as unacceptable, and we have or will obtain on or before completion a commonhold unit information certificate;

(vi) we have received satisfactory evidence that the buildings insurance is in place, or will be on completion, for the sum and in the terms required by you;

(vii) if the Property is to be purchased by the Borrower:

(a) the contract for sale provides for vacant possession on completion;

(b) the seller has owned or been the registered owner of the Property for not less than six months; and

(c) we are not acting on behalf of the seller;

(viii) we are in possession of:

(a) either a local search or local search insurance; and

(b) such other searches or search insurance as are appropriate to the Property, the mortgagor and any guarantor, in each case in accordance with your instructions;

(ix) nothing has been revealed by our searches and enquiries which would prevent the Property being used by any occupant for residential purposes; and

(x) neither any principal nor any other individual in the firm giving this certificate nor any spouse, child, parent, brother or sister of such a person is interested in the Property (whether alone or jointly with any other) as mortgagor.

WE:

(a) undertake, prior to use of the mortgage advance, to obtain in the form required by you the execution of a mortgage and a guarantee as appropriate by the persons whose identities have been checked in accordance with paragraph (1) above as those of the Borrower, any other person in whom the legal estate is vested and any guarantor; and, if required by you:

(i) to obtain their signatures to the forms of undertaking required by you in relation to the use, occupation or physical state of the Property;

(ii) to ask the Borrower for confirmation that the information about occupants given in your mortgage instructions or offer is correct; and

(iii) to obtain consents in the form required by you from any existing or prospective occupier(s) aged 17 or over of the Property specified by you or of whom we are aware;

(b) have made or will make such Bankruptcy, Land Registry or Land Charges Searches as may be necessary to justify certificate no. (2)(i) above;

(c) will within the period of protection afforded by the searches referred to in paragraph (b) above:

(i) complete the mortgage;

(ii) arrange for the issue of a stamp duty land tax certificate if appropriate;

(iii) deliver to the Land Registry the documents necessary to register the mortgage in your favour and any relevant prior dealings; and

(iv) effect any other registrations necessary to protect your interests as mortgagee;

(d) will despatch to you such deeds and documents relating to the Property as you require with a list of them in the form prescribed by you within ten working days of receipt by us of the title information document from the Land Registry;

(e) will not part with the mortgage advance (and will return it to you if required) if it shall come to our notice prior to completion that the Property will at completion be occupied in whole or in part otherwise than in accordance with your instructions;

(f) will not accept instructions, except with your consent in writing, to prepare any lease or tenancy agreement relating to the Property or any part of it prior to despatch of the title information document to you;

(g) will not use the mortgage advance until satisfied that, prior to or contemporaneously with the transfer of the Property to the mortgagor, there will be discharged:

  (i) any existing mortgage on property the subject of an associated sale of which we are aware; and

  (ii) any other mortgages made by a lender identified by you secured against a property located in England or Wales where you have given either an account number or numbers or a property address;

(h) will notify you in writing if any matter comes to our attention before completion which would render the certificate given above untrue or inaccurate and, in those circumstances, will defer completion pending your authority to proceed and will return the mortgage advance to you if required; and

(i) confirm that we have complied, or will comply, with your instructions in all other respects to the extent that they do not extend beyond the limitations contained in the Solicitors' Code of Conduct 2007, 3.19 (Conflict of interests – types of instruction which may be accepted).

OUR duties to you are limited to the matters set out in this certificate and we accept no further liability or responsibility whatsoever. The payment by you to us (by whatever means) of the mortgage advance or any part of it constitutes acceptance of this limitation and any assignment to you by the Borrower of any rights of action against us to which the Borrower may be entitled shall take effect subject to this limitation.

Signature box

SIGNED on behalf of THE CONVEYANCERS	....
NAME of Authorised Signatory	....

QUALIFICATION of Authorised Signatory	....
DATE of Signature	....

Guidance to rule 3 – Conflict of interests

Conflict is defined – 3.01

1. Conflict is defined as a conflict between the duties to act in the best interests of two or more different clients, or between your interests and those of a client. The definition appears in 3.01(2). This will encompass all situations where doing the best for one client in a matter will result in prejudice to another client in that matter or a related matter.

2. The definition of conflict in 3.01(2) requires you to assess when two matters are "related". Rule 3.01(3) makes it clear that if the two matters concern the same asset or liability, then they are "related". Accordingly, if you act for one client which is negotiating with publishers for the publication of a novel, an instruction from another client alleging that the novel is plagiarised and breaches copyright would be a related matter.

3. However, there would need to be some reasonable degree of relationship for a conflict to arise. If you act for a company on a dispute with a garage about the cost of repairs to a company car, your firm would not be prevented from acting for a potential bidder for the company, even though the car is a minor asset of the company and would be included in the purchase. If you act for a client selling a business, you might conclude that your firm could also act for a prospective purchaser on the creation of an employee share scheme which would cover all the entities in the purchaser's group, this work perhaps requiring the future inclusion of the target within the scheme and consideration as to whether this raised any particular issues.

4. In each case, you will need to make a judgement on the facts. In making this judgement, you might want to consider the view of your existing client where you are professionally able to raise the issue with him or her. You should also take care to consider whether your firm holds any confidential information from your existing client which would be relevant to the new instructions and if so, to ensure that you comply with rule 4 (Confidentiality and disclosure).

You are or your firm is permitted to act with clients' consent in defined circumstances of conflict subject to suitable safeguards

5. This reflects the fact that there may be circumstances in which, despite peripheral or potential conflict, the clients' best interests are served by you,

or your firm, being able to act for two or more clients who are able to give informed consent. The circumstances in which you could act despite a conflict are set out in 3.02.

6.   Two different situations are defined. These are in 3.02(1) and (2):

(a)   (i)   Rule 3.02(1) deals with the situation where the clients have a "common interest", they all want to continue to instruct you and it would be disproportionate, for example, in terms of cost and general disruption to their matter, to require them to instruct separate solicitors.

(ii)   For there to be a "common interest" there must be a clear common purpose and a strong consensus on how it is to be achieved. However, it will be for you to decide objectively on the facts in each case whether there is a "common interest" and it is appropriate to act. In making this decision, you should always consider whether the clients will be represented even-handedly with equal weight being given to the instructions from each.

(iii) The "common interest" might arise, for example, where you are acting for several members of a family in relation to their affairs or acting for various individuals in the setting up of a company. Any areas of conflict must be substantially less important to all the clients than their common purpose and may, for example, relate to slightly different views on how the common purpose is to be achieved. It will be your duty to keep the differences under review with the clients and to decide if the point has been reached when it would be untenable to continue to represent all of them in a fair and open manner or without any of them being prejudiced.

(iv)   There exist some multi-party complex commercial transactions, where sophisticated users of legal services, who have a common purpose, may expect a firm to act for two or more parties, because this will facilitate efficient handling of the matter (taking into account amongst other things the desire to complete the transaction quickly, the availability of necessary experience/expertise and the overall costs). Indeed in many cases it may already be accepted business practice for firms to act in this manner. An example is acting for different tiers of lenders (for example senior lenders and mezzanine lenders) and/or different parties (for example arrangers/underwriters and bond/security trustees) in entering into a financing transaction where there is already an agreed or commonly understood structure with regard to the ranking of their respective claims, the content of their respective obligations and associated commercial issues.

(v)   While accepted business practice can be considered as a factor in determining whether an appropriate common purpose exists, you and your firm should always exercise caution when proposing to act in accordance with 3.02 and should be mindful of the residual test of reasonableness referred to in 3.02(3).

(vi) In some situations it might be possible for you to consider whether the retainer could be limited to those areas where there is no conflict with the clients seeking separate advice on any areas of conflict. This could only be done where the conflict did not undermine the overriding common purpose (see below for further guidance on limiting retainers).

(vii) In some circumstances it might be possible that, while a conflict would prevent you from acting for another party on all aspects of a matter, a mandate limited to a specific issue where there is common purpose might be accepted. For example, you may be retained by the owner of a company to advise on its disposal. In that case you would not generally be able to advise another party on the purchase of the company. However, in the hope and anticipation of a successful sale a seller client which is a sophisticated user of legal services might agree that you should also accept a limited retainer to provide competition law advice to the prospective purchaser regarding the filings for competition law purposes that would be required in the event that the two businesses were combined.

(viii) When acting under this exception, especially in family situations, you need to consider the developing legal position. Courts are likely to make a presumption of undue influence where one of the parties who is considered vulnerable through age or other circumstances places trust and confidence in the other party. In any situation of doubt it may well be in the best interests of the clients that they are separately represented.

(b)   (i)   Rule 3.02(2) is intended to apply to specialised areas of legal services where the clients are sophisticated users of those services and conclude that rather than seek out new advisers they would rather use their usual advisers in the knowledge that those advisers might also act for competing interests. An "asset" is not necessarily physical, and can include a contract or a business opportunity. Examples where this exception might apply include:

      (A)   acting on insolvencies so that a firm can act for more than one creditor;

3

(B)   acting for competing bidders, and/or for those involved with the funding of bidders, for a business being sold by auction; and

(C)   acting for competing tenderers submitting tenders to perform a contract.

(ii)   The wording of 3.02(2) is sufficiently wide to permit other transactional work in the commercial field where clients can give consent. Solicitors and their firms should exercise considerable caution when proposing to act in accordance with 3.02(2) in categories of work where to do so is not already accepted business practice.

(iii) Rule 3.02(2) should not be applied to disputes over assets other than in the context of corporate restructurings and insolvencies.

7.   Reasonableness is an important rider to 3.02. There may be situations where, despite compliance with 3.02, it would still not be reasonable to act. The apparent unequal bargaining position of the parties, concerns about the mental stability of one of the parties, a family arrangement where an elderly parent is providing security for their son's or daughter's business loan, and the importance of one of the clients to the firm may all be situations where instructions to act for both or all parties should be declined. Having accepted instructions you must be satisfied that you can act even-handedly for both or all clients and that, taking into account any limitations in a specific retainer, you do not favour one at the expense of the other(s).

8.   The criterion against which reasonableness will be judged is whether one client is at risk of prejudice because of the lack of separate representation. In relation to all situations where you are proposing to act for two or more clients under the provisions of 3.02, the onus will be on you to demonstrate why it was reasonable to act for all the clients at the time the instructions were accepted. Above all, you must be satisfied that unfettered advice can be given, without fear or favour, to the clients. You must also keep under review whether it remains reasonable to continue to act for them. You should also have regard to 1.04 (Best interests of clients) which requires you to act in the best interests of each of your clients.

9.   (a)   Rule 3.02(4) places obligations on you to discuss with the clients the implications of you, or your firm, continuing to act for all of them. You must be satisfied that the clients understand the issues and that their consent is independently and freely given. You should consider setting out in your initial terms of business letter the issues discussed in relation to the conflict of interests and how that might affect your ability to represent both or all of the clients as the matter progresses. Extreme caution will be required where one of the clients is

particularly vulnerable due to mental health, language or other problems affecting their understanding of the issues, although where a litigation friend acts for a person who lacks capacity they will be able to consent on that person's behalf. Similarly, you must always be alert to situations where a client might be consenting under duress or undue influence and in those circumstances must insist on separate representation. For the avoidance of doubt, and for evidential purposes, you should always keep a written record of all discussions with the clients about the implications of your acting for them. You must always obtain all the clients' written consent on each occasion when acting under either of the exceptions.

(b) Where seeking informed consent under 3.02(1)(b) you should identify by name the other clients you or your firm propose(s) to act for, or be able to do so when their identities are known. Provided that you do this and comply with the requirements of 3.02(4), the obligation to obtain "informed" consent in 3.02(1)(b) will have been satisfied. Where consent is sought under 3.02(2), you need to comply with the requirements of 3.02(4) but you need not identify by name the other clients you or your firm propose(s) to act for.

10. When acting for two or more clients on a matter, or a related matter, there may be circumstances where you will have to cease acting for one or both clients. This may be in circumstances where no conflict was apparent when accepting instructions but a conflict subsequently arose or when acting under one of the exceptions and it becomes impossible to fulfil the conditions set out in 3.02. In these circumstances it is important to try and limit the disruption that will inevitably be caused for the clients. One way of doing this is to discuss and agree with the clients at the outset what will happen if a conflict arises and agree which client the firm would continue to represent where this is possible.

11. The rule does not specifically deal with potential or future conflict, although it does make clear that a significant risk of conflict should prevent a solicitor from acting. You should always be cautious, therefore, about accepting instructions where the possibility of future conflict is evident. The risks should be explained to the clients about the problems and expense which the requirement for future separate representation could bring.

Limited/defined retainers

12. There may be situations where, when acting for two or more clients, it is appropriate to continue to advise them but necessary to make clear that there are defined areas of conflict on which you cannot advise, and one or more of them may need separate advice. Your retainer with your clients will, when these situations arise, need to be limited to exclude those areas

of work or advice. Care must always be taken, however, to ensure that the clients understand:

(a)   exactly what you are proposing to deal with on their behalf; and

(b)   those contested areas which are to be excluded from the retainer.

13. A limited retainer would be unlikely to be appropriate in any situation where one of the clients was disadvantaged in some way as against the other. This might be because of an unequal bargaining position or because one had some form of disability. In any situation where you agree to act for two or more clients by limiting the retainer it is important that you keep all developments under review to ensure that it remains appropriate to continue to act.

Professional embarrassment

14. There may be some circumstances in which you should refuse instructions when, although there is no actual conflict of interests as defined in rule 3, you might feel unable to do your best for a client because of some form of professional embarrassment. It may be, for example, that if you have acted for a client in the past and accept instructions to act against that client you may feel inhibited in doing your best for the new client because of the past relationship with the former client. If so, the instructions from the new client should be refused as you would, otherwise, be in breach of core duties 1.03 (Independence) and 1.04 (Best interests of clients).

15. There may also be situations where you and your firm are asked to act with consent, using an information barrier in accordance with rule 4 (Confidentiality and disclosure), but the information you hold and which you cannot disclose to your client is of such a nature that it would cause severe embarrassment to your firm if, or when, it later came to light that your firm held such information. It may be, for example, that you are asked to act for a client on the acquisition of a business in circumstances where confidential information is held by your firm that the business has a serious problem with its accounts. Similarly, it may be that you are asked to prepare an employment contract for a company which is planning to recruit an individual who is known, confidentially, to be under investigation for fraud. In those circumstances you and your firm would be seriously embarrassed acting for a client who you knew was wasting legal fees on an outcome the client would not want to pursue if in possession of the knowledge held by your firm. It could be argued that you are not acting in the best interests of the client (see 1.04 (Best interests of clients)) or that you are damaging public confidence in the profession (see 1.06 (Public confidence)).

16. Where professional embarrassment is not a factor and the circumstances which would otherwise prevent you from acting in 4.03 (duty not to put

confidentiality at risk by acting) do not arise, it will be a purely commercial decision as to whether you should act against the interests of another client or former client, provided there is no conflict as defined in 3.01 or 3.02.

In-house practice

17. If you are employed as an in-house lawyer your employer is your client. The nature of this relationship may cause problems because you do not have the same freedom as a firm would have to decline instructions. There may be occasions, for example, when you are asked to advise your employer in situations where conflict or potential conflict arises between your interests and the interests of your employer. These include:

    (a) where your personal interests as an employee may conflict with the interests of your employer who wants advice on a course of action which could be detrimental to you as an employee where, for example, a merger could lead to your redundancy;

    (b) where your employer asks you to do something which would place you in breach of your professional obligations, for example, to file a document with the court which you know contains false information; or

    (c) where your employer may act against your advice and, for example, engage in criminal activity which may require you to take action against your employer.

18. In relation to situations where your personal interests may conflict with a course of action proposed by your employer you need not necessarily be excluded from advising your employer. Your employer will usually be aware of exactly how you will be affected by its proposals, and if you are able to give objective advice on the legal issues where your expertise is required you would normally be free to do so. There may, however, be situations where you are so affected by the advice you are asked to give that you feel your objectivity and independence are impaired and in those situations you would have to ask your employer to seek other advice, either internally or externally. What is important in these situations is that there is transparency about your interests. Beyond that, you will have to make a judgement about whether you feel you have the necessary objectivity to advise.

19. If your employer was unaware of your interests – and, therefore, the potential for conflict – the position would be different. If, for example, you had a large shareholding in another company and your employer's proposed action could adversely affect the value of those shares then you would either have to disclose your interest or explain that a conflict prevented you from advising on that issue.

3

20. In situations where you are asked to act contrary to your professional obligations then you should not compromise your position and you must refuse to carry out instructions which would have this result, even if ultimately this led to the loss of your job.

21. There may be situations where there is a positive legal obligation on you to take action against your employer where, for example, your employer is engaging in money laundering or where there are "whistle blowing" obligations. Legal issues of this nature are beyond the remit of this guidance. They are situations where your relationship with your employer has reached the stage where you would need to consider the advisability of seeking legal advice on your own position.

22. Finally, as an in-house lawyer you are, under rule 13 (In-house practice), able to act for a limited number of other bodies and individuals. For example, if employed by a company, you may act for a holding, associated or subsidiary company of that company employer. If you do so you must ensure that you do not act in any situation where there would be a conflict between the interests of your employer and the other company for whom you are also acting (see 13.01 and 13.03). Similarly, if employed in local government you may act, for example, for local councillors in certain circumstances, provided you can comply with rule 3.

Co-defendants

23. In publicly funded cases, regulations require that one solicitor be appointed to act for all co-defendants in a legal aid case unless there is, or is likely to be, a conflict. The purpose of this is to ensure economy in the use of public funds by ensuring that a single solicitor represents co-defendants where it is proper to do so. The professional conduct obligations which deal with conflicts of interest have always prevented a solicitor or firm acting for two or more clients where there is a conflict or significant risk of a conflict arising between the interests of two or more clients. A solicitor can act, however, for co-defendants where conflict is not a factor. The difficulty often lies, however, in spotting potential conflict and deciding whether it is sufficiently real to refuse instructions.

24. Your starting point should always be your fundamental professional obligation to act in each client's best interests. Can you discharge this obligation to each client? This means first asking each client if they are aware of any actual or potential conflict between them and then, if they indicate that there is no such conflict, asking yourself whether you feel there are any constraints on the advice you would want to give to one client, or on the action you would want to take on that client's behalf, which are likely to arise because you act for another co-defendant.

25. A conflict of interest arises wherever there is a constraint of that sort, for example where it is in the best interests of client A:

(a) to give evidence against client B;

(b) to make a statement incriminating client B;

(c) to implicate client B in a police interview;

(d) to provide prejudicial information regarding client B to an investigator;

(e) to cross-examine client B in such a manner as to call into question his or her credibility;

(f) to rely upon confidential information given by client B without his or her consent; or

(g) to adopt tactics in the course of the retainer which potentially or actually harm client B.

26. If these obligations actually come into conflict when acting for two or more clients you will have to cease to act for one and often both. This can cause considerable disruption and expense, which is why the rules require that you should not accept instructions if there is a significant risk of this happening.

27. Many criminal clients will, of course, have retained you at the police station prior to a police interview and are thus not at that stage defendants. The obligations referred to above apply at this early stage, and you must be satisfied that accepting instructions on behalf of a client prior to a police interview does not place you in conflict with another client who is also to be interviewed. In order to assess whether you can act for both clients it is important that you do not interview the clients together and that you get instructions which are as full as possible from the first client before any substantive contact with the second client. However, never let the police deter you from seeing the second client because they think there is a conflict – that decision must be yours.

28. A further consideration when taking instructions at the police station, especially out of office hours when an immediate conflict check is not possible, is that the firm may already act for another defendant in that matter or information obtained at the police station may be relevant to another client on an unrelated matter. For example, the firm may be acting in divorce proceedings for a wife where violence is alleged and information that her husband has been charged with an offence involving violence would be relevant and may make it impossible to continue acting for the wife. This highlights the importance of carrying out a conflict check at the earliest opportunity.

29. When considering accepting instructions from more than one client in the same matter you need to assess not only whether there is a conflict at the outset, but whether events are likely to arise which will prevent you from

continuing to act for one or both at a later stage in the proceedings. In almost all cases there will be some possibility of differences in instructions between the clients but the rules do not prevent you acting unless the risk of conflict is significant. Assessing the risk is often not easy. It is also important that where you have accepted instructions from co-defendants you remain alert to the risk of conflict arising as the case progresses.

30. When considering whether there is an actual conflict there are obvious indicators such as whether the clients have differing accounts of the important relevant circumstances of the alleged crime or where one seems likely to change his or her plea. There are also less obvious indicators. These would include situations where there is some clear inequality between the co-defendants which might, for example, suggest that one client is acting under the influence of the other rather than on his or her own initiative. If you are acting for both this may make it difficult for you to raise and discuss these issues equally with them. In trying to help one, you might be undermining the other. If you believe you are going to be unable to do your best for one without worrying about whether this might prejudice the other you should only accept instructions from one.

31. The risk of future conflict can be an even more difficult issue to assess. It may be that you have two clients who are pleading not guilty and who are apparently in total agreement on the factual evidence. Should they both be found guilty, you need to consider at the outset whether you would be able to mitigate fully and freely on behalf of one client without in so doing harming the interests of the other. It may be that one has a long list of convictions and is considerably older than the other. If so, it may be that the younger client with a comparatively clean record was led astray or pressurised into committing the crime and would want you to emphasise this in mitigation. If there is a significant risk of this happening you should not accept instructions from both.

32. Even where care is taken when accepting instructions from more than one client in the same matter there will inevitably be situations where a conflict subsequently arises. This will commonly happen where one defendant changes his or her plea or evidence. A decision will then have to be taken as to whether it is proper to continue to represent one client or whether both will have to instruct new firms. In making this decision you need to consider whether in the changed circumstances your duty to disclose all relevant information to the retained client will place you in breach of your duty of confidentiality to the other client. In other words, you need to decide whether you hold confidential information about the departing client which is now relevant to the retained client. If you do have such information then you cannot act for either client.

33. Following changes to regulations affecting publicly funded cases, some practitioners have reported pressure from some court clerks on solicitors to

represent co-defendants even where there is a clear risk of conflict. Similar pressure has been applied by police at police stations prior to interviews. However, the professional rules of conduct preclude you acting for both clients in those circumstances, and the regulations are not intended to put solicitors in a position where they are asked to act contrary to their professional responsibilities. If asked by the court for your reasons why you cannot act for both defendants, you must not give information which would breach your duty of confidentiality to your client(s). This will normally mean that you can say no more than that it would be unprofessional for you to continue to act.

34. For the avoidance of doubt, you cannot resolve a conflict by instructing another firm or counsel to undertake the advocacy on behalf of one client. Neither can you pass one of the clients to another member of your firm. The rules make it quite clear that your firm cannot act for clients whose interests conflict.

35. Any decision to act, or not to act, for co-defendants should be recorded with a brief note of the reasons.

Mediation

36. There is no objection to your acting as a conciliator and mediator between parties in a dispute. However, in so acting you should have regard to the appropriate codes of practice such as those issued by the Law Society from time to time. These codes provide detailed guidance on dealing with conflict when acting as mediators.

Local authority client

37. If tendering for local authority work, your firm will need to consider how frequently the range of work is likely to give rise to conflicts between existing clients and the local authority, for example, in housing and custody matters where the firm acts against the local authority.

Insolvency practice

38. If you are a licensed insolvency practitioner you must consider whether any relationship which you have, or your firm has, with clients or others might affect your independence and create a conflict preventing you accepting an appointment to administer an insolvent estate or bankruptcy. See also rule 17 (Insolvency practice).

Your interests conflicting with the client's – 3.01(2)(b)

39. There are no circumstances where you can act for a client whose interests conflict with your own interests. The situations outlined in 3.02 where you can act for two or more clients whose interests conflict have no application

in this situation. This is because of the fiduciary relationship which exists between you and your client which prevents you taking advantage of the client or acting where there is a conflict or potential conflict of interests between you and your client. Examples appear below.

40. In conduct there is a conflict of interests where you in your personal capacity sell to, or buy from, or lend to, or borrow from, your client. In all these cases you should insist the client takes independent legal advice. If the client refuses you must not proceed with the transaction.

41. You should never enter into any arrangement or understanding with a client or prospective client prior to the conclusion of a matter under which you acquire an interest in the publication rights with respect to that matter. This applies equally to non-contentious business.

42. Whilst you are entitled to take security for costs you should be aware of the risk of the court finding undue influence. Before you do take a charge over a client's property it is advisable, therefore, to suggest the client consider seeking independent legal advice. Such advice would not normally be essential unless the terms of the proposed charge are particularly onerous or would give you some unusual benefit or profit. It is, however, important always to ensure that the client understands that a charge is being taken and the effect of such a charge.

43. You are not able to secure costs by a first legal charge over your client's property if this means that you are entering into a regulated mortgage contract as a lender. A regulated mortgage contract is an investment which is regulated by the Financial Services Authority (FSA). It arises where the lender provides credit to an individual or trustee, and it is secured by a first legal mortgage on land which is in the United Kingdom, and at least 40% of the land is, or is to be, used as a dwelling by the borrower or, where the borrower is a trustee, by a beneficiary of the trust or by a related person. You must be authorised by the FSA in order to secure your costs in this way. Detailed guidance on this is in the booklet "Financial Services and Solicitors" available from the Professional Ethics Guidance Team.

44. You must always disclose with complete frankness whenever you have, or might obtain, any personal interest or benefit in a transaction in which you are acting for the client. In such circumstances, you must insist that the client receives independent advice.

45. Independent advice means both legal advice and, where appropriate, competent advice from a member of another profession, e.g. a chartered surveyor.

46. Your interests referred to in this rule may be direct (for example, where you seek to sell to or buy property from the client or lend to, or borrow from, the client), or indirect (for example, where your business interests lead you to recommend the client to invest in a concern in which you are interested).

47. This rule applies, therefore, not only where you are personally interested in a transaction, but equally where another person working in your firm has an interest of which you are aware and it impairs your ability to give independent and impartial advice.

48. The interests envisaged by this rule are not restricted to those of a primarily economic nature only. For example, if you become involved in a sexual relationship with a client you must consider whether this may place your interests in conflict with those of the client or otherwise impair your ability to act in the best interests of the client.

49. If you are a director of a company for which you act, or own shares in the company, you must consider whether you are in a position of conflict when asked to advise the company upon steps it has taken or should take. It may sometimes be necessary to resign from the board or for another solicitor (including a solicitor from the same firm if appropriate) to advise the company in a particular matter where your own interests conflict, or are likely to conflict. If acting for a company in which you have a personal interest you should always ensure that your ability to give independent and impartial advice is not, for that reason, impaired.

50. If you hold a power of attorney for a client you must not use that power to gain a benefit which, if acting as a professional adviser to that client, you would not be prepared to allow to an independent third party. This applies regardless of the legal position, for example, as to whether you could lend the donor's money to yourself.

51. You are free to negotiate your terms of business, including costs, with your clients. This includes negotiating conditional fees which are subject to statutory regulation. In all these negotiations you are not acting for the client. There may be situations, however, where the terms of business are particularly unusual and it would be prudent for you to suggest the client seeks independent advice. It would be advisable to do so if, for example, as part, or all, of your remuneration you are to receive shares in a company you are setting up on behalf of your client.

52. You need to consider whether the conditional fee agreement involves you in insurance mediation activities, such as arranging and/or advising on after the event insurance contracts, etc. Solicitors who carry on insurance mediation activities either need to be able to comply with the Solicitors' Financial Services (Scope) Rules 2001 or be authorised by the FSA. Detailed guidance is in the booklet *Financial Services and Solicitors* available from the Professional Ethics Guidance Team.

53. You must always be careful to ensure that any settlement achieved for a client, or any advice given in a non-contentious matter conducted on a contingency fee basis, is in the client's best interests and not made with a view to your obtaining your fee.

3

54. Where you discover an act or omission which would justify a claim against you, you must inform the client, and recommend they seek independent advice. You must also inform the client that independent advice should be sought in cases where the client makes a claim against you, or notifies an intention to do so. If the client refuses to seek independent advice, you should not continue to act unless you are satisfied that there is no conflict of interest. See 20.09 (Dealing with claims).

Accepting gifts from clients – 3.04

55. Rule 3.04 does not prevent you accepting a client's gift but does require the client to take independent advice where the gift is significant, or significant as compared with the client's likely estate and the reasonable expectations of prospective beneficiaries.

56. Rule 3.04 allows you to prepare a will for a family member under which you receive a significant gift without requiring the client to seek independent advice on that gift. However, extreme caution should always be exercised in these circumstances as your ability to give independent, dispassionate advice could easily be undermined by your relationship with others within, and outside, the family. The risk of conflict, therefore, is very high. If you are to receive a significant gift from the estate you need also to consider the reasonable expectations of the other prospective beneficiaries, who are likely to be your relatives. If, having taken these reasonable expectations into account, it appears that you are to receive a benefit which is in any way disproportionately large you should always ensure that the client is separately advised on that gift. "Prospective beneficiaries" in the context of this rule means others who would be reasonably expected to benefit because of their relationship to the client and their reasonable expectations would be dependent on the closeness of that relationship. An objective test would be applied in the event of a complaint.

57. There are other factors which should be taken into account when preparing a will for a family member under which you benefit. It may also be far easier for a close family member to talk through their proposals for their will with someone who has no personal interest in its contents and who is unlikely to be offended by any suggestions they might wish to make. Finally, your relative's bequests are secure from allegations of undue influence if their will is drawn by someone totally independent and who does not take a benefit from it. "Family member" is not defined in 3.04 to allow a flexible approach to be taken. Co-habitants are not included in the exception to independent advice because their legal position is less secure than those related by blood, marriage or adoption.

58. A "significant amount" for the purposes of 3.04 cannot be quantified because the particular circumstances of the proposed gift must be taken into account. In general, however, anything more than a token gift will be

considered significant. If, therefore, anything more than a token amount is accepted without the client having separate advice (other than where you are acting for a family member as permitted by 3.04) you may be exposed to allegations of misconduct.

59. When considering whether a gift is of a "significant amount" the date of preparation of the document is relevant when determining the size of the estate.

60. If more than one gift is made to members of a firm, for example, £1,000 to each of the partners in the firm, they should be amalgamated for the purpose of establishing whether the gift is "significant".

61. The implications of 3.04 need to be made clear to all members of your firm who take instructions from clients, whether solicitors or not. Supervision is important to ensure compliance.

62. Where you are given money or property to distribute for the benefit of others, such as in a secret trust, this is not considered to be a "gift" for the purposes of 3.04. However, care should be taken to ensure that records are kept confirming the arrangement and to ensure that the transaction is not one which could contain a potential for money laundering.

Public office or appointment leading to conflict – 3.05

63. Examples of the public offices and appointments which 3.05 covers are:

   (a) local councillor;

   (b) judicial appointments;

   (c) justices and justices' clerks;

   (d) the Gambling Commission;

   (e) coroners;

   (f) police authority;

   (g) the Legal Services Commission's Regional Legal Services Committees; and

   (h) Criminal Injuries Compensation Authority.

64. Where you hold (or a member of your firm or family holds) any of these, or similar, offices or appointments it will be up to you in every case to consider:

   (a) whether any political or other interest which you may have in connection with the office or appointment may conflict with, or affect, your duty to act in the best interests of any of your clients (including your ability to advise impartially and independently);

(b)   whether any duties which arise from your office or appointment conflict with, or affect, your duty to act in the best interests of your clients;

(c)   whether the terms of appointment, or any statutory provisions, restrict your ability to act in any particular matter; and

(d)   whether there is likely to be a public perception that you have, or your firm has, been able to obtain an unfair advantage for your client(s) as a result of the office or appointment.

65. Where you are aware that a member of your firm or family has accepted an appointment it is important for you to consider whether there is likely to be a public perception of your firm gaining an unfair advantage for your client(s).

ADR and conflict – 3.06

66. You may provide ADR services as part of your practice or through a separate business. For more information on separate businesses see rule 21 (Separate businesses).

67. Rule 3.06 also applies when you provide ADR services through a separate business.

68. "ADR service" means the service provided by you when acting as an independent neutral, for example, as mediator, conciliator or arbitrator.

69. The SRA Board recommends that those who offer ADR services comply with a code of practice such as the Law Society's Code of Practice for Civil and Commercial Mediation and Code of Practice for Family Mediation.

Acting for seller and buyer in conveyancing, property selling and mortgage related services

70. Rules 3.07 to 3.15 set out the limited circumstances in which you may act for more than one party in conveyancing, property selling or mortgage related services. They apply to all types of conveyancing transaction, commercial and residential.

71. The general rule is that separate representation is required because conveyancing is an area where the risk of a conflict arising between two parties is high and where any conflict may affect a conveyancing chain.

72. When judging whether or not a transaction is "at arm's length", you need to look at the relationship between the parties and the context of the transaction. A transaction may be regarded as not "at arm's length", even if it is at market value or is stated to be on arm's length terms. A transaction would not usually be at arm's length, for example, if the parties are:

(a)   related by blood, adoption or marriage, or living together;

(b) the settlor of a trust and the trustees;

(c) the trustees of a trust and its beneficiary or the beneficiary's relative;

(d) personal representatives and a beneficiary;

(e) the trustees of separate trusts for the same family;

(f) a sole trader or partners and a limited company set up to enable the business to be incorporated;

(g) associated companies (i.e. where one is a holding company and the other is its subsidiary within the meaning of the Companies Act 1985, or two associated companies); or

(h) a local authority and a company within the meaning of 13.08(c).

73. Rules 10.06(3) and 10.06(4) deal with the prohibition on acting for more than one prospective buyer, or for seller and buyer where there is more than one prospective buyer. These provisions recognise the inevitable conflict of interests which makes it impossible to act for more than one prospective buyer, or for the seller and one of several prospective buyers. If you were already acting for seller and buyer (for example, both are established clients), you would be unable to continue acting for both if another prospective buyer were introduced during the course of the transaction. There is a significant inherent conflict in these circumstances. It would be impossible, for example, to reconcile the interests of both clients if it were in the seller's best interests to exchange with the other prospective buyer.

74. The test of whether a person is an "established client" is an objective one – is it reasonable to regard the person as an established client? A seller or buyer who instructs you for the first time is not an established client. A former client is not necessarily the same as an established client. There needs to be a degree of permanence in the solicitor–client relationship as exemplified by some continuity of instruction over time and the likelihood of future instruction. An individual related by blood, adoption or marriage to an established client, or who is living with an established client, counts as an established client. A person also counts as an established client if selling or buying jointly with an established client.

75. The consideration will only count as £10,000 or less if the value of any property given in exchange or part exchange is taken into account.

76. A builder or developer who acquires a property in part exchange, and sells it on without development, is not selling "as a builder or developer" within the meaning of 3.10(c) and 3.13(c).

77. If acting for seller and buyer under the provisions of 3.07 to 3.15, you would have to stop acting for at least one of the clients if a conflict were to arise during the course of the transaction. Clients should be made aware of the consequent disruption and additional expense involved in such

circumstances, and of the advantages of separate representation, before giving their written consent.

78. An RFL cannot undertake conveyancing. RELs may undertake conveyancing only if they are entitled to do so under regulation 12 of the European Communities (Lawyer's Practice) Regulations 2000 (SI 2000/1119).

3

79. The effect of 3.11 is as follows:

   (a) if providing mortgage related services to the buyer (either through your own firm or a SEAL – see 3.12 for the definition of a SEAL which allows participating authorised non-SRA firms but requires at least one participating firm to be a recognised body or recognised sole practitioner), you may also provide property selling services to the seller (either through your own firm or a SEAL) and do the seller's conveyancing; and

   (b) if providing property selling services to the seller through a SEAL (not your own firm), you may also provide mortgage related services to the buyer (either through your own firm or the SEAL) and do the buyer's conveyancing.

80. A SEAL may act for the seller and provide mortgage related services to the buyer; one of the participating firms may do the seller's conveyancing, and another participating firm may do the buyer's conveyancing.

Acting for lender and borrower in conveyancing transactions

81. There will be no breach of 3.16(2)(c) to (d) or 3.19 if the lender has certified that its mortgage instructions and documents sent pursuant to those instructions are subject to the limitations set out in 3.19 and 3.21, and certifies any subsequent instructions and documents in the same way. If there is no certification, when acting in a transaction involving the charge of property to be used solely as the borrower's private residence you must notify the lender that the approved certificate of title will be used and that your duties to the lender will be limited accordingly (see 3.20(b)). In other types of transaction, you should draw the lender's attention to the provisions of 3.19 and 3.21 and state that you cannot act on any instructions which extend beyond the matters contained in 3.19.

82. As an alternative to printing the approved certificate for each transaction, it is acceptable for a lender to use a short form certificate of title which incorporates the approved certificate by reference. The form must include, in the following order:

   (a) the title "Certificate of Title";

   (b) the contents of the details box in the order set out in the approved certificate (use of two columns is acceptable) but with details not required shaded out or stated not to be required; and

(c)   the wording "We, the conveyancers named above, give the Certificate of Title set out in the annex to rule 3 of the Solicitors' Code of Conduct 2007 as if the same were set out in full, subject to the limitations contained in it."

Administrative details, such as a request for cheque, may follow the Certificate of Title.

83. The approved certificate is only required for a transaction where the property is to be used solely as the borrower's private residence. The approved certificate need not, therefore, be used for investment properties such as blocks of flats, business premises such as shops (even if living accommodation is attached), or "buy to let mortgages" on properties which are not intended for owner-occupation.

84. You must inform the lender of the circumstances, in accordance with 3.18, so that the lender can decide whether or not to instruct you.

85. A lender's instructions (see 3.19(x)) may require a wider disclosure of your circumstances than 3.18 requires; and you must assess whether the circumstances give rise to a conflict. For example, there will be a conflict between lender and borrower if you become involved in negotiations relating to the terms of the loan. A conflict might arise from the relationship you have or your firm has with the borrower – for example, if you are, or your firm is, the borrower's creditor or debtor or the borrower's business associate or co-habitant.

86. In relation to 3.22(2), the limitations contained in 3.19 will not apply to the insertion into a recognised certificate of any information required by that certificate. For example, where the recognised certificate requires details of the parties' repairing obligations under a lease of the property, you may provide a summary of the relevant terms of the lease despite the general limitation contained in 3.19(i). However, any additions or amendments to the text of a recognised certificate to suit a particular transaction must not, to the extent to which they create an increased or additional obligation, extend beyond the limitations contained in 3.19.

87. Many lenders require their lawyer or licensed conveyancer to check the vires of corporate borrowers and that the correct procedures have been followed to ensure the validity of the mortgage. Rule 3.19(n) enables lenders to impose duties on their lawyer or licensed conveyancer in relation to the execution of the mortgage and guarantee. Within this context it is perfectly proper for a lender to require you to obtain such information as the circumstances may require in relation to the capacity of, or execution of documents by, the borrower, third party mortgagor or guarantor; for instance, by way of certified copy minutes or an opinion from a lawyer of

the relevant jurisdiction as to the validity and enforceability of the security or guarantee given by a foreign registered company. There is no reason why you should not assist corporate clients by drafting minutes or board resolutions. You should not, however, certify the validity or passing of resolutions unless you were present at the meeting and have verified that it was convened and held strictly in accordance with all relevant requirements.

3

88. Rule 3.19(u) allows you to accept instructions from a lender to carry out administrative arrangements in relation to any collateral security. This expression includes associated debentures, collateral warranties, second charges, rent assignments, charges over rent income and deeds of priority. The administrative arrangements necessarily include the preparation and execution of the relevant documents and subsequent registration.

Rule 4   Confidentiality and disclosure

Introduction

Rule 4 sets out provisions for dealing with the protection of clients' confidential information and the duty of disclosure owed to clients.

Rule 4 – Confidentiality and disclosure

4.01   Duty of confidentiality

You and your firm must keep the affairs of clients and former clients confidential except where disclosure is required or permitted by law or by your client (or former client).

4.02   Duty of disclosure

If you are a lawyer or other fee earner you must disclose to a client for whom you are personally acting on a matter, whether individually or as one of a group, or whose matter you are personally supervising, all information of which you are aware which is material to that client's matter regardless of the source of the information, subject to:

(a)   the duty of confidentiality in 4.01 above, which always overrides the duty to disclose; and

(b)   the following where the duty does not apply:

   (i)   where such disclosure is prohibited by law;

   (ii)   where it is agreed expressly that no duty to disclose arises or a different standard of disclosure applies; or

   (iii)   where you reasonably believe that serious physical or mental injury will be caused to any person if the information is disclosed to a client.

4.03   Duty not to put confidentiality at risk by acting

If you are a lawyer or other fee earner and you personally hold, or your firm holds, confidential information in relation to a client or former client, you must not risk breaching confidentiality by acting, or continuing to act, for another client on a matter where:

(a)   that information might reasonably be expected to be material; and

(b)   that client has an interest adverse to the first-mentioned client or former client, except where proper arrangements can be made to protect that information in accordance with 4.04 and 4.05 below.

4.04   Exception to duty not to put confidentiality at risk by acting – with clients' consent

(1) You may act, or continue to act, in the circumstances otherwise prohibited by 4.03 above with the informed consent of both clients but only if:

    (a)   the client for whom you act or are proposing to act knows that your firm, or a lawyer or other fee earner of your firm, holds, or might hold, material information (in circumstances described in 4.03) in relation to their matter which you cannot disclose;

    (b)   you have a reasonable belief that both clients understand the relevant issues after these have been brought to their attention;

    (c)   both clients have agreed to the conditions under which you will be acting or continuing to act; and

    (d)   it is reasonable in all the circumstances to do so.

(2) "Both clients" in the context of 4.04(1) means:

    (a)   an existing or former client for whom your firm, or a lawyer or other fee earner of your firm, holds confidential information; and

    (b)   an existing or new client for whom you act or are proposing to act and to whom information held on behalf of the other client is material (in circumstances described in 4.03 above).

(3) If you, or you and your firm, have been acting for two or more clients in compliance with rule 3 (Conflict of interests) and can no longer fulfil its requirements you may continue to act for one client with the consent of the other client provided you comply with 4.04.

4.05   Exception to duty not to put confidentiality at risk by acting – without clients' consent

You may continue to act for a client on an existing matter, or on a matter related to an existing matter, in the circumstances otherwise prohibited by 4.03 above without the consent of the client for whom your firm, or a lawyer or other fee earner of your firm, holds, or might hold, confidential information which is material to your client (in circumstances described in 4.03) but only if:

    (a)   it is not possible to obtain informed consent under 4.04 above from the client for whom your firm, or a lawyer or other fee earner of your firm, holds, or might hold, material confidential information;

    (b)   your client has agreed to your acting in the knowledge that your firm, or a lawyer or other fee earner of your firm, holds, or might hold, information material to their matter which you cannot disclose;

(c)   any safeguards which comply with the standards required by law at the time they are implemented are put in place; and

(d)   it is reasonable in all the circumstances to do so.

4.06   Waivers

In spite of 22.01(1) (Waivers), the Solicitors Regulation Authority Board shall not have power to waive any of the provisions of this rule.

Guidance to rule 4 – Confidentiality and disclosure

4

Introduction

1.   This rule draws together, and describes the interaction of, the obligations created by the duties of confidentiality and disclosure. It also reinforces the common law duty whereby you and your firm must not put confidential information obtained from one client or former client at risk by acting adverse to the interests of that client or former client in a matter where the confidential information would be material. The rule also establishes that where a conflict between these duties arises the duty of confidentiality is paramount. The rule does recognise that confidential information can be protected by the use of information barriers with the consent of the client and, in very limited circumstances, without that consent.

2.   The rule should be read in conjunction with rule 3 (Conflict of interests) as there are important cross-references contained in both the rules and the guidance.

The duty of confidentiality – 4.01 – general

3.   Rule 4.01 sets out your fundamental duty to keep all clients' affairs confidential. It is important to bear in mind the distinction between this duty and the concept of law known as legal professional privilege. The duty of confidentiality extends to all confidential information about a client's affairs, irrespective of the source of the information, subject to the limited exceptions described below. Legal professional privilege protects certain communications between you and your client from being disclosed, even in court. However, not all communications are protected from disclosure and you should, if necessary, refer to an appropriate authority on the law of evidence.

4.   The duty of confidentiality continues after the end of the retainer. After the client dies the right to confidentiality passes to the personal representatives, but note that an administrator's power dates only from the grant of the letters of administration.

5. Information received in the context of a joint retainer must be available between the clients. They must, however, all consent to any confidential information being disclosed to a third party. Information communicated to you when acting for one of the clients in relation to a separate matter must not be disclosed to the other client(s) without the consent of that client.

6. If you obtain information in relation to a prospective client you may still be bound by a duty of confidentiality, even if that prospective client does not subsequently instruct your firm. There may be circumstances, however, where you receive information where there is no real or genuine interest in instructing your firm and that information is unlikely to be confidential.

Insolvency

7. If a client becomes insolvent you will need to consider to whom you owe a duty of confidentiality. To some extent this will depend on whether your client is a company or an individual and you will need to refer to the relevant statutory authority, such as the Insolvency Act 1986. Where a statutory power overrides confidentiality you should consider carefully to what extent it is overridden. It may, for example, require you to disclose only certain categories of information or documents. You should ensure that any disclosure you make is strictly limited to what is required by the law.

Specific instances where confidentiality is required

8. (a) You must not disclose the contents of a will, even after the death of the testator, other than to, or with the consent of, the executor(s), until probate has been obtained.

    (b) You must not disclose the address of a client without the client's consent.

    (c) Where a lender asks for a conveyancing file and you have kept a joint file for both borrower and lender clients, you cannot, without the consent of the borrower, send the whole file to the lender, unless the lender can show to your satisfaction that there is a prima facie case of fraud. If the client does not consent, you should send only those parts of the file which relate to work done for the lender.

    (d) You cannot, without the consent of the relevant client (or, if applicable, its administrator or similar officeholder), sell book debts to a factoring company because of the confidential nature of your bill. If your firm grants, as security to a lender, a charge over your firm's book debts, you need to ensure that you protect clients' confidential information should the lender need to enforce the security. Further advice on this issue can be obtained from the Professional Ethics Guidance Team.

(e) You should only share office services with other businesses if confidentiality can be ensured.

(f) If you outsource services such as word processing, telephone call handling or photocopying you must be satisfied that the provider of those services is able to ensure the confidentiality of any information concerning your clients. This would normally require confidentiality undertakings from the provider and checks to ensure that the terms of the arrangements regarding confidentiality are being complied with. Whilst you might have implied consent to confidential information being passed to external service providers, it would be prudent to inform clients of any such services you propose to use in your terms of business or client care letters.

4

Disclosure of confidential information in exceptional circumstances

9. Despite your duty of confidentiality you may be required to disclose confidential information in certain circumstances. A number of statutes empower government and other bodies, for example HM Revenue and Customs, to require any person to disclose documents and/or information. In the absence of the client's specific consent, you should ask under which statutory power the information is sought, consider the relevant provisions and consider whether privileged information is protected from disclosure. You should only provide such information as you are strictly required by law to disclose.

10. There are reporting requirements in relation to money laundering which override the duty of confidentiality and these are set out in the Proceeds of Crime Act 2002, the terrorism legislation and the Money Laundering Regulations 2007. These often require difficult judgements to be made as to whether or not a situation has arisen which would require you to report information to the relevant authorities. You should, however, always be mindful of the importance of your duty of confidentiality to your client. If you are uncertain as to whether you should report confidential information you should consider seeking legal advice or contact the Professional Ethics Guidance Team for advice.

11. The Freedom of Information Act 2000 applies to the majority of public bodies and to local authorities. This Act establishes a right to know the content of records held by certain public bodies subject to certain exemptions such as legal professional privilege. The legal professional privilege exemption is conditional and can only be relied upon where the public interest in maintaining the exemption outweighs the public interest in disclosing the information. In some cases, disclosure of matters which are on legal files may be required by law under the Act. The Information Commissioner's website provides Awareness Guidance upon this area of the Act.

12. You may reveal confidential information to the extent that you believe necessary to prevent the client or a third party committing a criminal act that you reasonably believe is likely to result in serious bodily harm.

13. There may be exceptional circumstances involving children where you should consider revealing confidential information to an appropriate authority. This may be where the child is the client and the child reveals information which indicates continuing sexual or other physical abuse but refuses to allow disclosure of such information. Similarly, there may be situations where an adult discloses abuse either by himself or herself or by another adult against a child but refuses to allow any disclosure. You must consider whether the threat to the child's life or health, both mental and physical, is sufficiently serious to justify a breach of the duty of confidentiality.

14. In proceedings under the Children Act 1989 you are under a duty to reveal experts' reports commissioned for the purposes of proceedings, as these reports are not privileged. The position in relation to voluntary disclosure of other documents or solicitor–client communications is uncertain. Under 11.01, an advocate is under a duty not to mislead the court. Therefore, if you are an advocate, and have certain knowledge which you realise is adverse to the client's case, you may be extremely limited in what you can state in the client's favour. In this situation, you should seek the client's agreement for full voluntary disclosure, for three reasons:

(a)   the matters the client wants to hide will probably emerge anyway;

(b)   you will be able to do a better job for the client if all the relevant information is presented to the court; and

(c)   if the information is not voluntarily disclosed, you may be severely criticised by the court.

If the client refuses to give you authority to disclose the relevant information, you are entitled to refuse to continue to act for the client if to do so will place you in breach of your obligations to the court.

15. You should reveal matters which are otherwise subject to the duty to preserve confidentiality where a court orders that such matters are to be disclosed or where a warrant permits a police officer or other authority to seize confidential documents. If you believe that the documents are subject to legal privilege or that for some other reason the order or warrant ought not to have been made or issued, you should normally, without unlawfully obstructing its execution, discuss with the client the possibility of making an application to have the order or warrant set aside. Advice may be obtained from the Professional Ethics Guidance Team.

16. Occasionally you may be asked by the police or a third party to give information or to show them documents which you have obtained when

acting for a client. Unless the client is prepared to waive confidentiality, or where you have strong prima facie evidence that you have been used by the client to perpetrate a fraud or other crime and the duty of confidence does not arise, you should insist upon receiving a witness summons or subpoena so that, where appropriate, privilege may be claimed and the court asked to decide the issue. If the request is made by the police under the Police and Criminal Evidence Act 1984 you should, where appropriate, leave the question of privilege to the court to decide on the particular circumstances. Advice may be obtained from the Professional Ethics Guidance Team.

4

17. Certain communications from a client are not confidential if they are a matter of public record. For example, the fact that you have been instructed by a named client in connection with contentious business for which that client's name is on the public record is not confidential, but the type of business involved will usually be confidential.

18. You may reveal confidential information concerning a client to the extent that it is reasonably necessary to establish a defence to a criminal charge or civil claim by your client against you, or where your conduct is under investigation by the SRA, or under consideration by the Solicitors Disciplinary Tribunal.

19. In the case of a publicly funded client, you may be under a duty to report to the Legal Services Commission information concerning the client which is confidential and privileged.

Duty to disclose information to a client – 4.02

20. You have a duty to disclose all information material to your client's matter. Your duty is limited to information of which you are aware (and does not extend to information of which others in your firm may be aware) but is not limited to information obtained while acting on the client's matter. You will not be liable, therefore, for failing to disclose material information held by others within your firm of which you were unaware. There are, however, some circumstances where you should not disclose material information because it is not in the best interests of your client to do so or because disclosure is prohibited by law. These include situations where:

   (a) disclosure may be harmful to the client because of the client's physical or mental condition;

   (b) the provisions in the money laundering legislation effectively prohibit you from passing information to clients;

   (c) it is obvious that privileged documents have been mistakenly disclosed to you; or *must send back then turn a blind eye!!*

   (d) you come into possession of information relating to state security or intelligence matters to which the Official Secrets Act 1989 applies.

21. Rule 4.02 also prevents you from disclosing information where this would breach your firm's duty of confidentiality to another client. The duty of confidentiality will always override the duty of disclosure.

22. You cannot, however, excuse a failure to disclose material information because to do so would breach a separate duty of confidentiality. Unless the retainer with the client to which the information cannot be disclosed can be varied so that the inability to disclose is not a breach of duty (see note 25 below), you should refuse the instructions or, if already acting, immediately cease to act for that client. Any delay in ceasing to act is likely to increase the risk that you are liable for breach of duty.

23. You should not seek to pass the client to a colleague (who would not be bound by the same duty because he or she is personally unaware of the material information) unless the client agrees to this, knowing the reason for the transfer and, if you have already started to act for the client, agreeing that you are released from your duty to disclose up to the time when you personally cease to act for the client on that matter. Further, you should consider carefully whether, even if these conditions are satisfied, it is appropriate for any members of your firm to act. A firm which holds information which it cannot convey to a client but which, if known to that client, might affect the instructions to the firm in a material way will usually be in an invidious position and quite possibly unable to act in the best interests of the client – see rule 3 (Conflict of interests). See also note 15 of the guidance to rule 3.

24. The rule does not define "information which is material to that client's matter" but it must be information which is relevant to the specific retainer with the client and not just information which might be of general interest to the client. The information must also be more than of inconsequential interest to the client. It must, therefore, be information which might reasonably be expected to affect the client's decision making with regard to their matter in a way which is significant having regard to the matter as a whole.

25. The duty outlined above reflects and builds on the fiduciary duty which exists at common law. As 4.02(b)(ii) makes clear, however, you or your firm can expressly agree a different degree of duty. For example, a client might wish to instruct you because it knows that you act for other entities which operate in the same market and because it knows that you, therefore, understand the market. The client would not be surprised that you hold material market intelligence of a confidential nature from such other clients, and would not expect you to divulge it. The client might, therefore, agree that the usual duty to disclose would not apply.

Duties of confidentiality and disclosure conflicting – 4.03

26. Rule 4.03 sets out the duty not to put confidentiality at risk by acting for a client where to do so might put at risk the confidential information held by your firm for another client (or former client). The rule makes clear that the relevant circumstances of risk arise where:

    (a) the confidential information "might reasonably be expected to be material" to the client for whom you wish to act; and

    (b) the work for the client for whom you wish to act would be adverse to the interests of the client or former client to whom the duty of confidentiality is owed.

    The effect of note 26(b) is that you can act if the confidential information your firm holds is not reasonably expected to be material to your new client or is reasonably expected to be material to your new client but the interests of the clients are not adverse. The confidential information would, however, have to be protected and you and your firm would be answerable in law and conduct if it leaked.

27. The rule does not define adverse interest, but the intention is to mirror what is considered adverse for these purposes at common law (see *Bolkiah v KPMG* [1998] UKHL 52; [1999] 2 AC 222; [1999] 1 All ER 517; [1999] 2 WLR 215 and subsequent cases). Essentially, adversity arises where one party is, or is likely to become, the opposing party on a matter, whether in negotiations or some form of dispute resolution. For example, if your firm acted for a client in a criminal case in which the client was convicted of assault and the client's wife, unaware of the conviction, then wished you to represent her in divorce proceedings you would have to refuse the instructions. The confidential information held about the husband would be material to her case and, if so, her interests would be adverse to his.

28. In contrast, action which seeks to improve the new client's commercial position as against others generally within a particular sector would not be "adverse" to the interests of another client which is one such competitor. This should be the case even if there might be some risk that such a market competitor might seek to challenge the activities of the client before, for example, the competition authorities.

29. There may, however, be some circumstances where you are permitted to act under 4.03 but where other considerations will prevent you from doing so. It might be that you personally have confidential information from another client/former client which would be material to the new instruction but, since the instruction would not be adverse to the other client/former client, 4.03 does not bite. In this situation, the duty of confidentiality conflicts with your personal duty to disclose, and you should therefore not act, unless the new client has expressly agreed a lesser duty of disclosure (4.02(b)(ii)).

30. You may act, or continue to act, despite the prohibition in 4.03 if the confidential information can be protected through the use of appropriate safeguards in the circumstances set out in 4.04 and 4.05, and as more fully explained in the following guidance notes.

Acting with appropriate safeguards (information barriers) – 4.04 and 4.05

31. Rule 4.03 sets the basic standard that you should not normally act on a matter where material confidential information is held elsewhere in the firm and where the matter would be adverse to the interests of the client/former client to whom the duty of confidentiality is owed. To act in these circumstances might increase the risk that the confidential information could be put at risk. The firm can act if the confidential information is not material to the instructions. For guidance on the meaning of "material" see note 24 above.

32. Rules 4.04 and 4.05 set out two situations where you can act even when material confidential information is held by another member of the firm. Both recognise ~~for the first time~~ that it can be acceptable to use information barriers. The first situation is where the party to whom the duty of confidentiality is owed consents. The second situation is where ~~you are already acting and~~ consent has not been given or cannot be sought.

33. Where the client consents as envisaged by 4.04 there is scope for more flexibility in the arrangements for the information barrier as the safeguards can be discussed with, and agreed by, the client. It is important, nonetheless, that the safeguards are effective to avoid a real risk of disclosure. A firm will be liable if confidential information does leak in breach of that agreement.

34. Rule 4.04 requires "informed consent" and one of the difficulties with seeking such consent of the client is that it is often not possible to disclose sufficient information about the identity and business of the other client without risk of breaching that other client's confidentiality. You will have to decide in each case whether you are able to provide sufficient information for the client to be able to give "informed consent". Every situation will be different but generally it will be only sophisticated clients, for example, a corporate body with in-house legal advisers or other appropriate expertise, who will have the expertise and ability to weigh up the issues and the risks of giving consent on the basis of the information they have been given. If there is a risk of prejudicing the position of either client then consent should not be sought and you and your firm should not act. It may, however, be possible to give sufficient information to obtain informed consent even if the identity of the other client(s) and the nature of their particular interest(s) are not disclosed. Wherever possible you should try to ensure that the clients are advised of the potential risks arising from your firm acting before seeking their consent.

4

35. In the case of sophisticated clients (such as those referred to in note 34 above) only, it may be possible to seek consent to act in certain situations at the start of and as a condition of your retainer and to do so through standard terms of engagement. For example, a sophisticated client may give its consent in this way for a firm to act for a future bidder for that client if, when the bidder asks the firm to act, a common law compliant information barrier is put in place to protect any of the client's confidential information which is held by the firm and which would be material to a bidder.

36. Where the client does not consent or does not know about the arrangements, an extremely high standard in relation to the protection of confidential information must be satisfied. In this situation, as has been demonstrated in recent case law, the client can have the firm removed from acting with all the attendant disruption for the other client, if there is shown to be a real risk of confidential information being leaked. *act*

37. Where your firm holds material confidential information you may ~~not without consent take on new instructions adverse to the interests of the client or former client to whom the duty of confidentiality is owed (4.04). However, where you are already acting and discover that your firm has – or comes to possess – such information, you may continue to act on that matter, or a related matter,~~ in circumstances where the party to whom the duty of confidentiality is owed refuses consent or cannot be asked (4.05). This may be because it cannot be contacted or because making the request would itself breach confidentiality. You should always seek consent when you can reasonably do so.

38. Where under 4.04 your firm has erected an information barrier without the consent of the party to whom the duty of confidentiality is owed, the firm should try to inform that party as soon as circumstances permit, and outline the steps which have been taken to ensure confidentiality is preserved. If some material points (such as the name of the client to whose matter the confidential information might be relevant, or the nature of that matter) still cannot be divulged for reasons of confidentiality and it is reasonably supposed that that party would be more concerned at news of your retention than if fuller details could be given, it might be appropriate to continue to wait before informing that party. There may be circumstances, however, where it is impossible to inform that party.

39. Where two or more firms amalgamate, or one firm takes over another, the new firm needs to ensure that this does not result in any breach of confidentiality. If the firm holds confidential information that is material to a matter being handled for another client, the firm must be able to ensure that the confidential information is protected by ceasing to act for both clients, or ceasing to act for the client to whom the information is relevant, or by setting up adequate safeguards in accordance with either 4.04 or 4.05.

40. Confidential information may also be put at risk when partners or staff leave one firm and join another. This might happen where, for example, an individual joins a firm which is acting against one of the individual's former clients. An individual joining a new firm could not act personally for a client of the new firm where to do so would put at risk confidential information which he or she personally possesses about a client of the previous firm. In addition, the individual and the firm which the individual is joining must ensure that adequate safeguards are put in place in accordance with 4.04 or 4.05 to ensure that confidential information held by that individual is safeguarded.

Safeguards for information barriers

41. Rigid safeguards for information barriers have not been enshrined in the rules. Where 4.04 applies (i.e. consent has been given), it is for the firm to agree the appropriate safeguards, but it would normally be necessary to satisfy note 44(a) to (f). Some of note 44(g) to (n) may also be applicable. Where 4.05 applies, the firm must satisfy the requirements of common law and at least most, if not all, of note 44(a) to (n) might be essential.

42. If, at any stage after an information barrier has been established, it becomes impossible to comply with any of the terms, the firm may have to cease to act. The possibility of this happening should always be discussed when instructions are accepted so that the client is aware of this risk, or addressed with reasonable prominence in standard terms of engagement.

43. Firms will always need to consider whether it is appropriate in any case for an information barrier to be used, and also whether the size or structure of a firm means that it could not in any circumstances be appropriate. It is unlikely that, for example, safeguards could ever be considered adequate where:

  (a) a firm has only one principal and no other qualified staff;

  (b) the solicitor possessing, or likely to possess, the confidential information is supervised by a solicitor who acts for, or supervises another solicitor in the firm who acts for a client to whom the information is or may be relevant; or

  (c) the physical structure or layout of the firm is such that confidentiality would be difficult to preserve having regard to other safeguards which are in place.

44. The following note 44(a) to (f) would normally be appropriate to demonstrate the adequacy of an information barrier when you are proposing to act in circumstances set out in 4.04. It might also be appropriate to agree some or all of note 44(a) to (f) where you are acting with consent in accordance with 4.05:

(a)   that the client who or which might be interested in the confidential information acknowledges in writing that the information held by the firm will not be given to them;

(b)   that all members of the firm who hold the relevant confidential information ("the restricted group") are identified and have no involvement with or for the other client;

(c)   that no member of the restricted group is managed or supervised in relation to that matter by someone from outside the restricted group;

(d)   that all members of the restricted group confirm at the start of the engagement that they understand that they possess or might come to possess information which is confidential, and that they must not discuss it with any other member of the firm unless that person is, or becomes, a member of the restricted group, and that this obligation shall be regarded by everyone as an ongoing one;

(e)   that each member of the restricted group confirms when the barrier is established that they have not done anything which would amount to a breach of the information barrier; and

(f)   that only members of the restricted group have access to documents containing the confidential information.

The following arrangements may also be appropriate, and might in particular be necessary where acting in circumstances set out in 4.05:

(g)   that the restricted group is physically separated from those acting for the other client, for example, by being in a separate building, on a separate floor or in a segregated part of the offices, and that some form of "access restriction" be put in place to ensure physical segregation;

(h)   that confidential information on computer systems is protected by use of separate computer networks or through use of password protection or similar means;

(i)   that the firm issues a statement that it will treat any breach, even an inadvertent one, of the information barrier as a serious disciplinary offence;

(j)   that each member of the restricted group gives a written statement at the start of the engagement that they understand the terms of the information barrier and will comply with them;

(k)   that the firm undertakes that it will do nothing which would or might prevent or hinder any member of the restricted group from complying with the information barrier;

(l)   that the firm identifies a specific partner or other appropriate person within the restricted group with overall responsibility for the information barrier;

(m) that the firm provides formal and regular training for members of the firm on duties of confidentiality and responsibility under information barriers or will ensure that such training is provided prior to the work being undertaken; and

(n) that the firm implements a system for the opening of post, receipt of faxes and distribution of e-mail which will ensure that confidential information is not disclosed to anyone outside the restricted group.

"Member", in the context of this note, applies to principals and all staff members including secretaries, but does not apply to any staff member (not having any involvement on behalf of any relevant client) whose duties include the maintenance of computer systems or conflict/compliance procedures and who is subject to a general obligation of confidentiality in relation to all information to which he or she may have access in the course of his or her duties.

This guidance should not be read as a representation that compliance with note 44(a) to (n) above will necessarily be considered sufficient at common law.

45. Where a firm proposes to erect an information barrier (whether under 4.04 or 4.05) it must first inform the client for whom it acts – or wishes to act – on the matter to which the confidential information might be material. The firm should not act – or continue to act – without that client's consent, with that client understanding that the firm holds information which might be material and which will not be communicated to it; see 4.04(1)(a) and 4.05(b). Although the rule does not require consent to be in writing, it is recommended that this be obtained for evidential purposes to protect both your client's position and your own position.

Rule 5   Business management in England and Wales

Introduction

Rule 5 deals with the supervision and management of a firm or in-house practice, the maintenance of competence, and the internal business arrangements essential to the proper delivery of services to clients. "Supervision" and "management" refer, respectively, to the professional overseeing of staff and clients' matters; and to the overall direction and development of the firm or in-house practice and its day-to-day administration. The rule does not apply to your overseas practice but you must comply with 15.05.

Broadly, the rule aims to set out:

(a) responsibility for the overall supervision and management framework of your firm or in-house practice;

(b) the minimum requirements to be met in order to be "qualified to supervise";

(c) the minimum standards applying to supervision of clients' matters; and

(d) the minimum requirements in relation to those business arrangements considered to be essential to good practice and integral to compliance with supervision and other duties to clients.

Rule 5 – Business management in England and Wales

5.01   Supervision and management responsibilities

(1) If you are a recognised body, a manager of a recognised body or a recognised sole practitioner, you must make arrangements for the effective management of the firm as a whole, and in particular provide for:

(a) compliance by the firm and its managers with the duties of a principal, in law and conduct, to exercise appropriate supervision over all staff, and ensure proper supervision and direction of clients' matters;

(b) compliance with the money laundering regulations, where applicable;

(c) compliance by the firm and individuals with key regulatory requirements such as certification, registration or recognition by the Solicitors Regulation Authority, compulsory professional indemnity cover, delivery of accountants' reports, and obligations to co-operate with and report information to the Authority;

(d) the identification of conflicts of interests;

(e)   compliance with the requirements of rule 2 (Client relations) on client care, costs information and complaints handling;

(f)   control of undertakings;

(g)   the safekeeping of documents and assets entrusted to the firm;

(h)   compliance with rule 6 (Equality and diversity);

(i)   the training of individuals working in the firm to maintain a level of competence appropriate to their work and level of responsibility;

(j)   financial control of budgets, expenditure and cashflow;

(k)   the continuation of the practice of the firm in the event of absences and emergencies, with the minimum interruption to clients' business; and

(l)   the management of risk.

(2)   If you are a solicitor or REL employed as the head of an in-house legal department, you must effect supervision and management arrangements within your department to provide for:

(a)   adequate supervision and direction of those assisting in your in-house practice;

(b)   control of undertakings; and

(c)   identification of conflicts of interests.

5.02   Persons who must be "qualified to supervise"

(1)   The following persons must be "qualified to supervise":

(a)   a recognised sole practitioner;

(b)   one of the lawyer managers of a recognised body or of a body corporate which is a manager of the recognised body;

(c)   one of the solicitors or RELs employed by a law centre; or

(d)   one in-house solicitor or in-house REL in any department where solicitors and/or RELs, as part of that employment:

(i)   do publicly funded work; or

(ii)   do or supervise advocacy or the conduct of proceedings for members of the public before a court or immigration tribunal.

(2)   To be "qualified to supervise" under this paragraph a person:

(a)   must have completed the training specified from time to time by the Solicitors Regulation Authority for this purpose; and

(b)   must have been entitled to practise as a lawyer for at least 36 months within the last ten years; and must be able to demonstrate this if asked by the Solicitors Regulation Authority.

5.03   Supervision of work for clients and members of the public

(1)   If you are a recognised body, a manager of a recognised body or a recognised sole practitioner, you must ensure that your firm has in place a system for supervising clients' matters.

(2)   If you are an in-house solicitor or in-house REL and you are required to be "qualified to supervise" under 5.02(1)(c) or (d) above, you must ensure that your law centre or in-house legal department has in place a system for supervising work undertaken for members of the public.

(3)   The system for supervision under 5.03(1) and (2) must include appropriate and effective procedures under which the quality of work undertaken for clients and members of the public is checked with reasonable regularity by suitably experienced and competent persons within the firm, law centre or in-house legal department.

Guidance to rule 5 – Business management in England and Wales

Geographical scope of the rule

1.   Rule 5 applies only to practice from an office in England and Wales; but if you are a solicitor practising from an office outside England and Wales or an REL practising from an office in Scotland or Northern Ireland, you will need to comply with 15.05 in relation to that practice.

Guidance on 5.01 generally

2.   The term "arrangements" is used broadly in 5.01 to encompass all systems, procedures, processes and methods of organisation put in place to achieve the required outcome. There is no requirement that these take a particular form; the method of delivery is a matter for the firm. Evidence that appropriate arrangements are actually in place and are operating will be required to demonstrate compliance. It is anticipated that most well-run firms will already be complying.

3.   Factors to be taken into account in determining the appropriateness of a set of arrangements will include the size and complexity of the firm; the number, experience and qualifications of staff; and the nature of the work undertaken. Arrangements are unlikely to be considered appropriate unless they include a mechanism for periodic review of their effectiveness.

4.   The overarching responsibility for the management of the firm in the broadest sense – including, for example, practice development and business efficiency – rests with the recognised sole practitioner, or the managers of the recognised body and the recognised body itself.

5.   Firms will be expected to be able to produce evidence of a systematic and effective approach to management, and this may include the implementation by the firm of one or more of the following:

(a)   guidance issued from time to time by the SRA or the Law Society on the supervision and execution of particular types of work;

(b)   the firm's own properly documented standards and procedures;

(c)   the Lexcel standard or other practice management standards promoted from time to time by the Law Society;

(d)   the guidelines for accounting procedures and systems published as Appendix 3 to the Solicitors' Accounts Rules 1998;

(e)   external quality standards such as BS EN ISO 9000, Investors in People, or quality standards required by the Legal Services Commission in connection with undertaking publicly funded work; and

(f)   in the case of an in-house solicitor or in-house REL employed by a law centre, charitable or similar non-commercial advice service, management standards or procedures laid down by its management committee, the Law Centres Federation or equivalent "umbrella" organisation.

6.   The day-to-day management of a firm can be delegated to an employee who is suitably experienced and competent, and a fit and proper person to perform the role. Firms must be able to demonstrate this if required.

7.   Sections 41 to 44 of the Solicitors Act 1974 impose restrictions on the employment or remuneration of certain persons by a solicitor, REL or recognised body:

(a)   Under section 41 of that Act, permission must first be obtained from the SRA by any solicitor, REL or recognised body wishing to employ or remunerate a struck-off or suspended solicitor or REL. You can check with the SRA whether a solicitor or REL has been struck off or suspended.

(b)   Under section 43 of that Act, the Solicitors Disciplinary Tribunal or the SRA can order that a person who is or was involved in a legal practice may not be employed or remunerated in future by any solicitor, REL or recognised body without written permission. Such permission is given or withheld by the SRA. You can check with the SRA whether a section 43 order exists.

Compliance with duties in law and conduct, etc. – 5.01(1)(a)

8.   Principals are responsible in law and in conduct for their firms, including exercising proper control over their staff, and the rule lays these duties, as a

matter of conduct, on a recognised body and its managers and on a recognised sole practitioner. For example, if certain work is to be done by unqualified staff it may only be done at the direction and/or under the supervision of persons who are allowed by law to do that work themselves. (See sections 22(2A) and 23(3) of the Solicitors Act 1974, section 9(4) of the Administration of Justice Act 1985, section 84(2)(e) of the Immigration and Asylum Act 1999 and paragraphs 1(7), 3(3) and 4(2) of Schedule 3 to the Legal Services Act 2007.) Recognised bodies, managers of a recognised body and recognised sole practitioners must therefore ensure that arrangements are in place to satisfy these statutory requirements. This would mean, for example, that conveyancing work could not be supervised by a manager who is:

(a) an RFL, legal executive, patent agent, trade mark agent, law costs draftsman or non-lawyer; or

(b) an REL who is not qualified to do the work under regulation 12 of the European Communities (Lawyer's Practice) Regulations 2000 (SI 2000/1119).

5

9. Under the rule, recognised bodies, managers of a recognised body and recognised sole practitioners are responsible for the acts and omissions of all staff, admitted and unadmitted alike. The duty to supervise staff covers not only persons engaged under a contract of service, but also those engaged under a contract for services to carry out work on behalf of the firm, e.g. consultants, locums and outdoor clerks. You cannot avoid responsibility for work carried out by the firm by leaving it entirely to staff, however well qualified.

10. Responsibility for the overall supervision framework rests with the recognised body and its managers, or the recognised sole practitioner. This includes, for example, matching staff expertise with relevant work so that work is supervised by the most appropriate individuals. More detailed requirements for the day-to-day supervision of work for clients and members of the public are set out in 5.03.

11. Operationally, supervision can be delegated within an established framework of reporting and accountability. However, careful consideration should be given to the issues set out below.

12. If a firm has more than one office, the recognised body and its managers, or the recognised sole practitioner, must be able to demonstrate the adequacy of their arrangements throughout the firm. This includes supervision and management of staff not working from a conventional office – for example, homeworkers, teleworkers, those visiting clients, attending court, at a police station, at a consulting room open only for a few hours a week, or staffing a stand at an exhibition.

13. As a general guide, the lower the ratio of managers to offices and staff, or the greater the number of the offices and staff of a sole practice, the greater will be the onus on the recognised body and its managers, or the recognised sole practitioner, to demonstrate the adequacy of their supervision arrangements. For example, the more staff a recognised sole practitioner employs, the higher the degree of personal involvement he or she may be expected to take in the supervision process, especially if those staff are inexperienced and/or unqualified.

Money laundering – 5.01(1)(b)

14. See the Money Laundering Regulations 2007 (SI 2007/2157) (and any subsequent regulations) and any guidance on compliance issued by the Law Society.

Compliance with key regulatory obligations – 5.01(1)(c)

15. The purpose of 5.01(1)(c) is to foster collective responsibility for the governance of the firm by requiring you to establish arrangements which provide for compliance with key regulatory obligations. These include arrangements to ensure that:

(a) every solicitor in the firm holds a practising certificate (except in the rare case of a solicitor employee who is not required to hold a practising certificate – see 20.02) and that the practising certificate is renewed promptly when required;

(b) every lawyer in the firm who is required to be registered in the UK under the Establishment Directive (see rule 24) and is not registered with another UK regulatory body for lawyers, is registered as an REL and that registration is renewed promptly when required;

(c) every lawyer in the firm who is required under these rules to be an RFL (as a manager or shareowner of the firm) is registered as an RFL and that the registration is renewed promptly when required;

(d) every lawyer manager or shareowner in the firm is eligible under these rules to undertake that role (see rule 14);

(e) every manager in the firm who is entitled to be a manager only by virtue of approval under regulation 3 of the SRA Recognised Bodies Regulations has received such approval;

(f) every body corporate which is a manager or shareowner in the firm is entitled to undertake that role;

(g) if the firm is a partnership or body corporate it has obtained recognition as a recognised body, its recognition is renewed promptly every year when required, and it complies with the requirements of rule 14 (Recognised bodies);

(h)   the firm complies with the Solicitors' Indemnity Insurance Rules;

(i)   an accountant's report is delivered in accordance with the Solicitors' Accounts Rules; and

(j)   the firm notifies the SRA of any change in the place or places of business of the solicitors, RELs and RFLs in the firm (they have a legal obligation to do this, under section 84 of the Solicitors Act 1974).

16. Some of these obligations mirror personal obligations of each solicitor, REL, RFL or recognised body (such as to renew a practising certificate or renew registration). The fact that 5.01(1)(c) is aimed at a recognised body and its managers or a recognised sole practitioner will not relieve an individual solicitor, REL or RFL of responsibility in this regard. The precise nature of the arrangements is for the firm to decide. See 20.02 (Practising certificates).

5

17. If you are a sole practitioner or a manager in a firm then you are personally responsible for complying with the Solicitors' Accounts Rules, including the delivery of an annual accountant's report. You will be liable to disciplinary action if there is a failure to comply with those rules, even if you have delegated book-keeping to someone else in the firm. The nature of the disciplinary action will depend on the seriousness of the breach and the extent to which you knew or should have known of the breach. Similarly, in the case of a partnership or body corporate, the recognised body itself is directly responsible for complying with the Solicitors' Accounts Rules, including delivering an accountant's report, and is itself liable to disciplinary action.

18. If you are an in-house solicitor or in-house REL and you receive or hold client money you must comply with the Solicitors' Accounts Rules and must submit an accountant's report.

Identification of conflicts – 5.01(1)(d)

19. Firms must adopt a systematic approach to identifying and avoiding conflicts of interests, dealing with conflicts between the duties of confidentiality and disclosure, and maintaining client confidentiality. See also the guidance to rule 3 (Conflict of interests) and to rule 4 (Confidentiality and disclosure) for assistance in identifying the sort of issues your arrangements will need to address.

Compliance with the requirements of rule 2 on client care, costs information and complaints handling – 5.01(1)(e)

20. This provision is designed to ensure that compliance with 2.02, 2.03 and 2.05 is addressed at the level of the firm's systems and procedures. If you have appropriate arrangements for compliance but a member of staff fails to follow established procedures in a one-off case, you will nevertheless

have satisfied 5.01(1)(e). However, a serious breach or repeated "minor" breaches of 2.02, 2.03 or 2.05 might indicate a failure to put in place effective arrangements, as required under 5.01(1)(e).

Control of undertakings – 5.01(1)(f)

21. See 10.05 (Undertakings) and the guidance to it for assistance in identifying the sort of issues your arrangements will need to address.

Safekeeping of documents and assets – 5.01(1)(g)

22. The terms "documents" and "assets" should be interpreted in a non-technical way to include, for example, client money, wills, deeds, investments and other property entrusted to the firm by clients and others.

23. The detail of the firm's arrangements will be a matter for you to decide in all the circumstances. However, as a minimum requirement you must be able to identify to whom documents and assets belong, and in connection with which matter.

Equality and diversity – 5.01(1)(h)

24. For guidance on equality and diversity and avoiding discrimination, see the guidance to rule 6 (Equality and diversity).

The training of individuals working in the firm to maintain a level of competence appropriate to their work and level of responsibility – 5.01(1)(i)

25. "Competence" is the ability to perform a task or role to a required standard by the application of essential knowledge, skill and understanding. The purpose of 5.01(1)(i) is to ensure that the competence of everyone in the firm involved in the provision of legal services is addressed systematically, at management level. Consequently, 5.01(1)(i) focuses on effecting arrangements to "provide for" competence levels to be maintained, and leaves it to the firm to determine the best method of doing this. It is anticipated that most firms will already have such arrangements in place.

26. The nature of the arrangements will vary significantly depending on the work and level of responsibility of each individual. However, if a breach of 5.01(1)(i) is alleged, evidence may be required to demonstrate that issues of competence are addressed in the firm's procedures in relation to, for example, recruitment, ongoing work assessment and training.

Firms will also need to consider which staff might need training in some or all of the rules of conduct. The rules apply to employees (see rule 23), but the impact will vary depending on the nature of the work and the responsibility of the employee concerned. All employees will need to be aware of the need to keep clients' matters confidential.

27. Training is an integral element of maintaining competence. Rule 5.01(1)(i) assumes that arrangements will include provision for training, but does not lay down any specific requirements. Training can be of any kind relevant to the work or responsibilities of the individual, and can be delivered by any appropriate method. For example, it could include on-the-job learning, mentoring schemes, in-house training, individual study, etc. It need not be accredited under the compulsory continuing professional development scheme (CPD) or involve attendance at courses.

28. Rule 5.01(1)(i) does not relieve an individual of the duty to decline to act when unable to provide a competent service, or allow an individual to escape obligations under the CPD scheme.

29. Rule 5.01(1)(i) is limited to effecting suitable arrangements. Therefore, an isolated case of incompetence would not normally indicate a breach. However, if you do not address issues of competence systematically, at management level, in your firm's arrangements for recruitment, ongoing work assessment and training, you would breach 5.01(1)(i).

30. It should be noted that training for the purpose of becoming "qualified to supervise" under 5.02 must be of a kind specified by the SRA from time to time (see note 44 below).

Financial control of budgets, expenditure and cashflow – 5.01(1)(j)

31. Client money is more likely to be at risk in a firm where the recognised body and its managers, or the recognised sole practitioner, do not exercise adequate oversight of the firm's own financial arrangements. The purpose of 5.01(1)(j) is to ensure this is addressed in the overall management framework – not to prescribe particular financial systems or to prevent you from delegating day-to-day financial operations to suitable staff. It may also help firms to ensure that they are looking forward when undertaking their financial management, so that they will know they will be able to cover their commitments and plan their resources properly. It should be noted, however, that some accounting and management information systems do not assist in this regard, as they tend to deal only with historic information.

Continuation of the practice of the firm in the event of absences and emergencies, etc. – 5.01(1)(k)

32. There is a continuing duty to ensure that the practice of your firm will be carried on with the minimum interruption to clients' business even if you are absent. Your supervision and management arrangements must therefore provide for the running of the firm during any period of absence (for example, holiday or sick leave). The arrangements must ensure that any duties to clients and others can be fully met. If you are a sole practitioner or sole director you should make adequate provision for the running of the

practice, in the event that you die or become permanently disabled, by a solicitor (or REL) who is "qualified to supervise".

33. If you are away for a month or more, and you are the only person in the firm "qualified to supervise" under 5.02, the arrangements for complying with 5.01(1)(k) will normally need to include the provision of another person qualified to supervise.

34. Rule 23 of the Solicitors' Accounts Rules requires that a withdrawal from a client account cannot be made without a specific authority. This rule cannot be complied with if blank cheques are left for completion by staff at a later date, as signing a blank cheque is not giving a specific authority.

35. If you have not made adequate arrangements in advance to meet unforeseen circumstances, difficulties may arise in the conduct of clients' affairs and in the administration of your own business. For example, a client may attend the office asking for urgent assistance, an accountant's report must be submitted, a practising certificate must be applied for or indemnity cover must be obtained notwithstanding your absence. Consequently, if you are a sole practitioner or sole director, you should have an arrangement with another solicitor or REL (sufficiently experienced and entitled to practise) to supervise your firm until you return. You should notify your bank of these arrangements in advance, so that the solicitor or REL covering your absence can operate your client and office accounts.

36. If you are a sole practitioner and your absence lasts beyond the period covered by your practising certificate, you may be able to obtain permission from the SRA for another solicitor to complete your application for a practising certificate. Your name can only remain on your professional stationery as sole practitioner if you continue to hold a practising certificate.

37. If you are a sole practitioner and you are struck off or suspended, you must inform clients of the firm, your bank, insurers, and the SRA, and clients will need to be told how their matter will be affected. You will not be able to continue to practise. This means that, from the date of the striking off or suspension (at least until, for example, the suspension is lifted), your firm will need to be closed or otherwise disposed of, e.g. by being taken over by another solicitor or REL. It is not sufficient for another solicitor or REL to take over day-to-day management of the practice whilst you are suspended or struck off if you remain the proprietor of the firm because you will not be entitled to be a recognised sole practitioner. If the firm is taken over by another firm you cannot be employed or remunerated by that firm whilst suspended or struck off except with written permission from the SRA (see section 41 of the Solicitors Act 1974). Care will need to be taken in any correspondence relating to your former practice to ensure that your status is not misrepresented. For instance, if you are suspended you are a non-practising solicitor. If you are struck off you are no longer a solicitor.

38. If you are a sole practitioner and you decide to stop practising, you must inform clients so that they may instruct another firm. Failure to inform clients could amount to misconduct, inadequate professional service and/or negligence. If you are considering retirement, guidance can be obtained from the Professional Ethics Guidance Team.

Management of risk – 5.01(1)(l)

39. Firms should have arrangements in place for assessing the risks attaching to each area of their operation. The rule is aimed at ensuring risk is addressed in the firm's overall management framework. If a particular risk materialises which had not been foreseen in the firm's systems, this would not necessarily constitute a breach of 5.01(1)(l). Risk management arrangements are unlikely to be considered adequate unless they include periodic reviews of the firm's risk profile.

5

40. Ideally the scope of the arrangements should not be confined to risks arising from professional negligence, but should extend to client-related and business-related risks of all sorts. A non-exhaustive list might include complaints (including a complaints log); client-related credit risks and exposure; claims under legislation relating to such matters as data protection; IT failures and abuses; and damage to offices.

In-house practice – 5.01(2)

41. As the head of an in-house legal department you do not have to institute all the arrangements required under 5.01(1). However, you must under 5.01(2) institute arrangements to ensure that:

   (a) work done for members of the public is adequately supervised, and if unqualified staff within the department undertake work reserved to solicitors, they are supervised by a person qualified to do that work, and the work is done in the name of that qualified person;

   (b) undertakings given by members of the department, whether or not they are solicitors or RELs, are given appropriately and can be fulfilled (you will be primarily responsible in conduct for fulfilling such undertakings); and

   (c) conflicts of interests are identified.

Qualified to supervise – 5.02

42. The purpose of 5.02 is to protect the public by ensuring that there is at least one person responsible for running the firm (or law centre or in-house legal practice falling within 5.02(1)(c) or (d)) who has the right kind of experience. The responsibilities involved relate to the management of the firm rather than the supervision of particular work, so the person "qualified to supervise" under 5.02 does not have to be personally entitled

by law to supervise all work undertaken by the firm. However, an important part of that person's responsibilities would be to ensure that unqualified persons did not undertake reserved work except under the supervision of a suitably qualified person – see note 8 above.

43. Waivers may be granted in individual cases. An applicant must satisfy the SRA that the circumstances are sufficiently exceptional to justify a departure from the requirements of 5.02, bearing in mind its purpose. Applications should be made to the Professional Ethics Guidance Team.

44. The training presently specified by the SRA is attendance at or participation in any course(s), or programme(s) of learning, on management skills involving attendance or participation for a minimum of 12 hours. The courses or programmes do not have to be CPD accredited in order to satisfy the requirement. It is not normally necessary to check with the SRA before undertaking a course or programme unless the course is unusual and outside the mainstream of management training. Advice may be sought from the Professional Ethics Guidance Team.

Supervision of work for clients and members of the public – 5.03

45. Rule 5.03 is aimed firstly at a recognised body and its managers, or a recognised sole practitioner. Secondly, it applies to you if you are an in-house solicitor or in-house REL who acts for members of the public and fulfils the role of the person "qualified to supervise" under 5.02(1)(c) or (d).

46. A suitably experienced and competent person or persons must undertake the supervision required under 5.03. Such a person need not hold a particular qualification or have been in legal practice for a particular time; but in certain circumstances (for example, where a sole practitioner has more than one office) these may be relevant factors in determining compliance with 5.03.

47. Those supervising client matters under 5.03 would need to have sufficient legal knowledge and experience to be able to identify problems with the quality or conduct of the work; but might not need to be an expert in the area of work. The training, qualifications and experience of the member of staff whose matters are being checked under 5.03 will be relevant in assessing the level and type of expertise required by the person conducting the checks.

48. Rule 5.03 requires that work for clients is supervised wherever staff happen to be working, including at home or from "virtual" offices.

49. Supervision is an inherently internal function. The phrase "within the firm, law centre or in-house legal department" is included to ensure that supervision is not delegated outside your control but undertaken by someone who is genuinely part of the practice.

50. If a complaint is made, you will have to demonstrate that the work-checking procedures are "appropriate", "effective", and undertaken with "reasonable regularity". Relevant factors will include the size and complexity of the firm, law centre or in-house department; the nature of the work; the experience of the individuals undertaking the work, and their level of responsibility.

51. Rule 5.03 does not apply to business development and practice management work unrelated to work on client matters.

52. Supervising "work for clients and members of the public" embraces all aspects of the work, including the handling of client money and compliance with rule 2 (Client relations).

5

Rule 6   Equality and diversity

Introduction

Rule 6 is designed to prevent discrimination within your firm or in-house practice. The rule does not apply to overseas practice but solicitors practising overseas must comply with 15.06 (Equality and diversity) and 1.02 (Integrity). The duties contained in this rule are in addition to, and not in substitution for, your obligations to comply with anti-discrimination legislation.

Rule 6 – Equality and diversity

6.01   Duty not to discriminate

(1)   You must not in your professional dealings with the firm's managers and employees, other lawyers, clients or third parties discriminate, without lawful cause, against any person, nor victimise or harass them on the grounds of:

    (a)   race or racial group (including colour, nationality and ethnic or national origins);

    (b)   sex (including marital status, gender reassignment, pregnancy, maternity and paternity);

    (c)   sexual orientation (including civil partnership status);

    (d)   religion or belief;

    (e)   age; or

    (f)   disability.

(2)   You must take such steps, and make such adjustments, as are reasonable in all the circumstances in order to prevent any of your employees, partners, members, directors or clients who are disabled from being placed at a substantial disadvantage in comparison with those who are not disabled.

6.02   Evidence of breach

Where there has been a decision of a court or tribunal of the United Kingdom in proceedings to which you are a party, that you have committed, or are to be treated as having committed, an unlawful act of discrimination then that finding shall be treated as evidence of a breach of this rule.

6.03   Equality and diversity policy

If you are a recognised body, a manager of a recognised body or a recognised sole practitioner, you must adopt and implement an appropriate policy for preventing discrimination and harassment and promoting equality and diversity within your firm. You must take all reasonable steps to ensure that all employees, partners, members and directors are aware of, and act in compliance with, its provisions and that it is made available to clients, the Solicitors Regulation Authority and other relevant third parties where required.

6.04   In-house practice

If you have management responsibilities in in-house practice you must use all reasonable endeavours to secure the adoption and implementation of an appropriate policy for preventing discrimination and promoting equality and diversity within your department. You must take all reasonable steps to ensure that all staff within that department are aware of, and act in accordance with, its provisions.

6.05   Waivers

In spite of 22.01(1), the Solicitors Regulation Authority Board shall not have power to waive any of the provisions of this rule.

6.06   Meaning of terms

For the avoidance of doubt, unless otherwise defined in the rules, the terms used in this rule shall have the meanings assigned to them in law.

Guidance to rule 6 – Equality and diversity

1.   The information which follows is by way of clarification and guidance. Those parts which deal with legal issues are intended only to provide an overview of the law and not an interpretative explanation or redefinition of it. This is to guide you and is not intended to lay down a binding course of action.

Duty not to discriminate – 6.01

The scope of the rule

2.   You must, as a matter of general law, comply with the requirements set out in legislation in relation to discrimination and you should be aware that the provisions contained in this rule are in addition to, and not in substitution for, your legal duties.

3.   This rule places two distinct requirements upon you:

   (a)   not to discriminate against, without lawful cause, nor victimise or harass, in the course of your professional dealings, those groups of people, and in those circumstances, set out in 6.01(1); and (b)　to make reasonable adjustments to prevent the firm's managers, employees or clients, or the clients of an in-house solicitor or REL, who are disabled from being at a disadvantage in comparison with those who are not disabled.

4.　You should be aware that, whilst the provisions contained in this rule are based upon legislative provisions, this rule goes beyond the scope of the legislation in a number of key areas and in particular in relation to age discrimination.

In particular you should note that it requires you to refrain from discriminating against all of those persons referred to in 6.01(1) in all of the circumstances referred to. There is no limitation in this requirement to discrimination occurring only in particular circumstances. Thus, for example, whilst the law dealing with age discrimination currently applies only in relation to employment and vocational training, this rule applies to all of your professional dealings with barristers, other lawyers, clients or third parties.

Please note, however, that the provisions relating to reasonable adjustment for disability set out in 6.01(2) are limited to an adjustment for clients, employees and the firm's managers.

5.　The following points should be noted:

(a)　Discrimination based on age is now included in this rule, as are requirements not to discriminate on the basis of civil partnership status, gender reassignment, pregnancy, maternity and paternity.

(b)　This rule does not address, but you should nevertheless be aware of, discrimination-related employment issues such as those which relate to fixed-term and part-time workers, the requirements for flexible working, and provisions relating to participation in, or abstention from, trade union activities.

(c)　Although this rule does not address issues set out in the Human Rights Act 1998 you should be aware of these, especially if you are working in the public sector.

(d)　Whilst this rule does not apply to overseas practice, nevertheless you should be aware of the provisions set out in regulation 11 of the Employment Equality (Sex Discrimination) Regulations 2005 (SI 2005/2467) in relation to employment wholly or partly outside Great Britain and its applicability to sex discrimination and equal pay.

(e)　Although they are not specifically dealt with in this rule, nevertheless you should be aware of the provisions of the Racial and Religious Hatred Act 2006 in so far as they affect your practice.

(f)   The terms "employer" and "employment" in this guidance are used in their normal everyday sense and not as defined in rule 24 (Interpretation).

(g)   The term "without lawful cause" means that the discrimination has taken place in circumstances which are not dealt with in notes 11, 12 and 13 below where there is a permitted exception within the law or where circumstances are such that it is possible to justify why the discrimination has taken place.

What is discrimination?

6.   Discrimination occurs when one person is treated less favourably than another is treated, or would be treated, in the same or similar circumstances without legitimate reason.

7.   The grounds upon which a person must not be discriminated against are:

(a)   race or racial group (including colour, nationality and ethnic or national origin);

(b)   sex (including marital status, gender reassignment, pregnancy, maternity and paternity);

(c)   sexual orientation (including civil partnership status);

(d)   religion or belief;

(e)   age; or

(f)   disability.

These terms have the same meaning in this rule as they have in law.

8.   In particular you should note that:

(a)   discrimination on the grounds of race or racial group includes discrimination on the basis of colour, nationality and national or ethnic origin;

(b)   sex discrimination includes discrimination against:

(i)   a married person on the grounds of their marital status;

(ii)   a person who is about to undergo, is undergoing or has undergone gender reassignment;

(iii)   a woman on the grounds of pregnancy or maternity; and

(iv)   a man on the grounds of paternity;

(c)   you are subject to the provisions of the Equal Pay Act 1970;

(d)   sexual orientation applies equally to those who are heterosexual as it does to those who are lesbian, gay or bisexual; discrimination based on sexual orientation includes discrimination against a person because they are in a civil partnership; it should also be noted that discrimination can be on the grounds of perceived sexual orientation as well as actual sexual orientation;

(e) disability is widely defined and includes stress related illnesses (which do not need to be "clinically well-recognised" to be capable of founding a claim), progressive illnesses (such as HIV and cancer) from the time of diagnosis, illnesses which would be substantial if not controlled by drugs (such as insulin-dependent diabetes) and conditions such as learning disabilities or dyslexia which restrict a person's ability to interact or communicate;

(f) religion or belief includes philosophical beliefs similar to a religion (for example humanism); and

(g) age means any age, not just old age and can include discrimination based on the age of others, e.g. a person's spouse. It should also be noted that discrimination can be on the grounds of perceived age as well as actual age.

6

9. Discrimination can take a variety of forms including direct discrimination, indirect discrimination, harassment, victimisation, less favourable treatment and failure to make an adjustment. A brief summary of each of these is set out below although you should rely upon the meanings assigned to them by law when interpreting your duties under this rule.

10. (a) Direct discrimination occurs where one person treats another less favourably by reason of:

    (i) race or racial group (including colour, nationality and ethnic or national origins);

    (ii) their sex (including marital status, gender reassignment, pregnancy, maternity and paternity);

    (iii) sexual orientation (including their civil partnership status);

    (iv) religion or belief;

    (v) age; or

    (vi) disability,

and, in respect of age discrimination only, it cannot be shown that the treatment in question was justified.

To treat a person less favourably for other reasons, for example because they have not performed adequately, will not generally be regarded as discrimination amounting to professional misconduct unless the true reason for the treatment is, or includes, one of the matters referred to above.

(b) Indirect discrimination occurs where a provision, criterion, practice, requirement or condition (as appropriate) which is applied to everyone, has the effect of placing at a disadvantage a particular person, or group of people, by reason of:

(i) race or racial group (including colour, nationality and ethnic or national origins);

(ii) sex (including marital status, gender reassignment, pregnancy, maternity and paternity);

(iii) sexual orientation (including civil partnership status);

(iv) religion or belief; and

(v) age,

and it cannot be shown that to apply that provision, criterion, practice, requirement or condition in that way is a proportionate means for achieving a legitimate aim.

Note that the provisions relating to indirect discrimination are not applicable to discrimination on the grounds of disability.

Indirect discrimination can occur whether or not the person applying the provision, criterion, practice, requirement or condition intended to discriminate against the person or group of people affected.

(c) Harassment occurs when one person subjects another to "unwanted conduct that has the purpose or effect ... of creating an intimidating, hostile, degrading, humiliating or offensive environment" (section 4A(1) of the Sex Discrimination Act 1975, as amended by the Employment Equality (Sex Discrimination) Regulations 2005 (SI 2005/2467)), in other words threatening, abusive or insulting behaviour, words or actions which violate the other person's dignity or create a humiliating, intimidating or hostile environment. Harassment may involve physical acts or verbal and non-verbal communications and gestures. Harassment can also occur where it has the defined effect upon the victim, notwithstanding the harasser's intention – it is the effect which the harassment has upon the victim that is important. For example, remarks made humorously or without malicious intent can still constitute harassment if that is the effect which they had upon the person being harassed.

In determining whether harassment has occurred you should be aware that a series of minor acts or comments can constitute harassment as can a one-off act of sufficient severity. However, the acts complained of must be capable of amounting to harassment.

You should also be aware of the provisions of section 4A(1)(b) of the Sex Discrimination Act 1975 in respect of sexual harassment.

(d) Victimisation occurs when a person is treated less favourably because he or she:

   (i)   has asserted a right not to be discriminated against on one of the prohibited grounds set out in 6.01;

   (ii) has assisted another to assert a right not to be discriminated against on one of the prohibited grounds set out in 6.01; or

   (iii) has given evidence in a tribunal or court relating to the assertion of such a right.

   The protection applies only to assertions made in good faith.

(e) Less favourable treatment, as used in relation to disability discrimination, occurs when a person with a disability is treated in a detrimental way in circumstances when a person without that disability would not be so treated. Thus, for example, charging more to a disabled client than a client without a disability because their disability means that more time is required to obtain instructions could constitute less favourable treatment, as could offering less favourable terms or refusing to act.

6

(f) Failure to make reasonable adjustment is another concept used in relation to disability discrimination. You are under a duty to take such steps (adjustments) as are reasonable in all the circumstances to ensure that employment arrangements, arrangements for partners, members, directors and clients, the premises from which your business is undertaken and the service provided, do not put at a substantial disadvantage a person with a disability when compared with a person without that disability, without justification.

   The following points should be borne in mind when making a reasonable adjustment:

   (i)   the duty to make the adjustment stands alone and requires no other form of less favourable treatment or intention to discriminate;

   (ii) the duty is a positive one – it requires that you take active steps to ensure that a person with a disability can access employment opportunities or services as if they did not have that disability;

   (iii) the cost of making the adjustment is one which must be absorbed by you, where it is reasonable to do so, and not passed on to the disabled client by way of a disbursement, additional charge or less comprehensive service;

   (iv) the duty is to make a reasonable adjustment – if the adjustment is not reasonable then you may not be under a duty to make it;

(v)   the fact that the cost of the adjustment exceeds the charges or profits from the matter in question does not of itself make the adjustment unreasonable. A more relevant factor is the resources of the firm;

(vi)   an adjustment does not have to be a physical adjustment – it may simply be a change to working practices such as visiting a client at home if they are unable to access your premises; and

(vii) an adjustment is not always a one-off action – it may need to be made on numerous occasions, for example employing the services of a British Sign Language Interpreter when advising a client with profound hearing loss. So long as the adjustment continues to be reasonable, its cost must be absorbed by you.

Permitted exceptions and justifiable discrimination

11. There are situations in which it is permitted to discriminate without breach of the legislation or this rule. In some instances this will be by way of specific exceptions to the legislation, whilst in others it will depend upon the nature of the discrimination and the extent to which it can be justified. Although a brief explanation is given below, in both cases you should rely upon the meanings assigned to them by law when interpreting your duties under this rule.

12. There are permitted exceptions to the legislation variously referred to as Genuine Occupational Qualifications (GOQs) and Genuine Occupational Requirements (GORs). These apply in relation to discrimination on the basis of race, sex, sexual orientation, religion or belief, and age. The exception to the concept of GOQs and GORs is discrimination on the grounds of disability. This relies upon whether it can be shown that the discrimination in question was reasonable.

13. In certain circumstances you may be able to justify discriminating against a person even though it is on one of the prohibited grounds set out in 6.01.

(a)   Direct discrimination cannot be justified other than in relation to age discrimination (where it must be a proportionate means of achieving a legitimate aim).

(b)   With regard to indirect discrimination, it may be possible for you to show that a provision, criterion, practice, requirement or condition which is applied to everyone, but which places a person or group of people at a disadvantage, is justified. To do so, you would need to show, amongst other things, that:

(i)   it was imposed other than for the purposes of discriminating;

(ii)   it was appropriate and necessary to achieve the required aim; and

(iii)   the means of achieving that legitimate aim were appropriate and necessary.

Dealing with clients and third parties

14. You are generally free to decide whether to accept instructions from any client provided that your refusal to act is not based upon any of the grounds in 6.01. You should also note 11.04 (Refusing instructions to act as advocate) which limits the circumstances in which you can refuse to act as an advocate and 2.01 (Taking on clients) which deals with taking on clients.

15. You should instruct barristers on the basis of their skill, experience and ability and it is unlawful to instruct them, or avoid instructing them, on the basis of any of the grounds in 6.01, or to request or encourage a barrister's clerk to do so.

16. You should normally comply with a client's request to instruct a named barrister (subject to your duty to discuss the suitability of that barrister for a particular type of work). Where a client's instructions as to the choice of barrister are based on any of the grounds in 6.01, you should encourage the client to modify their instructions. If they refuse to do so, you should cease to act for them as aiding an unlawful act is prohibited.

6

17. In relation to the instruction of a barrister, in addition to the requirements of this rule, you are subject to provisions relating to the giving, withholding or acceptance of instructions contained in:

(a)   section 26A(3) of the Race Relations Act 1976;

(b)   section 35A(3) of the Sex Discrimination Act 1975;

(c)   section 7A(3) of the Disability Discrimination Act 1995;

(d)   regulation 12(4) of the Employment Equality (Religion or Belief) Regulations 2003 (SI 2003/1660);

(e)   regulation 12(4) of the Employment Equality (Sexual Orientation) Regulations 2003 (SI 2003/1661); and

(f)   regulation 15(4) of the Employment Equality (Age) Regulations 2006 (SI 2006/1031).

18. If you maintain lists or databases of contractors, agents and other third parties who are regarded as suitable to be instructed by others within the firm, you should ensure that those lists or databases:

(a)   are compiled on the basis only of their ability to undertake work of a particular type; and

(b)   do not contain any discriminatory bias based on any of the grounds in 6.01.

Partners and partnerships

19. In relation to a position as partner in a firm, you should not discriminate against partners or potential partners. In addition to the provisions of this rule, you should note that you are subject to provisions as to discrimination in relation to a position as partner contained in:

    (a) section 10 of the Race Relations Act 1976;

    (b) section 11 of the Sex Discrimination Act 1975 as amended by section 1(3) of the Sex Discrimination Act 1986;

    (c) sections 6A, 6B and 6C of the Disability Discrimination Act 1995;

    (d) regulation 14 of the Employment Equality (Religion or Belief) Regulations 2003 (SI 2003/1660);

    (e) regulation 14 of the Employment Equality (Sexual Orientation) Regulations 2003 (SI 2003/1661);

    (f) regulation 14 of the Employment Equality (Sex Discrimination) Regulations 2005 (SI 2005/2467); and

    (g) regulation 17 of the Employment Equality (Age) Regulations 2006 (SI 2006/1031).

20. You should also comply with the various provisions which prohibit discrimination after the end of a professional relationship and which apply to both staff and managers. This means, for example, that you should exercise care when giving a reference for someone so as to ensure that you do not permit that reference to be in any way discriminatory or to appear to have been influenced by issues of a discriminatory nature.

Evidence of breach – 6.02

21. Whilst decisions of unlawful discrimination by an employment tribunal are not binding on the SRA or the Solicitors Disciplinary Tribunal in determining whether an allegation of misconduct involving discrimination is well founded, such decisions are admissible in evidence in disciplinary proceedings. The SRA or the Tribunal must determine whether an allegation or decision of discrimination against you amounts to misconduct. The starting point for this will be that the decision represents a strong indication that misconduct has taken place and it will be for you to show why, despite the decision, there has not been misconduct.

Equality and diversity policy – 6.03

22. (a) In order to encourage you to abide by the provisions of this rule, and to assist you in ensuring that managers and employees do so too, it is a requirement that your firm adopts and implements an appropriate

written policy for promoting equality, preventing discrimination and dealing with any instances of discrimination which might arise.

(b)   To be appropriate the policy must:

(i)   be in writing;

(ii)   include such provisions as are relevant to your firm (having regard to its nature and size);

(iii) as a minimum, deal with the following core items:

(A)   how the firm plans to implement, communicate, monitor, evaluate and update the policy;

(B)   how the firm intends to ensure equality in relation to employees, managers, clients and third parties and the means by which it will monitor, evaluate and update any procedures and policies in relation to this;

(C)   how complaints and disciplinary issues are to be dealt with;

(D)   a requirement that all employees and managers comply with the provisions set out in 6.01; and

(E)   a commitment to the principles of equality and diversity and to observing legislative requirements;

(iv)   not contain any additional items which would conflict with the core items.

(c)   In adopting and implementing that policy you should be aware that:

(i)   account must be taken of the size and nature of your firm and any policy which you adopt and implement should contain provisions which are relevant to your firm;

(ii)   you must ensure that all managers and employees are aware of, and act in compliance with, the provisions contained in the policy. A policy which is not brought to their attention will not be an appropriate policy.

In order to demonstrate that the policy has been brought to the attention of managers and employees in an effective manner, you may wish to give consideration to providing staff with training and information about complying with equality and diversity requirements. Where a client, the SRA or other relevant third party requests a copy of the policy to be provided to them, you must do so within a reasonable period of time; and

(iii) since the equality and diversity needs of your practice may change from time to time, you should monitor the continuing appropriateness of your policy and make such changes as are necessary.

In-house practice – 6.04

23. If you are a solicitor or REL with management responsibilities in in-house practice then it is likely that you will not have the same opportunity to formulate, adopt and implement measures for preventing discrimination and promoting equality and diversity, as a sole practitioner or manager in a firm. You may, however, have an opportunity to influence those measures which are implemented, especially within your own department.

24. If you are practising in-house then you are required to use your best endeavours to secure the adoption and implementation of an appropriate policy for preventing discrimination and promoting equality and diversity within your department. You should also ensure, so far as you are able, that employees within your department are aware of, and act in compliance with, its provisions. However, where you are unable to do so, no burden of professional misconduct will be placed upon you.

25. If there is an allegation of misconduct based upon discrimination on any of the grounds listed in 6.01, and you have management responsibility, you will be required to show good reason why you were unable to secure the operation of an appropriate policy.

26. In all other respects you will be required to abide by the terms of this rule to the same extent as a solicitor in private practice.

Rule 7   Publicity

Introduction

You are generally free to publicise your firm or practice, subject to the requirements of this rule. The rule as it applies to your overseas practice is modified by 15.07.

Rule 7 – Publicity

7.01   Misleading or inaccurate publicity

Publicity must not be misleading or inaccurate.

7.02   Clarity as to charges

Any publicity relating to your, or your firm's, charges must be clearly expressed. In relation to practice from an office in England and Wales it must be clear whether disbursements and VAT are included.

7.03   Unsolicited approaches in person or by telephone

(1)   You must not publicise your firm or practice by making unsolicited approaches in person or by telephone to a member of the public.

(2)   "Member of the public" does not include:

(a)   a current or former client;

(b)   another firm or its manager;

(c)   an existing or potential professional or business connection; or

(d)   a commercial organisation or public body.

7.04   International aspects of publicity

Publicity intended for a jurisdiction outside England and Wales must comply with:

(a)   the provisions of rule 7 (and 15.07, if applicable); and

(b)   the rules in force in that jurisdiction concerning lawyers' publicity.

Publicity intended for a jurisdiction where it is permitted will not breach 7.04 through being incidentally received in a jurisdiction where it is not permitted.

7.05   Responsibility for publicity

You must not authorise any other person to conduct publicity for your firm or practice in a way which would be contrary to rule 7 (and 15.07, if applicable).

7.06   Application

(1) Rule 7 applies to any publicity you or your firm conduct(s) or authorise(s) in the course of setting up or carrying on the practice in relation to:

(a) the firm or your practice;

(b) any other business or activity carried on by you or your firm; or

(c) any other business or activity carried on by others.

(2) Rules 7.01 to 7.05 apply to all forms of publicity including the name or description of your firm, stationery, advertisements, brochures, websites, directory entries, media appearances, promotional press releases, and direct approaches to potential clients and other persons, and whether conducted in person, in writing, or in electronic form.

7.07   Letterhead, website and e-mails

(1) The letterhead, website and e-mails of a recognised body or recognised sole practitioner must show the words "regulated by the Solicitors Regulation Authority", and either

(a) the firm's registered name and number if it is an LLP or company, or

(b) if the firm is a partnership or sole practitioner, the name under which it is recognised by the Solicitors Regulation Authority, and the number allocated to it by the Authority.

(2) (a) The letterhead of a recognised sole practitioner must include the name of the sole practitioner.

(b) The letterhead of a recognised body which is a partnership of 20 or fewer partners, must include a list of the partners.

(c) The letterhead of a recognised body which is a partnership of more than 20 partners, must include either

(i) a list of the partners; or

(ii) a statement that a list of the partners is open to inspection at the office.

(d) The letterhead of a recognised body which is an LLP must include either

(i) a list of the members, identified as members; or

(ii) a statement that a list of the members is open to inspection at the office,

unless the LLP is practising under a name other than its corporate name and has 20 or fewer members, in which case the list must be on the letterhead.

(e) The letterhead of a recognised body which is a company with a sole director must include the name of the director, identified as director.

(f)   The letterhead of a recognised body which is a company with more than
      one director must include either

      (i)   a list of the directors, identified as directors; or

      (ii)   a statement that a list of the directors is open to inspection at the
             office.

(3) In a recognised body, if the managers include persons other than solicitors,
     any list referred to in this rule must:

     (a)   identify any solicitor as a solicitor;

     (b)   in the case of any lawyer or notary of an Establishment Directive state
           other than the UK:

           (i)   identify the jurisdiction(s) – local or national as appropriate –
                  under whose professional title the lawyer or notary is practising;

           (ii)   give the professional title(s), expressed in an official language of
                  the Establishment Directive state(s) concerned; and

           (iii) if the lawyer is an REL, refer to that lawyer's registration with the
                  Solicitors Regulation Authority;

     (c)   indicate the professional qualification(s) of any other lawyer and the
           country or jurisdiction of qualification of any RFL not included in (b)
           above;

     (d)   identify any individual non-lawyer as a non-lawyer; and

     (e)   identify the nature of any body corporate, if this is not clear from its
           name.

(4) Whenever an REL is named on the letterhead used by any firm or in-house
     practice, there must be compliance with 7.07(3)(b).

(5) In 7.07 "letterhead" includes a fax heading.

Guidance to rule 7 – Publicity

Geographical scope of the rule

1.   (a)   Rule 7 applies to publicity in connection with practice from any office,
           whether in England and Wales or overseas – but the provisions are
           amended by 15.07 for publicity in connection with overseas practice.

     (b)   Rule 7 does not apply to the website, e-mails, text messages or similar
           electronic communications of any practice you conduct from an office
           in an EU state other than the UK (see 15.07(2)).

     (c)   Rule 7.07 (Letterhead, website and e-mails) does not apply to a
           solicitor's practice conducted from an office outside England and

Wales or to an REL's practice conducted from an office in Scotland or Northern Ireland. However, you must comply with 15.07(3).

General

2. In the delivery of professional services, there is an imbalance of knowledge between clients and the public on the one hand, and the service provider on the other. Rule 7 addresses this in a number of ways – for example, by ensuring that clients and the public have appropriate information about you, your firm and the way you are regulated; and by prohibiting misleading publicity and inappropriate approaches for business.

Local law society involvement in dealing with minor breaches

3. In the case of breaches of the rule which are not serious, the SRA encourages local law societies to bring the breaches to the attention of the practitioners concerned. Serious or persistent cases should be reported to the SRA.

Identifying your firm

4. Rule 7.07(1), as amended on 31 March 2009, applies to the letterhead, fax heading, website and e-mails of a recognised body or recognised sole practitioner. The effect of the rule is that:

   (a) a sole practitioner must state his or her SRA number and the name under which he or she is recognised;

   (b) a partnership must state its SRA number and the name under which it is recognised; and

   (c) an LLP or company must state its registered number from Companies House and its corporate name.

Statutory requirements and voluntary codes

5. You must comply with the general law on advertising, including:

   (a) any regulations made under the Consumer Credit Act 1974, concerning the content of advertisements;

   (b) sections 20 and 21 of the Consumer Protection Act 1987, regarding misleading price indications;

   (c) the Business Names Act 1985, concerning lists of partners and an address for service on stationery, etc.;

   (d) the Companies (Trading Disclosures) Regulations 2008 (SI 2008/495) regarding the appearance of the company name and other particulars on stationery, etc.;

(e) the Consumer Credit (Advertisements) Regulations 1989 (SI 1989/1125), in relation to advertisements to arrange mortgages;

(f) the Control of Misleading Advertisements (Amendment) Regulations 2000 (SI 2000/914), in relation to comparative advertising;

(g) the Data Protection Act 1998;

(h) E-Commerce Directive 2000/31/EC and the Electronic Commerce (EC Directive) Regulations 2002 (SI 2002/2013); and

(i) the Privacy and Electronic Communications (EC Directive) Regulations 2003 (SI 2003/2426).

6. You should also have regard to the British Code of Advertising, Sales Promotion and Direct Marketing ("the Advertising Code"). The main principle of the Advertising Code is that media advertisements be legal, decent, honest and truthful. For further information see the website of the Advertising Standards Authority.

7. A breach of a statutory provision or the Advertising Code may also entail a breach of rule 7 or another rule of conduct, but would not necessarily do so. For example, an advert adjudged by the Advertising Standards Authority to be untruthful under the Advertising Code might also, in the context of a complaint, be found by the SRA to breach 7.01 (which requires that publicity is not misleading or inaccurate).

Responsibility for publicity – 7.05

8. Where you become aware of breaches of rule 7 in publicity conducted on your or your firm's behalf, you should take reasonable steps to have the publicity changed or withdrawn.

Clarity as to charges – 7.02

9. Publicity relating to charges must not be misleading or inaccurate, and must be clearly expressed. The following examples in notes 10 to 12 below will assist in complying.

10. Particular care should be taken when quoting fees which are intended to be net fees, i.e. fees which are reduced by the availability of commission (such as that on an endowment policy). Any fee quoted in these circumstances should be the gross fee.

11. The following are examples of publicity which would breach 7.01 and/or 7.02:

(a) publicity which includes an estimated fee pitched at an unrealistically low level;

(b) publicity which refers to an estimated or fixed fee plus disbursements, if expenses which are in the nature of overheads (such as normal postage and telephone calls) are then charged as disbursements; and

(c) publicity which includes an estimated or fixed fee for conveyancing services, if you then make an additional charge for work on a related mortgage loan or repayment, including work done for a lender – unless the publicity makes it clear that any such additional charge may be payable (e.g. by the use of a phrase like "excluding VAT, disbursements, mortgage related charges and fees for work done for a lender").

12. Offers of discounts could be misleading if there are no clear rates of charges included. Similarly, if you publicise a service or services as being "free", this should genuinely be the case and should not be conditional upon some other factor (e.g. receiving further instructions or some other benefit). If you publicise work as being done on a pro bono basis there must be no fees charged to the client, except where a conditional fee agreement is used and the only fees charged are those which the firm receives by way of costs from the client's opponent or other third party and which are paid to a charity under a fee sharing agreement.

Agreeing to donate fees to charity

13. If you publicise that you will donate all, or a percentage, of the firm's fees in respect of certain matters to charity, it would be misleading not to do so. The same applies if you agree to pay to a charity fees received by way of costs from your client's opponent or other third party where you act under a conditional fee agreement.

Name of firm

14. It would be misleading for a name or description to include the word "solicitor(s)", if none of the managers are solicitors.

15. It would be misleading for a sole principal to use "and partners" or "and associates" in a firm name unless the firm did formerly have more than one principal.

E-commerce, e-mail and websites

16. The E-Commerce Directive 2000/31/EC covers cross-border e-commerce within the EU, including e-mails and websites. It affects any firm with a website, because a website can be accessed from other member states.

17. The Electronic Commerce (EC Directive) Regulations 2002 (SI 2002/2013) implementing the Directive require you to give certain information to persons visiting your firm's website or receiving e-mails from the firm (other than certain activities outside the scope of the Directive, e.g. litigation). The information you will need to give includes:

(a)   details of the professional body with which the firm is registered – see note 18;

(b)   your professional title and the member state where it was granted – it is recommended that you either state that the partners/members/directors of the firm are solicitors of England and Wales (if that is the case) or list the professional title and jurisdiction of qualification (or state "non-lawyer") for each of the partners/members/directors; and

(c)   a reference to the professional rules applicable to the firm in the member state where you are established and the means to access them – see note 18.

18. If you are "established" in the UK (i.e. your office is in the UK), it is appropriate to say that the firm is regulated by the SRA. For the rules, you are recommended to provide a link to the SRA's website on **www.sra.org.uk/solicitors/code-of-conduct.page**. If you are "established" in another Establishment Directive state, the professional body will be the bar or law society with which you are registered under the Establishment Directive, and the applicable rules will be their rules. Of course, your firm may be "established" in more than one Establishment Directive state.

19. Any promotional material is publicity. E-mails sent to individuals, companies or organisations with the intention of promoting your practice are advertisements and therefore publicity. Any promotional material in a business e-mail – such as the name and description of the firm – will also be publicity. In these cases 7.01 to 7.07 will apply.

20. Rule 7.07(1) applies to the letterhead, fax heading, website and e-mails of a recognised body or recognised sole practitioner.

21. Rule 7.07(2)–(4), which applies only to letterheads and fax headings, reflects some of the provisions of the Business Names Act 1985 and the Companies (Trading Disclosures) Regulations 2008, which apply to "business letters". It is for the courts to determine whether or to what extent these Acts may apply to e-mails. However, the SRA's guess is that e-mails will only be "business letters" when they are formally set out as such and not when they are used as an alternative to a telephone call, telegram or telex. It would be prudent for you to ensure that third parties with whom you deal by e-mail are given your practising address at an early stage, together with the details which would normally appear on the firm's letterhead.

22. Rule 7.03 prohibits unsolicited approaches in person or by telephone to members of the public. E-mails do not fall within this prohibition. However, you should check the terms of your agreement with your internet

7

service provider as to the use of unsolicited e-mail, and in some jurisdictions the law prohibits unsolicited e-mail. See also note 33 below on data protection.

23. Websites are publicity and should comply with 7.01 to 7.07. See also notes 24 to 28 below.

24. If your website or e-mails are to include any financial promotion as defined in the Financial Services and Markets Act 2000, your firm will need to be authorised by the Financial Services Authority. See also notes 31 and 32 below.

International aspects of publicity – 7.04

25. The effect of the E-Commerce Directive is that there are two different regimes governing international e-publicity:

    (a) cross-border e-publicity within the EU; and

    (b) other cross-border e-publicity, i.e. the e-publicity of law firms established outside the EU, wherever it is accessed or received; and the e-publicity of law firms established in the EU, if it is accessed or received outside the EU.

26. Cross-border e-publicity within the EU is governed by the E-Commerce Directive and national implementing legislation. Other cross-border e-publicity is not. However, as a website can be accessed from anywhere, your firm's website will have to comply with the E-Commerce Directive and the relevant implementing legislation if your firm is established anywhere within the EU.

27. Rule 7.04 provides that publicity intended for a jurisdiction outside England and Wales must comply with rule 7 (or, in the case of overseas practice, 15.07) and with the rules in force in that jurisdiction concerning lawyers' publicity. Publicity intended for a jurisdiction where it is permitted will not breach this provision through being incidentally received in a jurisdiction where it is not permitted.

28. Websites can, of course, be accessed worldwide. The relevant factor is the jurisdiction or jurisdictions at which a website is targeted. For example, a website aimed at Australia must comply with rule 7 (if the solicitor's office is in England and Wales) or 15.07 (if the office is elsewhere), and any other restrictions in force in Australia concerning lawyers' publicity.

Mailshots

29. Unsolicited mailshots may be sent and may be targeted. However, you should note the data protection considerations discussed in note 33 below.

"Cold calling"

30. Rule 7.03(1) prohibits you from making unsolicited approaches, either in person or by telephone, to a "member of the public". This is intended to protect the public from the intrusiveness and pressure of unsolicited telephone calls and approaches in person. This rule, therefore, bans what is often termed "cold calling" and prohibits, for example, knocking on doors, approaching people newly arrived at ports of entry, approaching someone in the street, in a hospital or at the scene of an accident, or handing out leaflets in the street. The rule also prohibits approaching a member of the public (either in person, e.g. in the street, or by telephone) to conduct a survey which involves the collection of contact details of potential clients, or otherwise promotes your firm's practice.

A combination of 7.03, 7.05 (Responsibility for publicity) and 9.02 (Financial arrangements with introducers) means that you must not have a financial arrangement with an introducer in respect of business which has been obtained (either by that introducer or through an intermediary) by way of unsolicited face-to-face or telephone "cold calling".

This means that, if a member of the public has indicated in a general consumer survey that they may have a claim, you cannot contact them in person or by telephone unless:

(a) they have explicitly agreed to be contacted about making a claim; and

(b) their response to the questionnaire was not obtained as a result of an unsolicited approach, in person or by telephone, by your firm, or by any party authorised by your firm, or by any other party if your firm has a financial arrangement with the introducer.

Financial promotions

31. Under section 21 of the Financial Services and Markets Act 2000 an unsolicited communication which invites or induces a person to enter into an investment activity is a financial promotion, and cannot be made by an unauthorised person.

32. If you intend to make any form of unsolicited contact allowed under 7.03, where it relates to an investment activity you must consider carefully whether you are authorised to carry out the activity, and also consider whether your contact constitutes a financial promotion and whether you are authorised to make such an approach. Breach of the Act is a criminal offence.

Data protection

33. Rule 7.03(2)(a) permits unsolicited visits or telephone calls to a current or former client. Before contacting clients or former clients in order to

publicise your firm you should consider the requirements of the Data Protection Act 1998. It is advisable to give all clients the opportunity to refuse to receive direct marketing correspondence or contact – for example, in a terms of business letter. This applies to unsolicited mailshots to current or former clients as well as unsolicited approaches in person or by telephone. Under the Privacy and Electronic Communications (EC Directive) Regulations 2003 (SI 2003/2426), prior opt-in consent is needed for direct marketing by e-mail.

Naming non-partners

34. If non-partners are named on a partnership's letterhead, their status should be made clear. A printed line is not sufficient in itself to distinguish partners from non-partners in a list. A similar standard applies to a company or an LLP's letterhead.

Salaried partners

35. A manager who is held out on the letterhead of an unincorporated firm as a partner – even if separately designated as a "salaried" or "associate" partner – is treated by the SRA as a full partner and manager, and therefore must comply with the Solicitors' Accounts Rules and the Solicitors' Indemnity Insurance Rules. Holding out as a partner someone who is not entitled under rule 14 to be a partner will put you and your firm in breach both of rule 7 and rule 14.

"Partners" in an LLP

36. In the context of an LLP, it is permitted, if desired, to refer to members of the LLP as "partners", provided the firm complies with the provisions of the Companies Act 1985, the Companies Act 2006, the Business Names Act 1985 and 7.07(2) as regards the items that must appear on the firm's notepaper, including use of the word "members" in heading up or referring to the list of members.

37. Some firms may also wish to designate some non-members of the LLP as "partners". This is potentially misleading, so if a firm wishes to go down this path care must be taken to ensure that:

    (a) no non-member is designated as a "partner" unless he or she:

        (i) is a consultant or employee of the LLP with equivalent standing to a member; and

        (ii) is a practising lawyer, and would be entitled under rule 14 to become a member of the LLP;

    (b) appropriate explanatory wording (see note 38 below) appears on:

        (i) the firm's notepaper, faxes, e-mails, brochures and websites; and

    (ii)   any bill on which the word "partner" appears;

(c)   proper distinction is made between a member of the LLP and a person who is not a member but who is referred to as a "partner":

    (i)   in any agreement, terms of business letter or client care letter in which the word "partner" appears;

    (ii)   when addressing any client or third party who is not in receipt of a letter, fax or e-mail; and

    (iii)   in any formal context such as an affidavit, a statement to a court, or a communication with the Legal Services Commission.

38. Appropriate explanatory wording for a firm's notepaper, faxes, e-mails, brochures, websites or bills would be to the effect that:

> "We use the word 'partner' to refer to a member of the LLP, or an employee or consultant who is a lawyer with equivalent standing and qualifications."

If a firm wishes to refer to a list of "partners" as well as the statutory list of members, it is suggested that this might be done by way of some such wording as:

> "A list of the members of the LLP is displayed at the above address, together with a list of those non-members who are designated as partners."

39. Notes 36 to 38 above deal only with what is or is not professionally proper. They do not deal with any legal consequences for individuals or the firm if members or non-members are held out as "partners".

"Partners" in a company

40. In the context of practice carried on by way of a company, it may be desired to designate some participants in the practice as "partners". This is potentially misleading, so if you wish to go down this path care must be taken to ensure that:

(a)   the company complies with the provisions of the Companies Act 1985, the Companies Act 2006, the Business Names Act 1985 and 7.07(2) as regards the items that must appear on the firm's notepaper, including use of the word "directors" in heading up or referring to the list of directors;

(b)   no person is designated as a "partner" unless he or she:

    (i)   is a shareowner or director of the company, or a consultant in or employee of the company with equivalent standing; and

    (ii)   is a practising lawyer, and would be entitled under rule 14 to own shares in the company;

  (c) appropriate explanatory wording (see note 41 below) appears on:

    (i)   the company's notepaper, faxes, e-mails, brochures and websites; and

    (ii)   any bill on which the word "partner" appears; and

  (d) no misunderstanding arises as to the status of a "partner":

    (i)   in any agreement, terms of business letter or client care letter in which the word "partner" appears;

    (ii)   when addressing any client or third party who is not in receipt of a letter, fax or e-mail; or

    (iii)   in any formal context such as an affidavit, a statement to a court, or a communication with the Legal Services Commission.

41. Appropriate explanatory wording for a company's notepaper, faxes, e-mails, brochures, websites or bills would be to the effect that:

"We use the word 'partner' to refer to a shareowner or director of the company, or an employee or consultant who is a lawyer with equivalent standing and qualifications."

If you wish to refer to a list of "partners" as well as the statutory list of directors, it is suggested that this might be done by way of some such wording as:

"A list of the directors is displayed at the above address, together with a list of those persons who are designated as partners."

42. Notes 40 and 41 above deal only with what is or is not professionally proper. They do not deal with any legal consequences if shareowners or other participants are held out as "partners".

Identifying the qualifications of managers (and RELs)

43. Rule 7.07(3) and (4) sets out the requirements to be followed when an REL, an RFL, any other lawyer, a non-lawyer manager or a body corporate is named as a manager on a recognised body's letterhead, and whenever an REL is named in any capacity on a letterhead used by a firm or in-house practice. The following example illustrates how to comply:

"Paul van den Hoek, advocaat (Brussels), registered with the Solicitors Regulation Authority".

Naming staff

44. You may name staff on your letterhead. However, it would be misleading (and could involve a criminal offence) to use the word "solicitor" to refer to an individual who is not a solicitor of the Supreme Court of England and Wales.

45. A lawyer whose professional title is "solicitor" in another jurisdiction but who is not a solicitor of England and Wales can only be referred to in publicity as "solicitor" if the word is suitably qualified, for example by the name of that lawyer's jurisdiction of qualification.

Naming clients

46. The fact that you have acted for a client and details of the client's transactions are subject to the duty of confidentiality – see rule 4 (Confidentiality and disclosure) – and you will therefore normally need the client's consent before disclosing such information in any publicity.

Fee earner leaving a firm

47. It is not in itself misconduct for you to write to clients of a firm after leaving that firm, inviting their instructions. However, this cannot absolve you from any legal obligations arising out of your former contract of employment or partnership agreement.

7

Rule 8   Fee sharing

Introduction

Rule 8 restricts the persons and businesses with whom or with which you can share your professional fees. Broadly, you may not share fees with a non-lawyer unless the fee sharing is with a non-lawyer employee or manager in your firm, or in the strictly defined circumstances set out in this rule. Its purpose is to protect your independence and professional judgement in these situations for the ultimate public benefit.

In relation to European cross-border practice the restrictions on fee sharing are more stringent and you will need to refer to rule 16.

Rule 8 – Fee sharing

Generally: cannot share fees with non-lawyers

8.01   Fee sharing with lawyers and colleagues

Except as permitted under 8.02 below, you may only share or agree to share your professional fees with the following persons:

(a)   practising lawyers, and businesses carrying on the practice of lawyers;

(b)   non-lawyer managers or owners within your firm;

(c)   a retired manager, member, owner or predecessor, or the dependants or personal representatives of a deceased manager, member, owner or predecessor; *of the firm*

(d)   your genuine employee (this does not allow you to disguise as "employment" what is in fact a partnership which rule 12 prohibits);

(e)   your non-lawyer employer, if you are practising in-house and acting in accordance with rule 13 (In-house practice, etc.) or 15.13 (In-house practice overseas);

(f)   a law centre or advice service operated by a charitable or similar non-commercial organisation if you are working as a volunteer and receive fees or costs from public funds or recovered from a third party;

(g)   an estate agent who is your sub-agent for the sale of a property; or

(h)   a charity (as defined in rule 24 (Interpretation)), provided:

(i)   you remain in compliance with 1.02 (Integrity), 1.03 (Independence) and 1.04 (Best interests of clients);

(ii)   if requested by the Solicitors Regulation Authority to do so, you supply details of all agreements to share fees with a charity;

8

(iii) the operation of any such agreement does not result in a partnership;

(iv) any such agreement does not involve a breach of rule 9 (Referrals of business); and

(v) if you are employed in-house, you remain in compliance with 13.04 (Pro bono work).

8.02 Fee sharing with other non-lawyers

(1) You may share your professional fees with another person or business ("the fee sharer") if:

(a) the purpose of the fee sharing arrangement is solely to facilitate the introduction of capital and/or the provision of services to your firm;

(b) neither the fee sharing agreement nor the extent of the fees shared permits any fee sharer to influence or constrain your professional judgement in relation to the advice which you give to any client;

(c) the operation of the agreement does not result in a partnership prohibited by rule 12 (Framework of practice);

(d) if requested by the Solicitors Regulation Authority to do so, you supply details of all agreements which you have made with fee sharers and the percentage of your firm's annual gross fees which has been paid to each fee sharer; and

(e) your fee sharing agreement does not involve a breach of rule 9 (Referrals of business) or 15.09 (Overseas practice – referrals of business).

(2) "Fee sharer" means a person or business who or which shares your fees in reliance on (1) above and the expression includes any person or business connected to or associated with the fee sharer.

Guidance to rule 8 – Fee sharing

What is fee sharing?

1. Fee sharing is not defined in rule 8. It can have a variety of forms and includes relationships where you make a payment within a firm or to a third party by reference to a percentage of the fees charged to a client in respect of a particular case, or a percentage of your gross or net fees, or your profits.

Fee sharing with lawyers and colleagues

2. Sharing your fees within a firm, or with other lawyers or in the other circumstances listed in 8.01, does not represent a serious risk to your independence and is therefore permitted.

3. Rule 8.01 allows you to share fees with a business carrying on the practice of lawyers. This allows you to share fees with a legal disciplinary practice, or with a multi-disciplinary practice outside England and Wales.

Fee sharing with charities and other non-lawyers

4. Rule 8.01(h) permits you to share fees with a charity. This rule applies to charitable giving where you have agreed with your client or a charity that you will share all, or some, of your fees in respect of a particular matter or matters with a charity. This will include situations where you use a conditional fee agreement and agree to pay to a charity fees you receive by way of costs from your client's opponent or other third party. By contrast, where you decide to make a donation to a charity without any binding commitment to do so, this will not constitute fee sharing and is permitted.

5. If you act in accordance with a pro bono conditional fee agreement and you advance disbursements on behalf of your client, and these disbursements are received by way of costs from your client's opponent or from another third party, you may retain from the costs which are received the element which covers such disbursements. The terms of this arrangement will need to be set out in the conditional fee agreement.

6. You may share your fees with other third party non-lawyers in the strictly defined circumstances set out in 8.02. The aim of 8.02 is to give practitioners greater freedom of choice as to the methods available to fund their firms or to pay for services provided to their firms, subject to safeguards designed to protect the public interest. Rule 8.02 allows you to enter into agreements with third party non-lawyers which provide that, in return for the third party making available capital and/or a service to you, you make payment to the third party by reference to a percentage of your fees.

7. You must take account of the requirements of rule 1 (Core duties), specifically of the requirements of independence, integrity, and your duty to act in the best interests of the client. This means that although a fee sharer may properly require you to, for example, observe certain service delivery standards, it would be improper for the fee sharer to interfere with your professional judgement in relation to the advice given to clients.

8. If the fee sharing relationship involves referrals between you and the fee sharer, you must also comply with rule 9 (Referrals of business) or 15.09 (which relates to referrals of business overseas).

9. You must also comply with rule 12 (Framework of practice), which sets out the types of business through which solicitors, RELs, RFLs and recognised bodies may practise. Solicitors who do share fees in accordance with 8.02 should take care that they do not, even inadvertently, enter into an unauthorised partnership with the fee sharer.

10. You must comply with rule 3 (Conflict of interests) to ensure that there is no conflict between the interests of the client and your own interests by virtue of your agreement with the fee sharer. Should a fee sharer become your client, you should be particularly conscious of the need to ensure that conflicts of interests do not arise, and that the wish to avoid offending the fee sharer does not colour the actions taken and advice given in respect of other clients.

11. Rule 8.02 allows you to share fees with a non-lawyer third party, but only in return for the fee sharer providing capital and/or services to your firm. The rule does not permit the fee sharer to provide services to your client as part of the fee sharing agreement.

12. Examples of the kind of arrangements which 8.02 permits include:

    (a) A bank may provide a loan to your firm in return for a sum, in whole or part, calculated as a percentage of the gross fees of your firm. The fact that some clients of your firm are also customers of the bank would not, of itself, prevent the bank from sharing your fees.

    (b) A supplier of information and communications technology may provide computer hardware, software, back-up and training to your firm in return for a share of the firm's gross fees.

    (c) You may pay a supplier of an interactive web based will-writing package on the basis of a percentage of the fee for each will.

13. Although 8.02 does not specify any cap or limit on the amount of fees which you may share with third parties, you must ensure that the extent of the fees shared does not put at risk your duties to act independently and in clients' best interests – see rule 1 (Core duties). Firms should carry out an assessment of any risk to these core duties that could be created by any fee sharing arrangement, and take action to limit or manage that risk. In assessing whether a firm may have been in breach of these duties, particularly where the percentage of all fees shared is higher than 15% of gross fees, the SRA may ask for evidence of this risk assessment.

14. If you have a fee sharing relationship with a third party non-lawyer in accordance with 8.02, you may need to disclose the existence and nature of the fee sharing relationship to any client whose affairs are significantly and directly connected to it. Service delivery standards agreed with a fee sharer need not normally be disclosed. See also 2.02(2)(e) and notes 16 and 17 of the guidance to rule 2 (Client relations).

15. There would, for example, be no obligation to disclose to clients that the firm has a fee sharing relationship with a bank which has supplied a loan to the firm, even to those clients who obtain banking services from that same bank.

16. Rule 8.02 states that you must, if asked to do so, make available to the SRA details of any fee sharing agreement. This may, for example, include the percentage of gross fees which has been passed to the fee sharer(s) pursuant to an agreement made under 8.02.

17. The SRA will respect the commercial sensitivity of any information supplied to it.

18. You are not allowed to share fees with a non-lawyer "fee sharer" under 8.02 in your European cross-border activities, because it is prohibited by rule 16 (European cross-border practice). The following are prohibited by rule 16:

   (a) solicitors (wherever practising) sharing fees with a non-lawyer fee sharer situated in a CCBE state other than the UK; and

   (b) solicitors practising in a CCBE state other than the UK sharing fees with a non-lawyer fee sharer (wherever situated).

   Further information can be found in rule 16 (European cross-border practice) and notes 6 and 7 of the guidance to that rule.

8

Rule 9   Referrals of business

Introduction

Rule 9 applies when you receive referrals of business from, or make referrals to, third parties. Its purpose is to protect your independence. Additional provisions apply when you have a financial arrangement with an introducer. In relation to European cross-border practice the restrictions on financial arrangements with introducers are more stringent and you will need to refer to rule 16. The rule does not apply to your overseas practice but you must comply with 15.09.

Rule 9 – Referrals of business

9.01   General

(1)   When making or receiving referrals of clients to or from third parties you must do nothing which would compromise your independence or your ability to act and advise in the best interests of your clients.

(2)   You must draw the attention of potential introducers to this rule and to the relevant provisions of rule 7 (Publicity).

(3)   This rule does not apply to referrals between lawyers (including businesses carrying on the practice of lawyers).

(4)   You must not, in respect of any claim arising as a result of death or personal injury, either:

(a)   enter into an arrangement for the referral of clients with; or

(b)   act in association with,

any person whose business, or any part of whose business, is to make, support or prosecute (whether by action or otherwise, and whether by a solicitor or agent or otherwise) claims arising as a result of death or personal injury, and who, in the course of such business, solicits or receives contingency fees in respect of such claims.

(5)   The prohibition in 9.01(4) shall not apply to an arrangement or association with a person who solicits or receives contingency fees only in respect of proceedings in a country outside England and Wales, to the extent that a local lawyer would be permitted to receive a contingency fee in respect of such proceedings.

(6)   In 9.01(4) and (5) "contingency fee" means any sum (whether fixed, or calculated either as a percentage of the proceeds or otherwise howsoever) payable only in the event of success in the prosecution or defence of any action, suit or other contentious proceedings.

9.02   Financial arrangements with introducers

The following additional requirements apply when you enter into a financial arrangement with an introducer:

(a)   The agreement must be in writing and be available for inspection by the Solicitors Regulation Authority.

(b)   The introducer must undertake, as part of the agreement, to comply with the provisions of this rule.

(c)   You must be satisfied that clients referred by the introducer have not been acquired as a result of marketing or publicity or other activities which, if done by a person regulated by the Solicitors Regulation Authority, would be in breach of any of these rules.

(d)   The agreement must not include any provision which would:

(i)   compromise, infringe or impair any of the duties set out in these rules; or

(ii)   allow the introducer to influence or constrain your professional judgement in relation to the advice given to the client.

(e)   The agreement must provide that before making a referral the introducer must give the client all relevant information concerning the referral, in particular:

(i)   the fact that the introducer has a financial arrangement with you; and

(ii)   the amount of any payment to the introducer which is calculated by reference to that referral; or

(iii)   where the introducer is paying you to provide services to the introducer's customers:

(A)   the amount the introducer is paying you to provide those services; and

(B)   the amount the client is required to pay the introducer.

(f)   If you have reason to believe that the introducer is breaching any of the terms of the agreement required by this rule, you must take all reasonable steps to ensure that the breach is remedied. If the introducer continues to breach it you must terminate the agreement.

(g)   Before accepting instructions to act for a client referred under 9.02 you must, in addition to the requirements contained in 2.02 (Client care), 2.03 (Information about the cost) or 2.05 (Complaints handling), give the client, in writing, all relevant information concerning the referral, in particular:

(i)   the fact that you have a financial arrangement with the introducer;

(ii) the amount of any payment to the introducer which is calculated by reference to that referral; or

(iii) where the introducer is paying you to provide services to the introducer's customers:

(A) the amount the introducer is paying you to provide those services; and

(B) the amount the client is required to pay the introducer;

(iv) a statement that any advice you give will be independent and that the client is free to raise questions on all aspects of the transaction; and

(v) confirmation that information disclosed to you by the client will not be disclosed to the introducer unless the client consents; but that where you are also acting for the introducer in the same matter and a conflict of interests arises, you might be obliged to cease acting.

(h) You must not enter into a financial arrangement with an introducer for the referral of clients in respect of criminal proceedings or any matter in which you will act for the client with the benefit of public funding.

(i) For the purpose of this rule:

(i) "financial arrangement" includes:

(A) any payment to a third party in respect of referrals; and

(B) any agreement to be paid by a third party introducer to provide services to the third party's customers; and

(ii) "payment" includes any other consideration but does not include normal hospitality, proper disbursements or normal business expenses.

So you can be bought dinner in return

9.03 Referrals to third parties

(1) If you recommend that a client use a particular firm, agency or business, you must do so in good faith, judging what is in the client's best interests. *p.105*

(2) You must not enter into any agreement or association which would restrict your freedom to recommend any particular firm, agency or business.

(3) Paragraph (2) above does not apply to arrangements in connection with any of the following types of contracts:

(a) regulated mortgage contracts;

(b) general insurance contracts; or

(c) pure protection contracts.

(4) The terms "regulated mortgage contracts", "general insurance contracts" and "pure protection contracts" in (3) above have the meanings given in 19.01(4).

(5) Where you refer a client to a firm, agency or business that can only offer products from one source, you must notify the client in writing of this limitation.

(6) If a client is likely to need an endowment policy, or similar life insurance with an investment element, you must refer them only to an independent intermediary authorised to give investment advice.

Guidance to rule 9 – Referrals of business

General

1. You must not allow the requirements of an introducer, nor your wish to avoid offending an introducer, to affect the advice you give to your clients. Neither must you become so reliant on an introducer as a source of work that this affects the advice you give to your client. It is therefore recommended that your firm conducts regular reviews of your referral arrangements to ensure that this is not happening. Factors you should consider in reviewing your arrangements are:

    (a) whether you have complied with the provisions of rule 9;

    (b) whether you have given referred clients independent advice, which has not been affected by the interests of the introducer; and

    (c) the amount and proportion of your firm's income arising as a result of each referral arrangement.

2. You should always retain control of the work you do for clients. No arrangement with an introducer should affect your duty to communicate directly with the client to obtain or confirm instructions, in the process of providing advice and at all appropriate stages of the transaction.

3. Note that rule 9 does not apply to referrals between lawyers, and that this includes an authorised non-SRA firm, or a multi-disciplinary practice overseas.

Financial arrangements with introducers

4. Rule 9 permits you to pay for referrals, and to be paid by an introducer to provide services to the introducer's customers, subject to conditions. These conditions apply whenever you make a payment, or give other consideration, to a third party who refers clients to you, unless you can show that the payment is wholly unconnected with the referral of any client to you. The conditions also apply regardless of how the payment (or other consideration) is described. For example, the conditions would apply to the

payment of administrative or marketing fees, payments described as "disbursements" which are not proper disbursements, and panel membership fees. Equally, you will not be able to avoid the requirements of the rule by, for example, making the payment to an intermediary who, in turn, has an arrangement with the introducer. When investigating complaints the SRA will consider the substance of any relationship rather than the mere form.

5. "Other consideration" might include, for example, the provision of services and secondment of staff to the introducer, or an agreement to purchase services or products from the introducer (where such a purchase is a condition of referrals being made).

Disclosure – by you

6. Where a payment is made to an introducer in relation to each client referred by the introducer, either as a fixed amount or as a proportion of the fee charged to the client, the amount of the payment must be disclosed to each client. Where a payment to an introducer is more general in nature (for example, it may be a fixed, annual or monthly fee), clients referred by the introducer should be informed that you are making a payment and of the nature of the financial arrangement (or other consideration given). If the client asks for more information about the overall amount of payments made, you should supply such information as you are able. In any case where it is reasonably possible for you to calculate how much of the payment to an introducer relates to a particular client, you must disclose the amount.

7. Where you are being paid by an introducer to provide services to the introducer's customers, both you and the introducer are required to disclose both the amount the introducer is paying you to provide services to the client and the amount the introducer is charging the client for your services. This will enable the client to ascertain whether, and if so how much, the introducer is charging for making the referral and to make an informed decision whether to accept the referral on that basis.

8. You may need to disclose to the client other information, apart from the payment, concerning the nature of the referral agreement. (See 2.02(2)(e).)

9. The requirement that you should make disclosure before accepting instructions will normally mean that you should write to the client as soon as you are asked to act for the client, rather than waiting until the first interview with the client. If time does not permit this, disclosure should be made at the beginning of the interview and confirmed in writing.

Disclosure – by the introducer

10. Rule 9.02(e) requires the introducer to provide the client with all information concerning the referral. It will therefore be necessary for you to agree the nature of this information with the introducer. See note 6 above on disclosure of payments. It is recommended that you ask referred clients on a regular basis what information the introducer has provided about the referral arrangement. You should keep written records of checks made with clients for evidential purposes.

Publicity

11. Rule 9.02(c) requires you to be satisfied that the introducer has not acquired the client as a consequence of marketing, publicity or other activities which, if done by a person regulated by the SRA, would have been in breach of these rules (particularly rule 7 (Publicity)). Three requirements of rule 7 are particularly important for you to bear in mind in the context of payments for referrals:

   (a) the general ban on misleading or inaccurate publicity;

   (b) the prohibition of unsolicited approaches in person or by telephone to a "member of the public" (see 7.03); and

   (c) the requirement that you must not authorise a third party to publicise your firm in a way which would be contrary to rule 7.

Duty to monitor/terminate referral agreements

12. You will be expected to have made suitable enquiries about the way in which an introducer publicises your firm. If you become aware of possible breaches of rule 9 or rule 7 (Publicity), you must bring these to the attention of introducers, and if necessary must terminate a referral agreement.

Improper constraints

13. Rule 9.02(d)(ii) aims to prevent the introducer from influencing or constraining your professional judgement in respect of advice given to clients. For example, the choice of an expert or the decision to instruct counsel are integral to your role in advising the client. See also notes 16 and 17 of the guidance to rule 2 (Client relations) regarding arrangements with introducers which may constrain your professional judgement. See also note 7 to rule 1.03 (Independence).

Excepted work

14. Rule 9.02(h) prohibits you having a financial arrangement with an introducer in respect of criminal proceedings, or in any matter in which you

will act for the client with the benefit of public funding. You would, however, not be prohibited from continuing to act for a referred client if there was a subsequent unanticipated need to obtain public funding or to represent the client in criminal proceedings. In this situation you should retain evidence as to how those circumstances had arisen.

"Normal hospitality"

15. What amounts to "normal hospitality" (see 9.02(i)(ii)) will depend on the circumstances in every case. For example, corporate entertainment, dinners or lunches are acceptable and would not amount to payment for a referral, provided these are proportionate to the relationship with a business contact/introducer.

"Normal business expenses"

16. "Normal business expenses" (see 9.02(i)(ii)) are payments for services provided to your firm which are totally unrelated to the referral of any client. So, for example, you would not be prevented from accepting referrals from the company with which you place your firm's indemnity or buildings insurance, or from the accountant who prepares your annual report or tax return.

Referral to third parties

17. Any referral to a third party will be subject to rule 1 (Core duties) and 9.01, as well as 9.03. You must therefore do nothing in respect of such referrals which would compromise your independence or ability to act or advise in the best interests of each of your clients. Any agreement you enter into in respect of regulated mortgage contracts, general insurance contracts (including after the event insurance contracts) or pure protection contracts will need to provide that referrals will only be made where this is in the best interests of the particular client and the contract is suitable for the needs of that client.

18. Rule 19 (Financial services) deals with referrals in relation to financial services.

19. Rule 2.06 (Commissions) applies in relation to commission received for the introduction of clients.

European cross-border practice

20. Rule 16 (European cross-border practice) prohibits you from making payments for referrals to non-lawyers when undertaking cross-border activities (see 16.06 and notes 12 and 13 of the guidance to rule 16).

Rule 10   Relations with third parties

Introduction

Rule 10 draws together a variety of obligations linked by the need to deal with third parties in a proper manner. The rule as it applies to your overseas practice is modified by 15.10.

Rule 10 – Relations with third parties

10.01   Not taking unfair advantage

You must not use your position to take unfair advantage of anyone either for your own benefit or for another person's benefit.

10.02   Agreeing costs with another party

When negotiating the payment of your client's costs by another firm's client or a third party, you must give sufficient time and information for the amount of your costs to be agreed or assessed.

10.03   Administering oaths

You can administer oaths or affirmations or take declarations if you are authorised to do so. You must not do so where you or your firm is acting for any party in the matter.

10.04   Contacting other party to a matter

You must not communicate with any other party who to your knowledge has retained a lawyer, or a business carrying on the practice of lawyers, to act in a matter, except:

(a)   to request the name and address of the other party's lawyer;

(b)   where it would be reasonable to conclude that the other party's lawyer has refused or failed for no adequate reason either to pass on messages to their client or to reply to correspondence, and has been warned of your intention to contact their client direct;

(c)   with that lawyer's consent; or

(d)   in exceptional circumstances.

10.05   Undertakings

(1)   You must fulfil an undertaking which is given in circumstances where:

(a) you give the undertaking in the course of practice;

(b) you are a recognised body, a manager of a recognised body or a recognised sole practitioner, and any person within the firm gives the undertaking in the course of practice;

(c) you give the undertaking outside the course of practice, but as a solicitor; or

(d) you are an REL based at an office in England and Wales, and you give the undertaking within the UK, as a lawyer of an Establishment Directive profession, but outside your practice as an REL.

(2) You must fulfil an undertaking within a reasonable time.

(3) If you give an undertaking which is dependent upon the happening of a future event, you must notify the recipient immediately if it becomes clear that the event will not occur.

(4) When you give an undertaking to pay another's costs, the undertaking will be discharged if the matter does not proceed unless there is an express agreement that the costs are payable in any event.

10.06 Dealing with more than one prospective buyer in a conveyancing transaction

(1) Each time a seller of land, other than in a sale by auction or tender, either:

(a) instructs you to deal with more than one prospective buyer; or

(b) to your knowledge:

(i) deals directly with another prospective buyer (or their conveyancer); or

(ii) instructs another conveyancer to deal with another prospective buyer;

you must, with the client's consent, immediately inform the conveyancer of each prospective buyer, or the prospective buyer if acting in person.

(2) If the seller refuses to agree to such disclosure, you must immediately stop acting in the matter.

(3) You must not act for both the seller and any of the prospective buyers.

(4) You must not act for more than one of the prospective buyers.

10.07 Fees of lawyers of other jurisdictions

(1) If in the course of practice you instruct a lawyer of another jurisdiction you must, as a matter of professional conduct, pay the lawyer's proper fees unless the lawyer is practising as a lawyer of England and Wales; or

(a) you have expressly disclaimed that responsibility at the outset, or at a later date you have expressly disclaimed responsibility for any fees incurred after that date;

(b)   the lawyer is an REL or is registered with the Bar of England and Wales under the Establishment Directive; or

(c)   the lawyer is an RFL based in England and Wales and practising in a firm.

(2)   If in the course of practice you instruct a business carrying on the practice of a lawyer of another jurisdiction you must, as a matter of professional conduct, pay the proper fees for the work that lawyer does, unless:

(a)   you have expressly disclaimed that responsibility at the outset, or at a later date you have expressly disclaimed responsibility for any fees incurred after that date; or

(b)   the business is a firm.

Guidance to rule 10 – Relations with third parties

Not taking unfair advantage – 10.01

1.   Rule 10.01 does not only apply to your actions which arise out of acting for a client. For example, if you are personally involved in a road accident and use your position as a solicitor unfairly to harass or intimidate the other motorist, you would breach 10.01.

2.   Particular care should be taken when you are dealing with a person who does not have legal representation. You need to find a balance between fulfilling your obligations to your client and not taking unfair advantage of another person. To an extent, therefore, 10.01 limits your duty to act in the best interests of your client. For example, your duty may be limited where an unrepresented opponent provides badly drawn documentation. In the circumstances you should suggest the opponent finds legal representation. If the opponent does not do so, you need to ensure that a balance is maintained between doing your best for the client and not taking unfair advantage of the opponent's lack of legal knowledge and drafting skills.

10

3.   You should take care, when dealing with an unrepresented third party, that any help given does not inadvertently create a contractual relationship with that party. For further information see *Cordery on Solicitors*. See also note 3 of the guidance to rule 2 (Client relations). You should also be careful, when dealing with unqualified persons, that you are not involved in possible breaches of the Solicitors Act 1974, in terms of the prohibitions relating to reserved work. For further details see 20.01 (Reserved work and immigration work) and the guidance to that rule.

4.   There may be situations where it is inappropriate for you to use your professional title in advancing your personal interests. You should consider public confidence in the profession – see 1.06 (Public confidence).

5. It would be unfair to demand anything that is not recoverable through the proper legal process. This would include a letter of claim and any other communication with another party to the action. For instance, where you are instructed to collect a simple debt, you should not demand from the debtor the cost of the letter of claim, since it cannot be said at that stage that such a cost is legally recoverable.

6. The following are some further examples of how you should act in order to ensure you comply with 10.01 and core duty 1.02 (Integrity):

    (a) If a person sends you documents or money subject to an express condition, you should return the documents or money if you are unwilling or unable to comply with the condition.

    (b) If you are sent documents or money on condition that they are held to the sender's order, you should return the documents or money to the sender on demand.

    (c) If you ask anyone to supply copies of documents, you should expect to pay a proper charge for them.

Agreeing costs with another party – 10.02

7. Rule 10.02 applies to all types of work. Its application is clear in litigation matters but will also commonly be relevant to other matters, such as where a landlord's solicitor's costs for dealing with a request for a licence to assign a lease are to be paid by the tenant.

8. You should expect to supply information about the basis of charging (for example an hourly rate or an estimate of the total amount) together with an indication of the nature of the elements of the work done or to be done.

Administering oaths – 10.03

9. You may administer oaths if you are:

    (a) a solicitor with a current practising certificate – see section 81(1) of the Solicitors Act 1974; or

    (b) an REL, under the Establishment Directive.

10. When administering oaths or affirmations or taking declarations, you must ensure the giver:

    (a) is present;

    (b) signs the document in your presence or, if the document is already signed, confirms that the signature is their own and that any attachments are correct; and

(c) appears to understand what they are doing and that the purpose is to confirm that the contents of the document and any attachments are true.

11. You are not responsible for the contents of the document, but if you have a good reason to believe that the contents may be false, you should not proceed.

12. You must not administer an oath where you or your firm are acting for a party in the matter or where you or your firm are otherwise interested in it. This prohibition can be found in section 81(2) of the Solicitors Act 1974 and other related legislation. The effect of these provisions would, for example, prevent you from administering an oath for your spouse where it arises out of a personal matter.

13. When the document has already been signed, it is sufficient for you to accept the giver's word that it is their signature, unless there is clear evidence to the contrary.

Contacting other party to a matter – 10.04

14. Rule 10.04 requires that you do not contact another party to a matter, subject to exceptions, if that party is represented by a lawyer or a business carrying on the practice of a lawyer. It is not intended to prevent you from dealing with other types of representative, if appropriate. If you are asked to deal with such a representative you should ensure that you are not involved in possible breaches of the Solicitors Act 1974 (see note 3 above) and that to do so is in your client's best interest. For example, where the other party is disabled and vulnerable you may well think it appropriate to deal with a representative from a specialist advice organisation or a disability charity. To do so, may mean that the matter is dealt with more efficiently and that you derive some protection from an allegation that you are acting in breach of 10.01 (Not taking unfair advantage). On the other hand, you would be unlikely to want to deal with a person purporting to represent another party who clearly does not have the relevant knowledge or skill.

10

15. Where an enquiry agent has been instructed, the agent may serve documents direct where the other party's lawyer has refused to accept service, but should not take a statement or in any other way communicate with the other party.

16. Care should be taken if you are instructed in a dual capacity. For example, if you are additionally instructed as an estate agent for the seller, you may contact the buyer, but solely about estate agency matters.

17. The other party's lawyer may consent explicitly to your contacting their client, or this may be implied, such as when a protocol is being followed or where it has been agreed that certain documents be sent to all parties.

18. It is not always easy to establish why another lawyer involved in a matter is not responding to correspondence. If you reasonably consider that the other lawyer may be refusing or failing to take instructions from their client, or may be refusing or failing to communicate your requests or correspondence to their client, then a warning should give them the opportunity to object if an incorrect conclusion has been drawn. If there is no valid objection, then you should be able to advance the matter by directly contacting the other client.

19. It is recommended that any communications permitted by 10.04 between you and another lawyer's client be in writing.

20. Rule 10.04 extends to your contact with the in-house lawyers of organisations. For example, if you are acting for a client in a matter concerning a local authority, and you have express or implied notice that the authority's solicitor has been instructed to act in the matter, you must not discuss that matter directly with another officer of the authority, the relevant lead member, any individual councillor or any political group on the authority. You can be involved in political lobbying of a relevant officer or lead member, individual councillors or a political group on the local authority on behalf of a client, even if you know that the authority's solicitor has been instructed to deal with the legal issues.

21. Where the other party is an organisation, you will not breach 10.04 by contacting employees who are not responsible for the giving of instructions because they are not regarded as the client for the purpose of 10.04. However, you should have regard to any contractual obligations employees may have to their employer. It may be appropriate to notify the employer or its lawyer of your intention to contact the employee. This would enable the employee to be advised as to the appropriate response.

22. Lawyers employed by organisations such as the SRA or the Land Registry may properly deal with represented clients when carrying out a statutory function.

23. There may be other situations where it becomes necessary to communicate directly with a represented client. Rule 10.04(d) refers to these as "exceptional circumstances". Such circumstances would include where you are contacted by the client of another lawyer. Care should be taken to avoid taking unfair advantage of this situation but it is acceptable for you to deal with that client's request, if appropriate, and explain that in future they should contact you through their own lawyer.

Undertakings – 10.05

24. An undertaking is any statement, made by you or your firm, that you or your firm will do something or cause something to be done, or refrain from doing something, given to someone who reasonably relies upon it (see rule

24 (Interpretation)). It can be given orally or in writing and need not include the word "undertake". However, it is recommended that oral undertakings be confirmed or recorded in writing for evidential purposes.

25. An agreement to pay a trading debt such as your electricity bill is not normally an undertaking. Once an undertaking is given and the recipient has relied upon it, it can only be withdrawn by agreement.

26. You are not obliged to give or accept undertakings.

27. In 10.05(1)(b) "person within the firm" includes anyone held out by the firm as representing the firm, as well as locums, agents, consultants and other employees.

28. It is important that there be a time frame within which an undertaking should be fulfilled. In the event that no specific time is referred to when the undertaking is given, fulfilment "within a reasonable time" will be expected. What amounts to a "reasonable time" will depend on the circumstances but the onus is on the giver to ensure that the recipient is kept informed of the likely timescale and any delays to it.

29. Failure to fulfil an undertaking may result in disciplinary action.

30. If an undertaking requires the recipient to take certain steps and the recipient fails to do so, the giver may ask the SRA to give notice to the recipient that unless these steps are taken within a period of time it will not then consider a complaint.

31. All undertakings given by solicitors and RELs can be enforced by the court. (See court rules for the appropriate procedure to be followed.) The SRA will not investigate complaints of breaches of undertakings given to the court unless the court makes a complaint to the SRA.

32. Where you undertake to pay the costs of another party or a professional agent's costs, unless a specific amount is agreed, the term "costs" will mean "proper costs". This allows you to request an assessment of the costs by the court.

10

33. If a complaint is made to the SRA concerning an alleged breach of an undertaking and it is found that the undertaking was procured by fraud, deceit or, in certain circumstances, innocent misrepresentation, the SRA is unlikely to take any action in respect of the alleged breach.

34. The SRA will generally interpret an ambiguous undertaking in favour of the recipient.

35. If you give an undertaking "on behalf" of a client it will usually fall within the definition of an undertaking (see rule 24 (Interpretation)) and its performance would, therefore, be your responsibility. If this is not what you intend, you should ensure that liability is disclaimed or it is made clear that you are simply informing the other party about your client's intentions.

36. A promise to give an undertaking is normally treated as an undertaking and will be binding.

37. Where an undertaking has been breached, the aggrieved party may seek compensation. Your firm's insurance as required by the Solicitors' Indemnity Insurance Rules should cover valid claims. If you are in in-house practice, you should consider whether your employer has appropriate insurance. You will remain personally liable in conduct, and may also be financially liable, regardless of whether you have adequate insurance.

38. An undertaking is binding even if it is to do something outside your control. For example, if you undertake to make a payment out of the proceeds of sale of an asset, unless you clearly state to the contrary, you will be expected to make the payment even if the fund (gross or net) is insufficient.

39. If you have received written instructions from your client that are expressed as irrevocable, they are nonetheless revocable, until you have acted on them in such a way as to change your personal position.

40. Certain areas of work, particularly conveyancing, involve the use of standard undertakings. Care should be taken when using standard undertakings to ensure that they suit the specific circumstances. For further details, please refer to a specialist publication.

41. Guidance on undertakings can be obtained from the Professional Ethics Guidance Team.

Dealing with more than one prospective buyer in a conveyancing transaction –
10.06

42. When you are acting for a seller and are asked to "deal" with more than one prospective buyer you must comply with 10.06. "Deal" means any communication you have with any of the relevant parties intended to progress the matter – for example, the sending of a draft contract or a plan of the property. Communicating information of an estate agency nature, such as sending out particulars of sale or showing prospective buyers around a property, would not amount to "dealing" for the purposes of 10.06. If you provide information for an estate agent or Home Information Pack provider only as part of the creation of a Home Information Pack, you will not have "dealt" with prospective buyers for the purpose of 10.06. However, providing additional information to buyers, either direct or through the estate agent or Home Information Pack provider, will normally amount to "dealing".

43. This requirement is sometimes known as the "contract races" rule. This has created the impression that when a transaction is proceeding under such terms, whichever party presents their contract ready for exchanging first is the "winner". In fact, the terms of the arrangement are entirely at the

discretion of the parties and speed may or may not be a factor. You should be careful to agree the terms of the arrangement.

44. If you are required to inform another conveyancer of your intention to proceed with two or more prospective buyers, you should do so immediately by the most suitable means. If the information is given in person or on the telephone, there is no requirement that the details be confirmed in writing but this is advisable.

45. Special care should be taken when dealing with unqualified conveyancers or unrepresented buyers. See notes 2 and 3 above.

Fees of lawyers of other jurisdictions – 10.07

46. Rule 10.07 does not apply when you merely introduce or refer a client to a lawyer of another jurisdiction. However, when you instruct such a lawyer, you will be accepting the liability to pay the lawyer's proper fees unless one of the exceptions in 10.07 applies. For example, if you do not hold money on account and your client is declared bankrupt, you may have to pay the lawyer's proper fee out of your own funds.

47. The fees of a lawyer of another jurisdiction may be regulated by a scale approved by the relevant bar association or law society. You can contact the International Unit of the Law Society for advice.

48. In the event that a dispute arises concerning the payment of the fees of a lawyer of a CCBE state, 16.07 and note 14 of the guidance to rule 16 (European cross-border practice) should be consulted and the necessary action taken before starting any proceedings.

10

Rule 11   Litigation and advocacy

Introduction

Rule 11 imposes additional duties on you if you are a firm or lawyer when exercising a right to conduct litigation or act as an advocate. "Court" in this rule has a wide meaning – see rule 24 (Interpretation). References to appearing or acting as an advocate apply when you are exercising rights of audience before any court, not just if you have been granted rights of audience in the higher courts. The rule only applies in a modified form to overseas practice – see 15.11.

Rule 11 – Litigation and advocacy

11.01   Deceiving or misleading the court

(1) You must never deceive or knowingly or recklessly mislead the court.

(2) You must draw to the court's attention:

    (a) relevant cases and statutory provisions;

    (b) the contents of any document that has been filed in the proceedings where failure to draw it to the court's attention might result in the court being misled; and

    (c) any procedural irregularity.

(3) You must not construct facts supporting your client's case or draft any documents relating to any proceedings containing:

    (a) any contention which you do not consider to be properly arguable; or

    (b) any allegation of fraud unless you are instructed to do so and you have material which you reasonably believe establishes, on the face of it, a case of fraud.

11.02   Obeying court orders

You must comply with any court order requiring you or your firm to take, or refrain from taking, a particular course of action.

11.03   Contempt of court

You must not become in contempt of court.

11.04   Refusing instructions to act as advocate

(1) You must not refuse to act as an advocate for any person on any of the following grounds:

(a)   that the nature of the case is objectionable to you or to any section of the public;

(b)   that the conduct, opinions or beliefs of the prospective client are unacceptable to you or to any section of the public; or

(c)   that the source of any financial support which may properly be given to the prospective client for the proceedings is unacceptable to you.

(2) You are not required to act as an advocate:

(a)   under a conditional fee agreement; or

(b)   if you reasonably consider that you are not being offered a proper fee having regard to:

(i)   the circumstances of the case;

(ii)   the nature of your practice; or

(iii) your experience and standing.

11.05   Appearing as an advocate

If you are appearing as an advocate:

(a)   you must not say anything which is merely scandalous or intended only to insult a witness or any other person;

(b)   you must avoid naming in open court any third party whose character would thereby be called into question, unless it is necessary for the proper conduct of the case;

(c)   you must not call into question the character of a witness you have cross-examined unless the witness has had the opportunity to answer the allegations during cross-examination; and

(d)   you must not suggest that any person is guilty of a crime, fraud or misconduct unless such allegations:

(i)   go to a matter in issue which is material to your client's case; and

(ii)   appear to you to be supported by reasonable grounds.

11.06   Appearing as a witness

You must not appear as an advocate at a trial or act in the litigation if it is clear that you, or anyone within your firm, will be called as a witness, unless you are satisfied that this will not prejudice your independence as an advocate, or litigator, or the interests of your client or the interests of justice.

11.07   Payments to witnesses

You must not make, or offer to make, payments to a witness dependent upon the nature of the evidence given or upon the outcome of the case.

11.08 Recordings of child witnesses' evidence

If you are acting in the defence or prosecution of an accused and you have in your possession a copy of an audio or video recording of a child witness which has been identified as having been prepared to be admitted in evidence at a criminal trial in accordance with the relevant provisions of the Criminal Justice Act 1991 or the Youth Justice and Criminal Evidence Act 1999, you must:

(a) not make or permit any person to make a copy of the recording;

(b) not release the recording to the accused;

(c) not make or permit any disclosure of the recording or its contents to any person except when, in your opinion, it is necessary in the course of preparing the prosecution, defence or appeal against conviction and/or sentence;

(d) ensure that the recording is always kept in a locked, secure container when not in use; and

(e) return the recording when you are no longer instructed in the matter.

Guidance to rule 11 – Litigation and advocacy

General

1. If you are a solicitor you are entitled to conduct litigation in any court. You are also entitled to exercise any right of audience which solicitors had immediately before 7 December 1989, provided that your exercise of that right is in compliance with these rules. You are entitled to exercise additional rights of audience in the higher courts if you have obtained a relevant higher courts advocacy qualification under the Higher Courts Qualification Regulations 2000, or if you had already acquired a relevant higher courts qualification from another regulator before becoming a solicitor.

2. If you are an REL you can conduct litigation or appear as an advocate provided you are instructed in conjunction with a solicitor or barrister who is entitled to perform that service. The role of the solicitor or barrister is not to supervise you or take responsibility for your work, but to assist the court in the event of a problem arising. You can appear as an advocate in those courts and cases in which all solicitors can exercise a right of audience. Like solicitors, you are eligible to acquire extended rights of audience by obtaining one of the solicitors' higher courts qualifications – or you may exercise a relevant higher courts qualification acquired from another regulator before registering with the SRA as an REL.

3. If you are an RFL you do not have any rights of audience or right to conduct litigation (or the right to supervise or assume responsibility for the

11

exercise of any such right) other than those rights which are not reserved by law to any category of persons but are open to any individual. The only exception to this is that you have litigation and advocacy rights before Asylum Support Adjudicators and the Asylum and Immigration Tribunal, or in a tribunal hearing an appeal from one of these, but only if you do the work as a manager or employee of a recognised body or as the employee of a recognised sole practitioner. See also 12.03 and notes 21–29 of the guidance to rule 12 (Framework of practice).

4. If you are a barrister, legal executive, patent agent, trade mark agent or a law costs draftsman you may also be entitled to exercise rights of audience or conduct litigation. When doing so you must comply with any professional obligations arising from such qualification and act within the limitations set by law, in addition to your obligations under these rules.

5. When acting for a client requiring advocacy services you should always consider whether the interests of the client would be best served by you, another lawyer from the same firm or another advocate providing these services. Factors to be taken into consideration include the nature and complexity of the case, your experience and ability, the cost of the advocacy service and the nature of your practice. See rule 2 (Client relations) and the guidance to it for fuller information on issues which you should discuss with your client when accepting instructions.

6. If you are a solicitor you are an officer of the court and you should take all reasonable steps to assist in the smooth running of the court but only insofar as this is consistent with your duties to your client. Difficulties are likely to arise, for example, where the defendant client absconds in a criminal case. If the client does fail to attend:

   (a) in relation to your duty of confidentiality you may properly state that you are without instructions, but may not disclose information about the client's whereabouts; and

   (b) in relation to your duty to act in the client's best interests, you may consider it appropriate to withdraw from the hearing where, having regard to the client's best interests, you believe you cannot properly represent the client. There may be cases where you would be able to proceed in the absence of your client, for example, where you may infer that the defendant expects you to continue to represent them, or where a legal point can be taken which would defeat the prosecution case.

   If you are an REL you are treated as if you were an officer of the court – see paragraph 21 of Schedule 4 to the Establishment Directive Regulations. Even if you are not a solicitor or REL, a similar standard of conduct is required of you in relation to litigation or advocacy as a manager or employee of a recognised body or as an employee of a recognised sole practitioner.

7. You should be cautious about communicating with judges outside the courtroom, in respect of matters in which you are appearing before them, unless you are invited to do so in the presence of the solicitor or counsel for the other side or party.

8. You should not agree to stand bail for your client except in very rare circumstances. By standing bail you risk becoming too closely involved with your client's situation and this may affect your ability to act independently. It is unlawful for you, or any other person, to be party to a bargain to indemnify a surety for bail.

Attending advocates at court

9. Whenever you instruct an advocate you will need to decide whether it is in the interests of your client and the interests of justice for you, or a responsible representative of your firm, to attend the proceedings. In reaching this decision you will need to consider what is necessary for the proper conduct of the case, taking into account the nature and complexity of the case and the capacity of the client to understand the proceedings. For example, you, or your representative, should normally attend:

(a) where the client is charged with an offence classified pursuant to section 75(2) of the Supreme Court Act 1981 as class 1 or 2 (such as murder, manslaughter or rape);

(b) in cases of complex or serious fraud;

(c) where the client may have difficulty in giving or receiving instructions or in understanding the proceedings, for example if the client is a child, has inadequate knowledge of English, or has a mental illness or some other disability;

(d) where the client is likely to disrupt proceedings if the advocate appears alone;

(e) where the advocate is representing more than one party to the hearing;

(f) where there are a substantial number of defence documents at a trial;

(g) where there are a large number of witnesses in the case;

(h) on the day on which the client is to be sentenced, particularly where the client is likely to receive a custodial sentence; or

(i) where issues are likely to arise which question the client's character or your conduct of the case.

11

10. Where you decide that an advocate should not be attended you should inform the advocate and deliver a full and detailed brief sufficiently early for the advocate to consider the papers and to decide whether it would be appropriate for the advocate to attend alone. You should also inform the client that the advocate will be unattended and how instructions may be given.

Statements to the media

11. You should exercise your professional judgement as to whether it is appropriate to make a statement to the media about your client's case and, if you do make a statement, about its content. In making these decisions you should consider:

    (a) whether it is in the client's best interests to do so;

    (b) whether the client has consented to this course of action; and

    (c) the legal position and, for example whether anything you say might be in contempt of court (see 11.03 and note 21).

Deceiving or misleading the court – 11.01

12. Rule 11.01 makes a distinction between deceiving the court, where knowledge is assumed, and misleading the court, which could happen inadvertently. You would not normally be guilty of misconduct if you inadvertently misled the court. However, if during the course of proceedings you become aware that you have inadvertently misled the court, you must, with your client's consent, immediately inform the court. If the client does not consent you must stop acting. Rule 11.01 includes attempting to deceive or mislead the court.

13. You might deceive or mislead the court by, for example:

    (a) submitting inaccurate information or allowing another person to do so;

    (b) indicating agreement with information that another person puts forward which you know is false;

    (c) calling a witness whose evidence you know is untrue;

    (d) not immediately disclosing a document you have become aware of during the course of a case, which should have been, but was not, disclosed;

    (e) attempting to influence a witness, when taking a statement from that witness, with regard to the contents of their statement; and

    (f) tampering with evidence or seeking to persuade a witness to change their evidence. To avoid such allegations it would be wise, when seeking to interview a witness for the other side, to offer to interview them in the presence of the other side's representative.

14. Whilst a person may call themselves by whatever name they choose, you must (in the context of court proceedings) be satisfied that the client is not adopting a different name or date of birth to avoid previous convictions becoming known to the court, or to deceive the court in any other way.

15. If you are acting for a defendant, you need not correct information given to the court by the prosecution or any other party which you know may allow the court to make incorrect assumptions about the client or the case, provided you do not indicate agreement with that information.

16. Where a client admits to having committed perjury or having misled the court in any material matter relating to ongoing proceedings, you must not act further in those proceedings unless the client agrees to disclose the truth to the court.

17. If, either before or during the course of proceedings, the client makes statements to you which are inconsistent, this is not of itself a ground for you to stop acting. Only where it is clear that the client is attempting to put forward false evidence to the court should you stop acting. In other circumstances it would be for the court, and not for you, to assess the truth or otherwise of the client's statement.

18. There are some types of information which you are obliged to disclose to the court, whether or not it is in the best interests of the client to do so. Failure to disclose such information could amount to a breach of 11.01. For example:

(a) The advocates on both sides must advise the court of relevant cases and statutory provisions. If one of them omits a case or provision or makes an incorrect reference to a case or provision, it is the duty of the other to draw attention to it even if it assists the opponent's case.

(b) Except when acting or appearing for the prosecution, if you know of facts which, or of a witness who, would assist the adversary you are not under any duty to inform the adversary, or the court, of this to the prejudice of your own client. However, if you know that a relevant document has been filed in the proceedings and is therefore notionally within the knowledge of the court, you must inform the judge of its existence.

19. You are permitted, even when acting as an advocate, to interview and take statements from any witness or prospective witness at any stage in the proceedings, whether or not that witness has been interviewed or called as a witness by another party. (However, see note 13(e) and (f) above.)

Obeying court orders – 11.02

20. You have a responsibility to ensure that you comply with any court order made against you. Similarly, you must advise your clients to comply with court orders made against them. If you are the recipient of a court order which you believe to be defective you are obliged under 11.02 to comply with it unless it is revoked by the court, or unless an application for a stay is pending. If your client is the recipient of an order you believe to be defective you must discuss with the client the possibility of challenging it and explain to the client the client's obligation to comply if the order is not overturned.

Contempt of court – 11.03

21. You could, for example, become in contempt of court by making a statement to the press which is calculated to interfere with the fair trial of a case which has not been concluded.

Refusing instructions to act as advocate – 11.04

22. In addition to complying with 11.04 you must comply with rule 6 (Equality and diversity) in your dealings with clients, staff, other lawyers and third parties.

23. Rule 11.04(2)(b) states that you may refuse to act if you are not being offered a proper fee. In the case of publicly funded matters this means that if the fee likely to be received from the Legal Services Commission is lower than your normal charging rate, you may decline to act.

Appearing as an advocate – 11.05

24. Rule 11.05 sets out a number of issues relating to the way in which you conduct yourself in court. There may be other restrictions, such as rules of court, which affect the way a case may be presented in court and you should familiarise yourself with these.

25. It is not the intention of 11.05 to prevent you robustly defending your client's position.

Appearing as a witness – 11.06

26. The circumstances in which it will be proper for you to appear as an advocate at a trial or act in litigation when you are also a witness will be extremely rare. Factors you will need to consider include:

    (a) the nature of the evidence you are being asked to give, its importance to the case and in particular whether it is likely to be contested or is purely formal;

    (b) whether the situation would give rise to a conflict between you or your firm and your client. For example, it would not be appropriate for you to give evidence for another party (or, in a criminal case, the prosecution); and

(c) how your client would be affected if, having already accepted instructions to act, you were to stop acting.

27. Provided the evidence is unlikely to be contested on a factual basis, it will normally be acceptable for you to act as an advocate if a member of your firm is to give evidence. For example, if an employee of your firm has advised a client at a police station, and is required to give evidence as to the reasons for advising the client to exercise the right to silence, it would not be improper for you to act as an advocate in the case.

28. You will need to consider your client's interests when asked to act in a matter in which there is a significant risk that you, or a member of your firm, will be called as a witness in the case. You should not accept instructions to act for a client in circumstances where you could not act if you had already been called – for example, if you had witnessed events which were material to the issue being tried. On the other hand there is always a degree of risk that events you witnessed at a police station, such as the client exercising the right to silence or an identity parade, will become an issue at the trial. However this would not normally prevent you appearing as an advocate.

29. Rule 11.06 would not normally prevent you giving evidence at a pre-trial hearing, for example by making a witness statement which is purely concerned with procedural issues, provided your evidence is unlikely to be contested at the trial.

Payments to witnesses – 11.07

30. There is no objection to your paying reasonable expenses to witnesses and reasonable compensation for loss of time attending court.

Recording of child witnesses' evidence – 11.08

31. The SRA recommends that you use the following form of undertaking in order to comply with 11.08:

"I/We acknowledge receipt of the recording marked 'evidence of . . .'.

I/We undertake that whilst the recording is in my/our possession I/we shall:

(a) not make or permit any other person to make a copy of the recording;

(b) not release the recording to [*name of the accused*];

(c) not make or permit any disclosure of the recording or its contents to any person except when in my/our opinion it is necessary in the course of preparing the prosecution, defence, or appeal against conviction and/or sentence;

(d)   ensure that the recording is always kept in a locked, secure container when not in use; and

(e)   return the recording to you when I am/we are no longer instructed in the matter."

32. Recordings should preferably be delivered to third parties by hand but where this is not possible the recording should be sent by recorded delivery. To avoid the risk of theft the contents of the package should not be apparent from the outside. If you personally collect, or a member of staff personally collects, a recording, you or they should be able to produce a proper form of identification.

33. Although 11.08 does not specifically define "locked, secure container" a locked car cannot be considered as such and a recording should never be left unattended in a car.

34. You may be asked to give an undertaking in the form recommended by the Home Office, which is similar to that recommended by the SRA. As with the giving of any undertaking, you should first ensure that you can comply with its terms.

Rule 12   Framework of practice

Introduction

This rule sets out the types of business through which solicitors, RELs, RFLs and recognised bodies may practise. The rule restricts the types of business available in order to reflect statutory provisions and to ensure that clients and the public have the protections provided for by statute.

Rule 12 – Framework of practice

12.01   Solicitors

Practice from an office in England and Wales

(1) You may practise as a solicitor from an office in England and Wales in the following ways only:

   (a) as a recognised sole practitioner or the employee of a recognised sole practitioner;

   (b) as a solicitor exempted under 20.03(2) from the obligation to be a recognised sole practitioner;

   (c) as a manager, employee, member or owner of:

      (i) a recognised body; or

      (ii) a body corporate which is a manager, member or owner of a recognised body;

   (d) as a manager, employee, member or owner of:

      (i) an authorised non-SRA firm; or

      (ii) a body corporate which is a manager, member or owner of an authorised non-SRA firm,

      provided that all work you do is either of a sort authorised by the firm's approved regulator, or done for the firm itself, or within 13.02 (Work colleagues), 13.03 (Related bodies) or 13.04 (Pro bono work);

   (e) as the employee of another person, business or organisation, provided that you undertake work only for your employer, or as permitted by rule 13 (In-house practice, etc.).

12

Practice from an office outside England and Wales

(2) You may practise as a solicitor from an office outside England and Wales in the following ways only:

   (a)   as a sole practitioner (including a recognised sole practitioner);

   (b)   as the employee of a sole principal who is a lawyer;

   (c)   as a manager, employee, member or owner of a recognised body, provided that if any of the body's managers or owners are non-lawyers and the office is in an Establishment Directive state other than the UK, the rules for local lawyers would permit a local lawyer to practise through a business of that composition and structure;

   (d)   as a manager, employee, member or owner of a business which has no office in England and Wales and meets all the following conditions:

      (i)   the business carries on the practice of law;

      (ii)   a controlling majority of the managers and the owners are lawyers and/or bodies corporate in which lawyers constitute a controlling majority of the managers and owners;

      (iii)   if any of the business's managers or owners are non-lawyers and any manager or owner is subject to the rules for local lawyers, the composition and structure of the business complies with those rules; and

      (iv)   if any of the business's managers or owners are non-lawyers and the office is in an Establishment Directive state, the rules for local lawyers would permit a local lawyer to practise through a business of that composition and structure;

   (e)   as the employee of another person, business or organisation, provided that you undertake work only for your employer, or as permitted by 15.13 (In-house practice overseas).

12.02　RELs

If you are an REL:

Practice from an office in England and Wales

(1)   You may practise as an REL from an office in England and Wales in the following ways only:

   (a)   as a recognised sole practitioner or the employee of a recognised sole practitioner;

   (b)   as an REL exempted under 20.03(2) from the obligation to be a recognised sole practitioner;

   (c)   as a manager, employee, member or owner of:

      (i)   a recognised body; or

      (ii)   a body corporate which is a manager, member or owner of a recognised body;

(d) as a manager, employee, member or owner of:

   (i)   an authorised non-SRA firm; or

   (ii) a body corporate which is a manager, member or owner of an authorised non-SRA firm,

   provided that all work you do is either of a sort authorised by the firm's approved regulator, or done for the firm itself, or within 13.02 (Work colleagues), 13.03 (Related bodies) or 13.04 (Pro bono work);

(e) as the employee of another person, business or organisation, provided that you undertake work only for your employer, or as permitted by rule 13 (In-house practice, etc.).

Practice from an office in Scotland or Northern Ireland

(2) You may practise as an REL from an office in Scotland or Northern Ireland in the following ways only:

(a) as a sole practitioner (including a recognised sole practitioner);

(b) as the employee of a sole principal who is a lawyer;

(c) as a manager, employee, member or owner of a recognised body;

(d) as a manager, employee, member or owner of a business which has no office in England and Wales and meets all the following conditions:

   (i)   the business carries on the practice of law;

   (ii) a controlling majority of the managers and the owners are lawyers and/or bodies corporate in which lawyers constitute a controlling majority of the managers and owners; and

   (iii) if any of the business's managers or owners are non-lawyers, the professional rules governing a solicitor of that jurisdiction would allow such a solicitor to practise through a business of that composition and structure;

(e) as the employee of another person, business or organisation, provided that you undertake work only for your employer, or as permitted by 15.13 (In-house practice overseas).

12.03   RFLs

12

Practice in the capacity of an RFL

(1) Your practice as a foreign lawyer in the capacity of an RFL is confined to practice as:

(a) the employee of a recognised sole practitioner;

(b) a manager, employee, member or owner of:

    (i)   a recognised body; or

    (ii)   a body corporate which is a manager, member or owner of a recognised body;

(c)   a manager, employee, member or owner of:

    (i)   an authorised non-SRA firm; or

    (ii)   a body corporate which is a manager, member or owner of an authorised non-SRA firm,

in which case all the work you do must be of a sort authorised by the firm's approved regulator, or done for the firm itself, or within 13.02 (Work colleagues), 13.03 (Related bodies) or 13.04 (Pro bono work).

Practice in another capacity than as an RFL

(2)   If you provide services as a foreign lawyer in any of the following ways in England and Wales or elsewhere, you will not be practising in the capacity of an RFL and you must not be held out or described in that context as an RFL, or as regulated by or registered with the Law Society or the Solicitors Regulation Authority:

(a)   as a sole principal; or

(b)   as a manager, member or owner of any business or organisation other than a recognised body or an authorised non-SRA firm; or

(c)   as a manager, member or owner of a body corporate which is a manager, member or owner of any business or organisation other than a recognised body or an authorised non-SRA firm; or

(d)   as the employee of any business or organisation other than a recognised sole practitioner, a recognised body or an authorised non-SRA firm.

(3)   If you have a practice under (1) above, and another business under (2) above, the latter is a "separate business" for the purpose of these rules and you must therefore comply with rule 21 (Separate businesses).

Scope of practice

(4)   Whether or not you are practising in the capacity of an RFL you must not:

(a)   be held out in any way which suggests that you are, or are entitled to practise as, a lawyer of England and Wales;

(b)   undertake the following reserved work in England and Wales:

    (i)   advocacy in open court;

    (ii)   the conduct of court litigation;

    (iii) the administration of oaths and statutory declarations;

(c) undertake advocacy in chambers in England and Wales, except under instructions given by a person qualified to direct reserved work;

(d) undertake the following reserved work in England and Wales, except at the direction and under the supervision of a person qualified to direct reserved work:

   (i) the preparation of court documents;

   (ii) the preparation of instruments and the lodging of documents relating to the transfer or charge of land;

   (iii) the preparation of papers on which to found or oppose a grant of probate or a grant of letters of administration;

   (iv) the preparation of trust deeds disposing of capital,

   unless you also have an appropriate legal qualification as a lawyer of England and Wales.

(5) If you are not practising in the capacity of an RFL you must not give immigration advice or provide immigration services in the UK unless:

   (a) you are entitled under the Immigration and Asylum Act 1999 to do that work in your own right; or

   (b) you do the work under the supervision of a person who is not a solicitor, an REL or an RFL but is entitled under the Immigration and Asylum Act 1999 to do that work.

12.04 Recognised bodies

Practice from an office in England and Wales

(1) A recognised body may practise from an office in England and Wales in the following ways only:

   (a) as a stand-alone firm;

   (b) as a manager, member or owner of another recognised body; or

   (c) as a manager, member or owner of an authorised non-SRA firm, in which case the services you provide must all fall within the scope of the firm's authorisation;

   (d) as an executor, trustee or nominee company, or a company providing company secretarial services, owned and operated by another recognised body or by a recognised sole practitioner.

12

Practice from an office outside England and Wales

(2) A recognised body may practise from an office outside England and Wales in the following ways only:

   (a) as a stand-alone firm, provided that if any of the body's managers or owners are non-lawyers and the office is in an Establishment Directive state other than the UK, the rules for local lawyers would permit a local lawyer to practise through a business of that composition and structure;

(b) as a manager, member or owner of a business which has no office in England and Wales and meets all the following conditions:

    (i) the business carries on the practice of law;

    (ii) a controlling majority of the managers and the owners are lawyers and/or bodies corporate in which lawyers constitute a controlling majority of the managers and owners;

    (iii) if any of the business's managers or owners are non-lawyers and any manager or owner is subject to the rules for local lawyers, the composition and structure of the business complies with those rules; and

    (iv) if any of the business's managers or owners are non-lawyers and the office is in an Establishment Directive state other than the UK, the rules for local lawyers would permit a local lawyer to practise through a business of that composition and structure;

(c) as an executor, trustee or nominee company, or a company providing company secretarial services, owned and operated by another recognised body or by a recognised sole practitioner.

12.05   Managers and employees authorised by another approved regulator

(1) If you are a manager or employee of a recognised body or an employee of a recognised sole practitioner and you are not a solicitor but you are authorised by an approved regulator other than the SRA, you must not:

(a) be held out in any way which suggests that you are, or are entitled to practise as, a solicitor;

(b) undertake the following reserved work in England and Wales, unless authorised by your approved regulator to do so:

    (i) advocacy in open court;

    (ii) the conduct of court litigation;

    (iii) the administration of oaths and statutory declarations;

(c) undertake advocacy in chambers in England and Wales, unless authorised by your approved regulator or acting under instructions given by a person qualified to direct reserved work;

(d) undertake the following reserved work in England and Wales, unless authorised by your approved regulator or acting under the supervision of a person qualified to direct reserved work:

    (i) the preparation of court documents;

    (ii)   the preparation of instruments and the lodging of documents relating to the transfer or charge of land;

    (iii)   the preparation of papers on which to found or oppose a grant of probate or a grant of letters of administration;

    (iv)   the preparation of trust deeds disposing of capital;

(e)   (i)   undertake the conduct of immigration tribunal proceedings in the UK or advocacy before an immigration tribunal in the UK unless you are authorised by your approved regulator or the Immigration Services Commissioner to do that work;

    (ii)   prepare documents in the UK for immigration tribunal proceedings unless you are authorised by your approved regulator or the Immigration Services Commissioner to do that work or acting under the supervision of a person qualified to direct reserved work; or

(f)   give immigration advice or undertake immigration services in the UK which are not within (b) to (e) above, unless you are authorised by your approved regulator or the Immigration Services Commissioner to do that work, or acting under the supervision of an individual working in the firm who is authorised under statute to do that work.

12.06   Managers and employees who are not lawyers

(1)   If you are a manager or employee of a recognised body or an employee of a recognised sole practitioner and you are not a lawyer of England and Wales, an RFL, or a lawyer of an Establishment Directive profession, you must not:

(a)   be held out in any way which suggests that you are, or are entitled to practise as, a lawyer of England and Wales;

(b)   undertake the following reserved work in England and Wales:

    (i)   advocacy in open court;

    (ii)   the conduct of court litigation;

    (iii)   the administration of oaths and statutory declarations;

(c)   undertake advocacy in chambers in England and Wales, except under instructions given by a person qualified to direct reserved work;

(d)   undertake the following reserved work in England and Wales, except at the direction and under the supervision of a person qualified to direct reserved work:

    (i)   the preparation of court documents;

    (ii)   the preparation of instruments and the lodging of documents relating to the transfer or charge of land;

    (iii)   the preparation of papers on which to found or oppose a grant of probate or a grant of letters of administration;

12

(iv)   the preparation of trust deeds disposing of capital;

(e)   (i)   undertake the conduct of immigration tribunal proceedings in the UK or advocacy before an immigration tribunal in the UK unless you are authorised by the Immigration Services Commissioner to do that work;

(ii)   prepare documents in the UK for immigration tribunal proceedings unless you are authorised by the Immigration Services Commissioner to do that work, or acting under the supervision of a person qualified to direct reserved work; or

(f)   give immigration advice or undertake immigration services in the UK which are not within (b) to (e) above, unless you are authorised by the Immigration Services Commissioner to do that work or you do the work under the supervision of an individual working in the firm who is authorised under statute to do that work.

Guidance to rule 12 – Framework of practice

1.   The Legal Services Act 2007 (the LSA) provided for significant changes to the regulation of lawyers, and the ways in which they can practise, to increase competition and facilitate access to justice for the public. The framework established by the LSA enables the SRA (as well as other regulators) to update and improve its regulation, and solicitors and RELs to increase the scope of their practice, by allowing:

(a)   the SRA

(i)   to permit and regulate legal disciplinary practices (LDPs),

(ii)   to approve non-lawyers as managers of firms,

(iii)   to apply firm-based regulation to all practices;

(b)   solicitors and RELs

(i)   to practise through an LDP with lawyers regulated by another approved regulator and/or with non-lawyers,

(ii)   to practise through an LDP regulated by another approved regulator.

2.   The lawyers of England and Wales (other than solicitors) who can practise in an LDP, and their approved regulators for the purposes of the LSA, are:

barrister   Bar Council (through the Bar Standards Board)

legal executive   Institute of Legal Executives (through ILEX Professional Standards Ltd)

licensed conveyancer   Council for Licensed Conveyancers

patent agent   Chartered Institute of Patent Attorneys (through the Intellectual Property Regulation Board)

trade mark agent   Institute of Trade Mark Attorneys (through the Intellectual Property Regulation Board)

law costs draftsman   Association of Law Costs Draftsmen

notary public   Faculty Office of the Archbishop of Canterbury.

Firms regulated by one of the other approved regulators are referred to in the rules as authorised non-SRA firms.

3.   A non-lawyer must be approved by the SRA under regulation 3 of the Recognised Bodies Regulations to be a manager of a recognised body.

4.   Rules 12, 13, 14 and 20 make up the framework rules which set out the ways in which individuals and bodies subject to the SRA's rules can practise, and restrictions upon those individuals and bodies. Rule 12 imposes restrictions on the type of firm through which you may practise if you are a solicitor, an REL, an RFL or a recognised body. It also sets out the restrictions on you if you are a manager or employee of a firm regulated by the SRA and you are a lawyer regulated by another approved regulator or are a non-lawyer. The ability to impose such restrictions on any individual or body in a firm providing legal services and, if necessary, enforce them enables the SRA to protect clients and the public interest as anticipated by the LSA.

5.   Rule 12 governs the types of business through which you may practise, but disgraceful conduct outside of practice may put you in breach of 1.06 (Public confidence) if you are a solicitor, an REL or an RFL, and 10.01 (Not taking unfair advantage) if you are a solicitor or an REL. Rule 10.05(1)(c) and (d), (2) and (3) (undertakings given outside the course of practice) apply to you if you are a solicitor or REL.

6.   The SRA's approach to regulation is primarily firm-based. The LSA facilitates this to ensure proper regulation of practices that can involve a variety of lawyers and non-lawyers. This approach does not prevent the SRA taking regulatory action against individuals, as well as firms, in appropriate cases. This could include action against anyone in the firm including non-lawyer managers and employees, as the requirements in the Code apply to all recognised bodies and their managers and employees, as well as to solicitor and REL sole practitioners and their employees (23.01(1)).

12

Solicitors – 12.01

England and Wales

7. The rule requires every private practice firm providing legal services to the public in England and Wales under the SRA's regulation to be a recognised body or a recognised sole practitioner. A solicitor can be a manager, employee, member or owner of a recognised body, or of a body corporate which is a manager, member or owner of a recognised body. "Manager" is the term used in the LSA to refer to a partner in a partnership, a member of an LLP or a director of a company. Owner is included, in addition to manager, as you may be a shareowner in a company but not hold a directorship. Member is included, in addition to owner, because holding a share (as member of the company) is not the same as owning the share – you could, for example, be holding the share as nominee.

8. A recognised body must be at least 75% owned and controlled by lawyers. Rule 14 does not prohibit layers of ownership of recognised bodies, but a body corporate with an ownership interest in a recognised body must itself be a recognised body, an authorised non-SRA firm with at least 75% ownership by lawyers, or a European corporate practice (as defined in rule 24) with similar ownership restrictions.

9. New partnerships, companies and LLPs must apply to the SRA for recognition of the firm before being able to practise (rule 14 deals with the composition, structure and services of recognised bodies and the Recognised Bodies Regulations set out the procedural and administrative requirements).

10. If you wish to practise on your own account, you must be authorised as a recognised sole practitioner by the SRA endorsing your practising certificate, before you can establish your firm (see 20.03 and the SRA Practising Regulations). There are limited exceptions in 20.03(2) permitting sole practice without such an endorsement, for example when practising entirely outside England and Wales, as a locum or when providing services to family and friends free of charge.

11. If you are practising as a manager, employee, member or owner of an authorised non-SRA firm, what you can do will depend on the type of work you want to do, and for whom you want to do it.

    (a) The services you can provide to the public are limited to those which are regulated by the firm's approved regulator. For example, as a partner in a firm regulated by the Council for Licensed Conveyancers (CLC) you could not carry out litigation on behalf of clients of the firm, as the CLC is not authorised to regulate this work. When you are providing services of a type regulated by the firm's approved regulator (whether to the public or to the firm itself), you will primarily be regulated by the firm's regulator, and you will in general be complying with that regulator's rules rather than the SRA's rules – see 23.01(2).

(b) Under rule 12.01(1)(d) you could also, however, provide services that are not regulated by the firm's approved regulator. As a partner in the CLC-regulated firm you could provide, say, litigation services to the firm itself or, subject to the limitations in rule 13, to colleagues, or to related bodies of the firm, or to clients on a pro bono basis. When providing services which are not regulated by the firm's approved regulator, you will be subject to all the SRA's rules.

12. Rule 13 (In-house practice, etc.) sets out the limited circumstances in which, if you are an in-house solicitor in England and Wales, you can provide services to persons other than your employer.

Outside England and Wales

13. If you are a sole practitioner and practise only from an office outside England and Wales, you will not need to be (and will not be able to be) a recognised sole practitioner. However, if your sole practice also has an office in England and Wales, you will need to be a recognised sole practitioner.

14. A solicitor may practise with other lawyers from an office outside England and Wales in almost any kind of partnership or body corporate, including, for example, through an overseas partnership with a separate legal identity. You can practise as a manager, employee, member or owner of such a firm, which may be an overseas legal practice or a recognised body.

15. If the firm is an overseas legal practice (i.e. it is practising entirely outside England and Wales):

(a) a controlling majority (i.e. more than 50%) of the managers *and* owners must be lawyers;

(b) if any of the managers or owners are non-lawyers, and the firm has an office in an Establishment Directive state, the composition and structure of the firm must comply with rules for local lawyers (even if there are no local lawyers in the firm);

(c) if any of the managers or owners are non-lawyers, and the firm has an office in any other jurisdiction, compliance with local rules with regard to the composition and structure of the firm is only necessary if any of the firm's managers are subject to those rules (either because they are local lawyers, or because the local law applies local rules to the firm).

16. If the firm is a recognised body (i.e. it also has an office or offices in England and Wales), *and* it has any non-lawyer managers or owners, *and* it has an office in any Establishment Directive state other than the UK, the

composition and structure of the firm must comply with rules for local lawyers (even if there are no local lawyers in the firm).

17. You may practise as an in-house solicitor outside England and Wales, within the limits set by 15.13 (In-house practice overseas).

Registered European lawyers (RELs) – 12.02

England and Wales

18. An REL is subject to the same restrictions as a solicitor in relation to practice from an office in England and Wales.

19. If you wish to practise on your own account, you must be authorised as a recognised sole practitioner by the SRA endorsing your certificate of registration, before you can establish your firm.

Outside England and Wales

20. The overseas provisions for an REL are the same as for a solicitor except that they apply only in Scotland and Northern Ireland. You are not subject to rule 12 in relation to practice from an office outside the UK.

Registered foreign lawyers (RFLs) – 12.03

England and Wales

21. Any foreign lawyer (whether based in England and Wales or elsewhere) must be registered with the SRA as an RFL to be a manager, member or owner of a recognised body, with the following exceptions:

    (a) a foreign lawyer who is also qualified as a lawyer of England and Wales does not have to be an RFL;

    (b) a member of an Establishment Directive profession – except that if the lawyer is not a national of an Establishment Directive state and will be based, or partly based, in England and Wales, he or she *does* have to be an RFL in order to be a manager, member or owner of a recognised body.

    Additional guidance on RFLs and multi-national practice can be found on our website.

22. There is no requirement to register as an RFL in order to be employed by a recognised body or a recognised sole practitioner but, if you are registered, you will be subject to SRA regulation in this capacity when working for an SRA regulated firm or an authorised non-SRA firm.

23. An RFL is subject to the same restrictions as a solicitor or REL in relation to practice from an office in England and Wales with two exceptions. Your registration as an RFL does not entitle you to practise:

    (a) as an RFL sole practitioner; or

    (b) as an in-house RFL.

24. Registration as an RFL is portable to the extent that it will enable you to be a manager, employee, member or owner of an authorised non-SRA firm, although your ability to work within such a firm will depend on the framework of practice requirements of the relevant approved regulator. You will be able to undertake work authorised by the firm's approved regulator (subject to any statutory limitations or requirements). Additionally you will be able to function as an in-house lawyer under rule 13, doing other work for the employer, related bodies, work colleagues and pro bono clients under the SRA's rules. For example, you might be an Australian solicitor employed to do conveyancing work for the clients of a firm authorised by the Council for Licensed Conveyancers. Under the SRA's authorisation of RFLs you could advise the firm and fellow employees on immigration issues, but would need to comply with rule 13 and all other SRA rules.

25. Rule 12.03(2) specifies the activities that will constitute practice in a capacity other than as an RFL. In effect, your registration as an RFL will not be relevant in the role of owner or employee of a business in England and Wales which is not regulated by the SRA or one of the other approved regulators. The SRA does not regulate any practice you might have outside the framework established under the LSA, so there must be no implication in such a context that you are an RFL, or that you or the business are regulated by or registered with the SRA or the Law Society. As your work in such a role is not regulated by the SRA, any implication that it is could, for example, lead to removal from the register of RFLs.

26. If you are practising as an RFL in an SRA regulated firm or in an authorised non-SRA firm, and at the same time you are involved in a separate legal practice as a foreign lawyer, this will be a separate business and you must comply with the requirements of 21.05.

27. Rules 12.03(4) and 12.03(5) set out a number of prohibitions relating to RFLs. For example:

    (a) whether or not you are practising as an RFL you cannot be held out or described in any way that suggests you are a lawyer of England and Wales, unless you have an appropriate additional qualification;

    (b) whether or not you are practising as an RFL you must not provide any reserved legal services unless you have an appropriate additional qualification or do the work under appropriate supervision;

    (c) if you are not practising as an RFL you must not give immigration

12

advice or provide (non-reserved) immigration services unless you have an appropriate additional qualification or authorisation or do the work under appropriate supervision.

28. Where, in order to satisfy statutory requirements, there is a need for an RFL doing reserved work to be supervised or directed by someone in the firm, this can only be undertaken by a person of equivalent or higher status. For example, it would not be appropriate for the work of an RFL manager to purport to be supervised or directed by an employee.

Outside England and Wales

29. The rules in general do not apply to an RFL in relation to practice outside England and Wales. However 15.01 makes clear that 1.06 (Public confidence) applies to an RFL's activities outside England and Wales, whether as a lawyer or in some other business or private capacity. Rule 15.01(1)(b)(iv) states that 12.03(2), (3), (4)(a) and (5) also apply to an RFL's activities outside England and Wales. Rule 12.03(2) applies to prohibit an RFL from being held out or described as an RFL or as regulated by or registered with the Law Society or the SRA when participating outside England and Wales in a legal practice which is not authorised by the SRA or any other approved regulator, or in an in-house practice. Rule 12.03(3) provides that when an RFL participates in England and Wales in a legal practice which is authorised by the SRA or another approved regulator, and also participates in a separate practice or business outside England and Wales, he or she must comply with 21.05 (Separate businesses). Rule 12.03(4)(a) provides that an RFL must not be held out outside England and Wales as a lawyer of England and Wales (unless of course the RFL does have such a qualification). Rule 12.03(5) applies in Scotland and Northern Ireland and provides that an RFL who is not practising in that capacity is subject to the prohibitions in note 27(c) above.

Recognised bodies – 12.04

England and Wales

30. A recognised body must have at least one office in England and Wales (see rule 14 for the composition and structure requirements for recognised bodies) and may be:

(a) a stand-alone firm which itself provides legal services to the public;

(b) a manager, member or owner of another recognised body or of an authorised non-SRA firm (but see below for the services you can provide);

(c) an executor, trustee or nominee company, or a company providing company secretarial services, which is owned and operated by another recognised body or recognised sole practitioner and is providing services in conjunction with that firm.

31. If the recognised body is a manager, member or owner of an authorised non-SRA firm it may only provide services through that firm which the firm is authorised to provide.

32. Recognised bodies can have a complex structure, involving multi-layered ownership by other legally qualified bodies (see rule 24). But note that a partnership cannot be a partner in another partnership which is a recognised body (although, as an exception, an overseas partnership with separate legal identity could be a partner in a partnership which is a recognised body). Non-lawyer participation in all recognised bodies is restricted to 25% as measured by three different indicators:

    (a)   numbers of managers;

    (b)   proportion of shares or other ownership rights;

    (c)   proportion of voting rights exercised or controlled.

Outside England and Wales

33. If a firm practises only from an office or offices outside England and Wales, it will not need to be (and will not be able to be) a recognised body. However, if the firm also has at least one office in England and Wales it must be a recognised body and can practise as such outside England and Wales.

34. Outside England and Wales the rules apply to a "solicitor-controlled recognised body" (and also to an "REL-controlled recognised body" in Scotland or Northern Ireland) – see the definitions in rule 24, and further details in 15.01(2) and 15.27.

35. A recognised body can practise outside England and Wales as a stand-alone firm or as a manager, member or owner of an overseas legal practice (i.e. one that practises entirely outside England and Wales). It may also of course practise as a manager, member or owner of another recognised body with an overseas office.

36. If the recognised body has any non-lawyer managers or owners, and it has an office in any Establishment Directive state other than the UK, see note 16 above.

37. If the recognised body is a manager, member or owner of an overseas legal practice which does not have an office in England and Wales, see note 15 above.

12

Managers and employees authorised by an approved regulator other than the SRA – 12.05

England and Wales

38. Rule 14 permits lawyers and firms authorised by another approved regulator to be owners and managers of a recognised body. Rule 12 sets out the ways in which such persons authorised by other approved regulators can and cannot practise as a manager or employee of a recognised body or as the employee of a recognised sole practitioner. The Code applies to such a manager or employee.

39. An individual authorised by another approved regulator cannot practise as a recognised sole practitioner regulated by the SRA as the SRA can only authorise and regulate sole solicitors and RELs. Likewise the SRA can only grant recognised body status to a firm with at least one solicitor or REL manager (or at least one manager which is a legally qualified body with a solicitor or REL manager) so, for example, a firm made up solely of licensed conveyancers or a mix of lawyers approved by other approved regulators cannot become a recognised body.

40. The restrictions in 12.05 establish that the following legal prohibitions on non-solicitors, which include those authorised by another approved regulator, will be treated as breaches of the Code:

    (a) you cannot be held out or described in any way that suggests you are, or are entitled to practise as, a solicitor; and

    (b) you must not provide any reserved legal services, unless, for example, authorised by your own approved regulator; or under the supervision and direction of a person qualified to direct such work; or are authorised by another regulator, such as the Office of the Immigration Services Commissioner, to do the work.

41. Where, in order to satisfy statutory requirements, there is a need for an individual doing reserved work to be supervised or directed by someone in the firm, this can only be undertaken by a person of equivalent or higher status. For example, it would not be appropriate for the work of a manager to purport to be supervised or directed by an employee.

Outside England and Wales

42. A lawyer of England and Wales who is an individual authorised by another approved regulator is subject to the rules in relation to practice outside England and Wales if he or she is a manager of a solicitor-controlled recognised body (and also if he or she is a manager of an REL-controlled recognised body in Scotland or Northern Ireland).

Non-lawyers – 12.06

England and Wales

43. From March 2009, non-lawyers can be owners and managers, as well as employees, of SRA-regulated firms. Rule 12 permits a non-lawyer to become a manager or employee of one of the practice vehicles permitted to solicitors, RELs and so on.

44. The position of non-lawyer employees changed in 2009 in that the SRA has direct powers of regulation over all employees and not just over solicitors and RELs. The guidance to rules 5 and 23 provides some more detail on this.

45. The purpose of rule 12.06 is to establish that the following legal prohibitions on non-lawyers will be treated as breaches of the Code. For example:

    (a) you cannot be held out or described in any way that suggests you are, or are entitled to practise as, a lawyer of England and Wales; and

    (b) you must not provide any reserved legal services, unless, for example, acting under the supervision and direction of a person qualified to direct such work (see also note 41 above), or are authorised by a regulator, such as the Office of the Immigration Services Commissioner, to do the work.

46. The LSA requires that any non-lawyer owners of practices must be approved by the SRA, and must also be managers. This means that a non-lawyer could only be a shareowner in a company (whether beneficially or as nominee) if he or she is also a director of the company (subject to a limited exception in 14.01(3)(e)).

Outside England and Wales

47. A non-lawyer manager is subject to the rules in relation to practice outside England and Wales if he or she is a manager of a solicitor-controlled recognised body (and also if he or she is a manager of an REL-controlled recognised body in Scotland or Northern Ireland). Non-lawyer employees, employed outside England and Wales, are not subject to the rules.

12

Rule 13   In-house practice, etc.

Introduction

Rule 12 (Framework of practice) allows a solicitor or an REL to practise in-house from an office in England and Wales as the employee of a business which is not a recognised sole practitioner, recognised body or authorised non-SRA firm, but subject to restrictions. The solicitor or REL may act only for the employer or in the circumstances set out in rule 13.

Rule 12 also provides that a solicitor, REL or RFL in an authorised non-SRA firm may do work which falls outside the firm's authorisation, but only if acting for the firm or within 13.02 (Work colleagues), 13.03 (Related bodies) or 13.04 (Pro bono work). The rule, except for 13.04, does not apply to your overseas practice, but you must comply with 15.13 (In-house practice overseas).

Rule 13 – In-house practice, etc.

13.01   Conditions applying at all times

(1) (a) You must not, as an in-house solicitor or REL, act for a client other than your employer under 13.02 to 13.12 if to do so would compromise:

    (i) your professional independence or integrity;

    (ii) your duty to act in the best interests of that client;

    (iii) your duty to comply with rule 3 (Conflict of interests);

    (iv) your duty to keep information about that client's affairs confidential from your employer (unless the other client consents to disclosure, or you are acting under 13.11 as the employee of a foreign law firm); or

    (v) your ability to discharge any other duty owed to that client under these rules.

  (b) (i) In order to act for a client other than your employer under 13.04, 13.07, 13.09 and 13.11, you must have professional indemnity insurance cover.

    (ii) In all other cases you must consider whether your employer has appropriate indemnity insurance or funds to meet any award made as a result of a claim in professional negligence against you, for which your employer might be vicariously liable. If not, you must inform the client in writing that you are not covered by the compulsory insurance scheme.

13

(2) If you are a solicitor, REL or RFL in an authorised non-SRA firm, you must comply with this rule as if you were an in-house solicitor or REL when, as:

(a) a manager or employee; or

(b) a manager or employee of a body which is a manager of the firm,

you do work of a type which is outside the scope of the firm's authorisation in accordance with rule 12, either for the firm itself or within 13.02 (Work colleagues), 13.03 (Related bodies) or 13.04 (Pro bono work).

13.02   Work colleagues

(1) Subject to the provisos in 13.02(2) below, you may act for a person who is, or was formerly:

(a) an employee, a manager, the company secretary, a board member or a trustee of the employer or authorised non-SRA firm;

(b) an employee, a manager, the company secretary, a board member or a trustee of a related body (within the meaning of 13.03(1) or 13.08(c) below) of the employer or authorised non-SRA firm; or

(c) a contributor to a programme or periodical publication, broadcast or published by the employer (or by a related body within the meaning of 13.03(1) or 13.08(c) below), but only where the contributor is a defendant or potential defendant in a defamation case.

(2) You may act under (1) above only if:

(a) the matter relates to or arises out of the work of the employee, manager, company secretary, board member, trustee or contributor in that capacity;

(b) the matter does not relate to a claim arising as a result of a personal injury to the employee, manager, company secretary, board member, trustee or contributor;

(c) you are satisfied that the employee, manager, company secretary, board member, trustee or contributor does not wish to instruct some other lawyer; and

(d) no charge is made for your work unless those costs are recoverable from another source.

(3) Where acting in a conveyancing transaction under (1)(a) or (b) above you may also act for a joint owner/buyer and for a mortgagee.

13.03   Related bodies

(1) You may act for:

    (a)   the employer's, or authorised non-SRA firm's, holding, associated or subsidiary company;

    (b)   a partnership, syndicate, LLP or company by way of joint venture in which the employer, or authorised non-SRA firm, and others have an interest;

    (c)   a trade association of which the employer or authorised non-SRA firm, is a member; or

    (d)   a club, association, pension fund or other scheme operated for the benefit of employees of the employer, or the employees or managers of the authorised non-SRA firm.

(2)   If you are employed in local government, (1)(a) and (b) above do not apply.

(3)   For the purpose of 13.04 to 13.07 references to your employer or authorised non-SRA firm include related bodies of the employer or authorised non-SRA firm as set out in (1) above, and "employment" and "employed" must be construed accordingly.

13.04   Pro bono work

(1)   You may, in the course of your practice, conduct work on a pro bono basis for a client other than your employer or authorised non-SRA firm provided:

    (a)   the work is covered by an indemnity reasonably equivalent to that required under the Solicitors' Indemnity Insurance Rules; and

    (b)   either:

        (i)   no fees are charged; or

        (ii)   a conditional fee agreement is used and the only fees charged are those which you receive by way of costs from your client's opponent or other third party and pay to a charity under a fee sharing agreement.

(2)   Paragraph (1) above does not permit you to conduct work on a pro bono basis in conjunction with services provided by your employer under 13.05 (Associations), 13.06 (Insurers), 13.07 (Commercial legal advice services) or 13.11 (Foreign law firms).

13.05   Associations

If you are employed by an association you may act for a member provided:

    (a)   the membership of the association is limited to persons engaged or concerned in a particular trade, occupation or activity or otherwise having a community of interest;

    (b)   the association is one formed bona fide for the benefit of its members and not formed directly or indirectly for your benefit or primarily for securing assistance in legal proceedings; and

(c)   there is no charge to the member in non-contentious matters, and in contentious matters the association indemnifies the member in relation to your costs and disbursements insofar as they are not recoverable from any other source.

13.06   Insurers

(1)   If you are employed by an insurer subrogated to the rights of an insured in respect of any matter you may act on behalf of the insurer in relation to that matter in the name of the insured, and also:

(a)   act on behalf of the insured in relation to uninsured losses in respect of the matter;

(b)   act in proceedings both for the insured and for a defendant covered by another insurer where the insurers have agreed an apportionment of liability; and/or

(c)   act in the matter on behalf of the employer and another insurer in the joint prosecution of a claim.

(2)   If you are employed by a legal expenses insurer you may, provided that the insured has given specific consent, act for an insured in any proceedings which are covered by the legal expenses insurance policy, provided that the proceedings do not include:

(a)   a personal injury claim (whether made by or for the insured); or

(b)   a civil claim for damages which:

(i)   exceeds the small claims limit from time to time in operation in the county court; and/or

(ii)   is allocated or re-allocated to the fast track or the multi-track.

13.07   Commercial legal advice services

If you are employed by a commercial organisation providing a telephone legal advice service you may advise enquirers, provided:

(a)   the advice comprises telephone advice only, together with a follow up letter to the enquirer when necessary; and

(b)   you are satisfied that there is indemnity cover reasonably equivalent to that required under the Solicitors' Indemnity Insurance Rules.

13.08   Local government

If you are employed in local government you may act:

(a)   for another organisation or person to which or to whom the employer is statutorily empowered to provide legal services, subject to the conditions in (b) to (g) below;

(b)　for a member or former member of the local authority, provided that:

　(i)　the matter relates to or arises out of the work of the member in that capacity;

　(ii)　the matter does not relate to a claim arising as a result of a personal injury to the member;

　(iii)　you are satisfied that the member does not wish to instruct some other lawyer; and

　(iv)　no charge is made for your work unless those costs are recoverable from some other source;

(c)　for a company limited by shares or guarantee of which:

　(i)　the employer or nominee of the employer is a shareholder or guarantor; or

　(ii)　you are, or an officer of the employer is, appointed by the employer as an officer of the company,

　provided the employer is acting in pursuance of its statutory powers;

(d)　for lenders in connection with new mortgages arising from the redemption of mortgages to the local authority, provided:

　(i)　neither you nor any other employee acts on behalf of the borrowers; and

　(ii)　the borrowers are given the opportunity to be independently advised by a qualified conveyancer of their choice;

(e)　for a charity or voluntary organisation whose objects relate wholly or partly to the employer's area, provided that there is no charge to the charity or voluntary organisation in non-contentious matters, and in contentious matters the employer indemnifies the charity or voluntary organisation in relation to your costs insofar as they are not recoverable from any other source;

(f)　for a patient who is the subject of a Court of Protection Order where you are acting for a work colleague (under 13.02 above) who is appointed as receiver for the patient; or

(g)　for a child or young person subject to a Care Order in favour of the employer on an application to the Criminal Injuries Compensation Authority.

13.09　Law centres, charities and other non-commercial advice services

(1)　If you are employed by a law centre or advice service operated by a charitable or similar non-commercial organisation you may give advice to and otherwise act for members of the public, provided:

(a)　no funding agent has majority representation on the body responsible

13

for the management of the service, and that body remains independent of central and local government;

(b)   no fees are charged save:

   (i)   where the client is publicly funded; or

   (ii)   where the organisation indemnifies the client in relation to your costs insofar as they are not recoverable from any other source;

(c)   all fees you earn and costs you recover are paid to the organisation for furthering the provision of the organisation's services;

(d)   the organisation is not described as a law centre unless it is a member of the Law Centres Federation; and

(e)   the organisation effects indemnity cover reasonably equivalent to that required under the Solicitors' Indemnity Insurance Rules.

(2)   Paragraph (1) above does not apply to an association formed for the benefit of its members.

13.10   The Crown, non-departmental public bodies, and the Legal Services Commission

If you are employed by the Crown, a non-departmental public body, or the Legal Services Commission (or any body established or maintained by the Legal Services Commission), you may give legal advice to, and act for, other persons if in doing so you are carrying out the lawful functions of the employer.

13.11   Foreign law firms

(1)   You may provide legal services to your employer's clients, subject to the conditions set out in (2) below, if you are a solicitor or an REL employed by:

(a)   a practising lawyer of another jurisdiction who:

   (i)   is not struck off or suspended from the register of foreign lawyers or the register of European lawyers; and

   (ii)   is not practising in that context as a solicitor or as an REL; or

(b)   a business whose managers and owners are all practising through that business as lawyers of jurisdictions other than England and Wales, and do not include any person who:

   (i)   is struck off or suspended from the register of foreign lawyers or the register of European lawyers; or

   (ii)   is practising through or in the context of that business as a solicitor or as an REL.

(2)   You must meet the following conditions if acting for anyone other than your employer.

(a) Even if you are qualified to do such work for your employer, you must not do, or supervise or assume responsibility for doing any of the following:

    (i) drawing or preparing any instrument or papers, or making any application or lodging any document relating to litigation reserved to qualified persons by the Solicitors Act 1974;

    (ii) exercising any right of audience, or right to conduct litigation before a court or immigration tribunal; or

    (iii) providing any immigration advice or immigration services, unless the employer, or a senior fellow employee, is registered with the Immigration Services Commissioner.

(b) You must ensure that the work is covered by professional indemnity insurance reasonably equivalent to that required under the Solicitors' Indemnity Insurance Rules.

(c) You must inform your client that your employer is not regulated by the Solicitors Regulation Authority and that the Authority's compulsory insurance scheme does not apply; and either give or confirm this information in writing, if you are a solicitor, and you are held out to a client as a solicitor (or as an English or Welsh lawyer) in connection with work you are doing for that client.

(d) You must ensure that if you are identified on the notepaper as a solicitor (or as an English or Welsh lawyer) the notepaper also states that your employer is not regulated by the Solicitors Regulation Authority.

(3) Paragraph (2)(c) and (d) above should also be read as referring to an REL being held out or identified as a lawyer, or under the REL's home title.

13.12   Regulatory bodies

If you are employed by a regulatory body you may in carrying out the function of the employer give legal advice to other persons and in the case of statutory functions may act generally for such persons.

Guidance to rule 13 – In-house practice, etc.

1. If you are a solicitor working in-house (whether in or outside England and Wales) you must comply with 20.02 (Practising certificates). Examples of situations where you will be practising as a solicitor, and will therefore need a practising certificate, include:

    (a) you are employed as a solicitor;

    (b) you are held out, on stationery or otherwise, as a solicitor for your employer;

    (c) you administer oaths;

13

(d)   you appear before a court or tribunal in reliance upon your qualification as a solicitor;

(e)   you instruct counsel;

(f)   you undertake work which is prohibited to unqualified persons by the Solicitors Act 1974 and under the forthcoming provisions of Part 3 of the Legal Services Act 2007, unless you are supervised by, and acting in the name of, a solicitor with a practising certificate or another qualified person;

(g)   your only qualification as a lawyer is that you are a solicitor, and:

    (i)   you are employed or held out as a lawyer;

    (ii)   you undertake work in another jurisdiction which is reserved to lawyers;

    (iii) you are registered in a state other than the UK under the Establishment Directive; or

    (iv) you are a registered foreign legal consultant in another jurisdiction.

2.   In England and Wales a number of statutory exceptions apply to qualify this. Certain in-house government solicitors are allowed to practise as solicitors without practising certificates. Some reserved work can be undertaken by non-solicitors working for local government, and therefore by non-practising solicitors working for local government. See also rule 20 (Rights and obligations of practice) and the guidance to it.

3.   A solicitor acting only as a justices' clerk in England and Wales is not practising as a solicitor and can instruct counsel without a practising certificate.

4.   Although the guidance to this rule will generally apply to practice in and outside England and Wales unless otherwise stated, the only provision of rule 13 which applies to practice outside England and Wales is 13.04 (Pro bono work). However, you must also comply with the provisions of 15.13 (which relates to in-house practice overseas) in relation to your in-house practice, if you are employed at an office outside England and Wales (or if you are an REL, employed at an office in Scotland or Northern Ireland).

5.   If you are an in-house solicitor or in-house REL you are personally bound by undertakings given in the course of your professional duties – see 10.05 (Undertakings) (or, if you practise overseas, 15.10(2)).

6.   When you act in your capacity as an in-house solicitor or in-house REL you should not communicate with third parties who you know are represented by another lawyer, except with that lawyer's consent. Any communication should be made through the lawyer acting for the third party.

7. You may use the stationery of, or stationery including the name of, your employer for professional work, provided:

    (a) the letterhead or the signature makes it clear that the stationery is being used by an in-house solicitor or in-house REL on legal professional business and that person is responsible for the contents of the letter; and

    (b) the stationery is being used for the business of the non-lawyer employer or for third parties in circumstances permitted by rule 13 or 15.13 (which relates to in-house practice overseas).

8. You may, as an in-house solicitor or in-house REL, use a style of stationery or description which appears to hold you out as a principal in a firm. However, if you are held out as a principal on notepaper and you hold or receive clients' money, you will be required to pay the full contribution to the Compensation Fund. Note that you should be careful not to hold out a non-existent entity as if it were regulated by the SRA. There is no objection to your stating "John Smith, solicitor, is regulated by the Solicitors Regulation Authority".

9. If you are an in-house solicitor the address of your employer's legal department is the place (or one of the places) where you practise and must therefore be notified to the SRA.

Accounts rules and accountants' reports

10. If you are an in-house solicitor or in-house REL employed in England and Wales, and you receive or hold clients' money, you must comply with the Solicitors' Accounts Rules 1998. If you pay in or endorse over a cheque made out in your favour, you receive clients' money and must deal with it in accordance with the relevant rules (see note (viii) to rule 35 of the Solicitors' Accounts Rules 1998). For the name of a client account, see rule 14(3) of the Solicitors' Accounts Rules 1998. Even if a cheque is simply endorsed over to your employer, you will need to keep a record (see rule 32 of the Solicitors' Accounts Rules 1998), submit an accountant's report, and pay the full contribution to the Compensation Fund. If you receive only your employer's money you can try to ensure that all cheques are made payable to the employer. If you are an in-house solicitor or in-house REL employed overseas, the Solicitors' Accounts Rules do not apply but you must comply with similar requirements which are set out in 15.27.

11. An in-house accountant (working for the same employer) may not prepare an accountant's report for an in-house solicitor or in-house REL (see rule 37(2)(a) of the Solicitors' Accounts Rules 1998).

12. If you only undertake a small number of transactions or handle a small volume of clients' money in a year, you can apply to the Caseworking and

13

Applications department of the SRA for a dispensation from the obligation to deliver an accountant's report. However, dispensations are not given as a matter of course.

13. If you are:

   (a) a solicitor or REL practising as an employee of:

      (i)   a local authority;

      (ii)   statutory undertakers;

      (iii) a body whose accounts are audited by the Comptroller and Auditor General;

      (iv)   the Duchy of Lancaster;

      (v)   the Duchy of Cornwall; or

      (vi)   the Church Commissioners;

   (b) a solicitor practising as the Solicitor of the City of London; or

   (c) a solicitor or REL carrying out the functions of:

      (i)   a coroner or other judicial office; or

      (ii)   a sheriff or under-sheriff,

   you need not comply with the Solicitors' Accounts Rules 1998 (see rule 5 of those rules) or submit an accountant's report. However, if you hold or receive client money, you must pay the full Compensation Fund contribution, but this will not apply if you come within note 13(c) and are not practising as a solicitor.

Separate practice through a firm

14. If you are an in-house solicitor or in-house REL you can also be a manager in a firm. However, you must effect indemnity insurance for the firm in accordance with the Solicitors' Indemnity Insurance Rules, and notify the SRA of the address of the firm.

15. The firm must not act for a private client where there is any conflict between the interests of that client and the interests of your employer.

16. For details regarding arrangements for the referral of clients, see rule 9 (Referrals of business).

17. If you hold or receive client money as a manager in a firm in England and Wales you must comply with the Solicitors' Accounts Rules 1998.

18. You may agree to reimburse your employer for that proportion of your salary and of the employer's other overhead expenses which is attributable to any work carried out in the employer's time for your firm, on the

employer's premises and/or with the assistance of staff and materials provided by the employer. You must make sure that this allowance for overheads is properly calculated, otherwise there could be a breach of rule 8 (Fee sharing).

Industrial action by in-house solicitors or in-house RELs

19. It is not professional misconduct for you to strike or take other industrial action, but you must have regard to your duties to the court and third parties. Before deciding to take such action you must:

   (a) ensure that no client for whom you act is prejudiced by the action in any crucial way, e.g. by missing a time limit;

   (b) ensure that steps are taken to cover all court engagements;

   (c) ensure compliance with your professional undertakings; and

   (d) promptly arrange to notify persons who may be affected by the proposed action.

Costs recovered from third parties

20. When you put forward a claim for costs against a third party, you must, as an in-house solicitor or in-house REL, have regard to the proper indemnity basis for costs.

21. Where you act for your employer, there is no presumption that it is any cheaper to employ an in-house lawyer than to retain a firm. The court will, therefore, normally regard it as proper for your bill to be drawn on the usual principles applicable to firms. There may, however, be special cases where it is clear that a bill drawn on this basis would improperly remunerate the employer and should therefore be disallowed (see *Henderson v Merthyr Tydfil UDC* [1900] 1 QB 434 and *Re Eastwood (deceased)* [1975] Ch 112). There seems no reason in principle why such an approach should not also be applicable to non-contentious business, or to matters where you act for someone other than the employer.

22. Under certain circumstances rule 13 allows you to act for someone other than your employer, as part of your employment. In such cases there will be no breach of rule 8 (Fee sharing) when you account to your employer for costs paid either by the client, the client's opponent or another third party (see rule 8). Similarly, there will be no breach of rule 8 if you conduct work on a pro bono basis in accordance with 13.04(1)(b)(ii) and fees received by way of costs from your client's opponent or other third party are paid to a charity under a fee sharing agreement.

13

Direct access to client

23. If you are the senior legal adviser of a company or a local authority you should have direct access to the board or to the council and its committees, and should try to ensure that your terms of employment provide for such access. "Direct access" does not mean that all instructions and advice must pass directly to and from the council, committee or board, but you must have direct access where necessary.

Insurers and commercial legal advice services

24. If you are employed as a solicitor or REL by an insurer which runs a commercial legal telephone advice service, the restrictions in 13.07 will not apply to prevent you acting for an insured under a legal expenses insurance policy in accordance with 13.06.

Law centres, charities and other non-commercial advice services

25. If you are employed as a solicitor or REL by a law centre or advice service operated by a charitable or similar non-commercial organisation, you can advise and act for members of the public provided you comply with 13.09. This contains important provisions relating to (for example) professional indemnity, the charging of fees, and the independence of the body responsible for the management of the service. A solicitor or REL who works as a volunteer for such an advice service must comply with the Solicitors' Indemnity Insurance Rules unless exempted by a waiver.

Foreign law firms

26. In-house practice in England and Wales includes any employment by a business which is not authorised by the SRA or some other approved regulator. As the in-house employee of a foreign law firm, you are not as free to act for your employer's clients as you would be if you were employed in England and Wales by a solicitor, an REL or a recognised body. Under 13.11 you may not do reserved work for clients, or (unless your employer is separately authorised) immigration work. You must also comply with special requirements as to insurance and "health warnings". Note also, that if you are employed by a foreign law firm and a principal, owner or director of the firm is a solicitor, 13.11 will not apply unless the solicitor is dually qualified and is practising only as a lawyer of another jurisdiction in the context of that business.

27. By contrast, employment *overseas* by a foreign law firm will not usually fall within the definition of in-house practice in rule 24 (Interpretation) if your employer is a lawyer or a law firm.

Practice as a manager or employee of an authorised non-SRA firm

28. If you are a solicitor, REL or RFL practising as a manager, employee, member or owner of an authorised non-SRA firm, neither rule 13, nor the bulk of the other rules in the Code, nor the Accounts Rules, will be relevant to you when you do work of a type which is within the scope of the firm's authorisation. See 23.01(2).

29. If you are a solicitor, REL or RFL practising as a manager, employee, member or owner of an authorised non-SRA firm, you must comply with rule 13, and all the other rules in the Code, and with the Accounts Rules, as if you were an in-house solicitor or REL when you do work of a type which is outside the scope of the firm's authorisation – see 13.01(2). Rule 12.01(1)(d) allows you to do such work for the firm itself, or if the work would come within 13.02 (Work colleagues), 13.03 (Related bodies) or 13.04 (Pro bono work).

30. Note that if you are a solicitor, REL or RFL and you are a manager, member or owner of an authorised non-SRA firm, or employed in such a firm in connection with the provision of any legal services, it must be:

    (a) in your capacity as a solicitor, REL or RFL, or

    (b) in the capacity of an individual authorised by an approved regulator other than the SRA, if you are so authorised, or

    (c) in both such capacities;

    except that if you are a solicitor who is a director of an authorised non-SRA firm or employed in such a firm in connection with the provision of any legal services, you must be practising in your capacity as a solicitor, even if also in some other capacity. See 20.04(2) and (3), as well as section 1A(d) of the Solicitors Act 1974.

13

Rule 14   Recognised bodies

Introduction

Under rule 12 (Framework of practice) solicitors and RELs must not provide services to the public in England and Wales except through a firm which is a recognised body or a recognised sole practitioner (both regulated by the Solicitors Regulation Authority) or through an authorised non-SRA firm (regulated by another approved regulator). Rule 14 governs the composition and structure of a recognised body and the services a recognised body may provide, and is to a large extent based on the requirements of sections 9 and 9A of the Administration of Justice Act 1985.

Rule 14 – Recognised bodies

14.01   Fundamental requirements for all recognised bodies

Services requirement

(1)   The business of a recognised body may consist only of the provision of:

    (a)   professional services of the sort provided by individuals practising as solicitors and/or lawyers of other jurisdictions; and

    (b)   professional services of the sort provided by notaries public, but only if a notary public is a manager or employee of a recognised body,

but this does not prevent a recognised body providing services within 21.03, or having an ownership interest in a company which is a separate business.

Relevant lawyer requirement

(2)   (a)   At all times at least one manager of a recognised body must be:

        (i)   a solicitor with a current practising certificate;

        (ii)   an REL; or

        (iii)   (in the case of a partnership or LLP) a body corporate which is a legally qualified body with at least one manager who is a solicitor with a current practising certificate or an REL.

    (b)   If an event which could not reasonably have been foreseen would put a recognised body in breach of the relevant lawyer requirement but within 28 days the situation is remedied, the recognised body will be deemed to have remained in compliance with the relevant lawyer requirement and to that extent will not be liable to have its recognition revoked under regulation 9.1(b) of the Recognised Bodies Regulations.

(c)   If the only, or last remaining, solicitor or REL whose role in the body ensures compliance with the relevant lawyer requirement:

(i)   is committed to prison in civil or criminal proceedings;

(ii)   becomes and continues to be unable to attend to the practice of the body because of incapacity caused by illness, accident or age;

(iii)   becomes and continues to be a person who lacks capacity under Part 1 of the Mental Capacity Act 2005;

(iv)   abandons the practice of the body; or

(v)   is made subject to a condition on his or her practising certificate or registration which would be breached by continuing to fulfil the role of relevant lawyer within the body,

the body must inform the Solicitors Regulation Authority within seven days and must within 28 days either ensure that the body can fulfil the relevant lawyer requirement without reference to that person, or cease to practise.

Management and control requirement

(3) (a)   At least 75% of the body's managers must be:

(i)   individuals who are, and are entitled to practise as, lawyers of England and Wales, lawyers of Establishment Directive professions or RFLs; or

(ii)   bodies corporate which are legally qualified bodies;

although a legally qualified body cannot be a director of a recognised body which is a company, as under 14.06(1) all the directors must be individuals.

(b)   Individuals who are, and are entitled to practise as, lawyers of England and Wales, lawyers of Establishment Directive professions or RFLs must make up at least 75% of the ultimate beneficial ownership of the recognised body.

(c)   Individuals who are, and are entitled to practise as, lawyers of England and Wales, lawyers of Establishment Directive professions or RFLs, and/or legally qualified bodies, must:

(i)   exercise or control the exercise of at least 75% of the voting rights in the recognised body; and

(ii)   if the recognised body is a company with shares, hold (as registered members of the company) at least 75% of the shares.

(d)   Every owner of the recognised body, and every person who exercises or controls the exercise of any voting rights in the body, must be:

(i)   an individual who is, and is entitled to practise as, a lawyer of

England and Wales, a lawyer of an Establishment Directive profession or an RFL;

(ii) a legally qualified body; or

(iii) an individual who is approved under regulation 3 of the Recognised Bodies Regulations and, subject to (e) below, is a manager of the body.

(e) An individual who is not entitled under (d)(i) above may be an owner of a recognised body without being a manager of the body if:

(i) the recognised body is a company which is wholly or partly owned by a partnership or LLP which is a legally qualified body;

(ii) the individual is approved under regulation 3 of the Recognised Bodies Regulations and is a manager of the partnership or LLP; and

(iii) the individual is precluded under the partnership agreement or members' agreement from exercising or authorising any vote in relation to the company.

(f) If an event which could not reasonably have been foreseen would put a recognised body in breach of the management and control requirement but within 28 days the situation is remedied, the recognised body will be deemed to have remained in compliance with the management and control requirement and to that extent will not be liable to have its recognition revoked under regulation 9.1(b) of the Recognised Bodies Regulations.

(g) If the only or last remaining lawyer of England and Wales, lawyer of an Establishment Directive profession or RFL whose role in the body ensures compliance with the management and control requirement:

(i) is committed to prison in civil or criminal proceedings;

(ii) becomes and continues to be unable to attend to the practice of the body because of incapacity caused by illness, accident or age;

(iii) becomes and continues to be a person who lacks capacity under Part 1 of the Mental Capacity Act 2005;

(iv) abandons the practice of the body; or

(v) is made subject to a condition on his or her practising certificate or registration which would be breached by continuing to fulfil that role,

the body must inform the Solicitors Regulation Authority within seven days and must within 28 days either ensure that the body can fulfil the management and control requirement without reference to that person, or cease to practise.

14.02   Duties in relation to compliance

(1) (a) A recognised body and its managers and employees must comply with rule 14.

(b) A recognised body must so far as possible ensure that its managers, members and owners comply with rule 14.

(c) A recognised body must not take on a new manager without first being satisfied of that manager's eligibility, by:

(i) checking that any solicitor has a practising certificate, that any REL or RFL is registered with the Solicitors Regulation Authority, and that the practising certificate or registration is not subject to a condition which would preclude that person becoming a manager;

(ii) obtaining (and retaining, for production to the Solicitors Regulation Authority if required), in respect of any lawyer authorised by an approved regulator but not by the SRA, written confirmation from the approved regulator to the effect that the lawyer is authorised by that approved regulator, entitled to practise and not subject to a condition or other restriction which would preclude that person becoming a manager;

(iii) obtaining (and retaining, for production to the Solicitors Regulation Authority if required), in respect of any individual who is entitled to be a manager only by virtue of approval under regulation 3 of the Recognised Bodies Regulations, written confirmation:

(A) from the Authority that the individual concerned is approved under regulation 3; and

(B) from the individual concerned, details of any event which the body will have to declare when next renewing its recognition, which has occurred in relation to that individual since he or she was last a manager of a recognised body renewing its recognition; and

(iv) in relation to any body corporate, making checks and obtaining (and retaining, for production to the Solicitors Regulation Authority if required) confirmations under (i) to (iii) above in respect of every individual who is a manager of or who has an interest in that body corporate.

(2) A manager of a recognised body:

(a) must so far as possible ensure that the body complies with rule 14;

(b) must ensure that the body complies with any condition imposed on its recognition; and

(c) must not cause, instigate or connive at any breach of these rules by the recognised body or any of its managers or employees.

(3) A solicitor, REL or RFL who is a member of, or the owner of a share in, a recognised body which is a company must not cause, instigate or connive at any breach of these rules by the recognised body or any of its managers or employees.

(4) A person employed to work in the practice of a recognised body must not cause, instigate or connive at any breach of these rules.

(5) The partners in a recognised body which is a partnership are responsible not only as managers but also, jointly and severally, as the recognised body.

14.03 Formation, office in England and Wales and registered office

Law of formation

(1) (a) A recognised body which is a partnership may be formed under the law of any country and may be a legal person.

(b) A recognised body which is an LLP must be incorporated and registered in England and Wales or in Scotland under the Limited Liability Partnerships Act 2000.

(c) A recognised body which is a company must be:

(i) incorporated and registered in England and Wales or in Scotland under Part I of the Companies Act 1985;

(ii) incorporated in an Establishment Directive state and registered as an oversea company under Part I of the Companies Act 1985; or

(iii) incorporated and registered in an Establishment Directive state as a societas Europaea.

Practising address in England and Wales

(2) A recognised body must have at least one practising address in England and Wales.

Registered office of a company or LLP

(3) A recognised body must have its registered office at a practising address in England and Wales if the recognised body is registered in England and Wales:

(a) under Part I of the Companies Act 1985;

(b) under the Limited Liability Partnerships Act 2000; or

(c) as a societas Europaea.

14.04   Recognised bodies which are partnerships

Who may be a partner

(1)   Provided that the fundamental requirements for all recognised bodies set out in 14.01 are met, a recognised body which is a partnership may have all or any of the following as a partner:

(a)   a lawyer of England and Wales (including a solicitor with a current practising certificate);

(b)   an REL;

(c)   an RFL;

(d)   an exempt European lawyer;

(e)   an individual approved under regulation 3 of the Recognised Bodies Regulations;

(f)   a body corporate which is a legally qualified body.

Change to the composition of the partnership

(2)   Recognition may continue despite a change in the composition of a recognised body which is a partnership, subject to (3) to (5) below.

(3)   (a)   A recognised body which is a partnership must cease to practise from the date of any failure to comply with 14.01(2)(a) or (b) (relevant lawyer requirement), and with 14.01(3)(a)–(e) or (f) (management and control requirement) which results from the change.

(b)   A recognised body which is a partnership must cease to practise from the date of any change which results in there being no remaining partner who was a partner before the change; the 28 day period under 14.01(2)(b) and 14.01(3)(f) does not apply.

(4)   If a partnership change results in there being only one remaining principal who or which needs to be recognised as a recognised sole practitioner but could not reasonably have commenced an application in advance of the change, the firm need not cease to practise if the remaining principal:

(a)   is a solicitor or REL;

(b)   notifies the Solicitors Regulation Authority within seven days;

(c)   is granted temporary emergency recognition.

(5)   (a)   Temporary emergency recognition may be granted for an initial period of 28 days and may be extended in response to a reasonable request by the applicant.

(b)   During the initial 28 day period, or such extended period as the Solicitors Regulation Authority may allow, the remaining principal must:

(i)   cease to practise, and notify the Solicitors Regulation Authority; or

  (ii) commence a substantive application for recognition as a recognised sole practitioner (or, if the remaining principal has taken on a new partner, as a recognised body) by submitting a completed application form, together with the prescribed fee and any Compensation Fund contribution required.

(c) Subject to (d) below, if an application has been commenced under (b)(ii) above, temporary emergency recognition must be extended pending determination of the application.

(d) In exceptional circumstances and for reasonable cause the Solicitors Regulation Authority may revoke a temporary emergency recognition at any time.

(e) The grant or extension of a temporary emergency recognition is without prejudice to the discretion of the Solicitors Regulation Authority to refuse a substantive application made under (b)(ii) above.

Partnership splitting into two or more firms

(6) Subject to (7) to (9) below, if a recognised body which is a partnership splits so that the recognised body will continue but one or more of the former partners intend to carry on as a separate firm, the separate firm must, before commencing practice, obtain recognition as a recognised body or a recognised sole practitioner.

(7) Following such a partnership split, the Solicitors Regulation Authority will if necessary decide which of the groups of former partners will continue to be covered by the existing recognition and which must apply for a new recognition, and may apportion recognition fees and Compensation Fund contributions between the groups. Any such decision will be without prejudice to the outcome of any legal dispute between the former partners.

(8) If the principal(s) in the new firm could not reasonably have commenced an application for recognition in advance of the change, the new firm may practise from the date of the split provided that the following conditions are met:

(a) the new firm is:

  (i) a partnership which complies with rule 14 of the Solicitors' Code of Conduct in its formation, composition and structure; or

  (ii) a solicitor or REL sole practitioner;

  and complies with the Solicitors' Indemnity Insurance Rules;

(b) the new firm notifies the Solicitors Regulation Authority within seven days; and

(c) the Solicitors Regulation Authority grants the firm temporary emergency recognition.

(9) (a)   Temporary emergency recognition may be granted for an initial period of 28 days and may be extended in response to a reasonable request by the applicant.

   (b)   During the initial 28 day period, or such extended period as the Solicitors Regulation Authority may allow, the new firm must:

      (i)   cease to practise, and notify the Solicitors Regulation Authority; or

      (ii)   commence a substantive application for recognition as a recognised body or recognised sole practitioner by submitting a completed application form, together with the prescribed fee and any Compensation Fund contribution required.

   (c)   Subject to (d) below, if an application has been commenced under (b)(ii) above, temporary emergency recognition must be extended pending determination of the application.

   (d)   In exceptional circumstances and for reasonable cause the Solicitors Regulation Authority may revoke a temporary emergency recognition at any time.

   (e)   The grant or extension of a temporary emergency recognition is without prejudice to the discretion of the Solicitors Regulation Authority to refuse a substantive application made under (b)(ii) above.

Only one active partner remaining

(10)   If a partner in a partnership which is a recognised body:

   (a)   is committed to prison in civil or criminal proceedings;

   (b)   becomes and continues to be unable to attend to the practice of the body because of incapacity caused by illness, accident or age;

   (c)   becomes and continues to be a person who lacks capacity under Part 1 of the Mental Capacity Act 2005;

   (d)   abandons the practice of the body; or

   (e)   is made subject to a condition on his or her practising certificate or registration which would be breached by continuing as a partner;

and this results in there being only one active partner, that partner must inform the Solicitors Regulation Authority within seven days.

Prohibition on creating third party interests

(11)   A partner in a partnership must not create any charge or other third party interest over his or her interest in the partnership.

14.05   Recognised bodies which are LLPs

Who may be a member

(1) Provided that the fundamental requirements for all recognised bodies set out in 14.01 are met, a recognised body which is an LLP may have all or any of the following as a member:

(a) a lawyer of England and Wales (including a solicitor with a current practising certificate);

(b) an REL;

(c) an RFL;

(d) an exempt European lawyer;

(e) an individual approved under regulation 3 of the Recognised Bodies Regulations;

(f) a body corporate which is a legally qualified body.

Minimum number of members

(2) (a) A recognised body which is an LLP must have at least two members.

(b) If an event which could not reasonably have been foreseen results in an LLP having fewer than two members, but within six months the situation is remedied, the LLP will be deemed to have remained in compliance with (a) above and to that extent will not be liable to have its recognition revoked under regulation 9.1(b) of the Recognised Bodies Regulations.

Prohibition on creating third party interests

(3) A member must not create any charge or other third party interest over the member's interest in the LLP.

14.06   Recognised bodies which are companies

Who may be a director

(1) Provided that the fundamental requirements for all recognised bodies set out in 14.01 are met, a recognised body which is a company may have all or any of the following as a director:

(a) a lawyer of England and Wales (including a solicitor with a current practising certificate);

(b) an REL;

(c) an RFL;

(d)   an exempt European lawyer;

(e)   an individual approved under regulation 3 of the Recognised Bodies Regulations.

Who may be a member or shareowner

(2) Provided that the fundamental requirements for all recognised bodies set out in 14.01 are met, a recognised body which is a company may have all or any of the following as a member or shareowner:

(a)   a lawyer of England and Wales (including a solicitor with a current practising certificate);

(b)   an REL;

(c)   an RFL;

(d)   an exempt European lawyer;

(e)   an individual approved under regulation 3 of the Recognised Bodies Regulations, who is also a director of the company;

(f)   a legally qualified body.

Prohibition on creating third party interests

(3) A member or shareowner must not create any charge or other third party interest over his or her interest in the company, except by holding a share as nominee for a non-member shareowner who is eligible to be a member or shareowner under (2) above.

Record of non-member shareowners

(4) (a)   A recognised body which is a company with shares must keep a record of any non-member shareowners, and retain the record for at least three years after their ownership ceases; and

(b)   a member who holds a share as nominee for a non-member shareowner must keep the recognised body informed of all facts necessary to keep an accurate and up-to-date record.

Death of member or shareowner of a company

(5) (a)   If a recognised body is a company with shares and a member or shareowner dies and is eligible to be a member or shareowner at the date of death, then, whether or not the personal representatives are themselves eligible to be members or shareowners, the personal representatives may replace the deceased member or shareowner in their capacity as personal representatives, provided that:

(i)   no vote may be exercised by or on behalf of a personal

14

representative (and no such vote may be accepted) unless all the personal representatives are eligible to be members or shareowners;

(ii) no personal representative may hold or own a share in that capacity for longer than 12 months from the date of death;

(iii) within 12 months of the death the recognised body must cancel or acquire the shares or ensure that they are held and owned by persons eligible to be members or shareowners, but without this resulting in RFLs being the only shareowners; and

(iv) no vote may be exercised by or on behalf of any personal representative (and no such vote may be accepted) after the 12 month period has expired.

(b) If, following the death of a member or shareowner, a company meets the requirements of (a) above the company will be deemed to have remained in compliance with (2) above as to membership and share ownership, and to that extent will not be liable to have its recognition revoked under regulation 9.1(b) of the Recognised Bodies Regulations.

Member or shareowner ceasing to be eligible to be a member or shareowner

(6) (a) If a recognised body is a company with shares and a member or shareowner ceases to be eligible to be a member or shareowner, or ceases to exist as a body corporate, then:

(i) no vote may be exercised or accepted on the shares held by or on behalf of that member or shareowner;

(ii) in the case of a member or shareowner becoming ineligible, a trustee in bankruptcy or liquidator may (whether or not eligible to be a member or shareowner) replace that member or shareowner in the capacity of trustee or liquidator for a period which must not exceed six months from the date the member or shareowner became ineligible; and

(iii) the company must cancel or acquire the shares within six months, or within that time ensure that the shares are held and owned by persons eligible to be members or shareowners, but without this resulting in breach of the relevant lawyer requirement or the management and control requirement in 14.01(2) or (3).

(b) If (a) above applies and a company meets its requirements, the company will be deemed to have remained in compliance with (2) above as to membership and share ownership, and to that extent will not be liable to have its recognition revoked under regulation 9.1(b) of the Recognised Bodies Regulations.

Member or shareowner becoming insolvent but not ineligible

(7) (a) If a recognised body is a company with shares and a member or

shareowner becomes insolvent but remains eligible to be a member or shareowner, then the trustee in bankruptcy or liquidator (whether eligible or not) may replace the insolvent member or shareowner in the capacity of trustee in bankruptcy or liquidator, provided that:

(i)   no vote may be exercised by or on behalf of a trustee in bankruptcy or liquidator (and no such vote may be accepted) unless the trustee or liquidator is eligible to be a member or shareowner;

(ii)   no trustee in bankruptcy or liquidator may hold or own a share in that capacity for longer than six months from the date of the insolvency;

(iii)   within six months of the insolvency the company must cancel or acquire the shares or ensure that they are held and owned by persons eligible to be members or shareowners, but without this resulting in breach of the relevant lawyer requirement or the management and control requirement in 14.01(2) or (3); and

(iv)   no vote may be exercised by or on behalf of any trustee in bankruptcy or liquidator (and no such vote may be accepted) after the six month period has expired.

(b)   If (a) above applies and a company meets its requirements, the company will be deemed to have remained in compliance with (2) above as to membership and share ownership, and to that extent will not be liable to have its recognition revoked under regulation 9.1(b) of the Recognised Bodies Regulations.

Court of Protection deputy

(8) (a)   A Court of Protection deputy appointed under section 19 of the Mental Capacity Act 2005 may be a member or shareowner in that capacity, without breach of these rules, provided that:

(i)   the person in respect of whom the deputy has been appointed remains eligible to be a member or shareowner; and

(ii)   if the deputy is not eligible to be a member or shareowner, no vote is exercised or accepted on the shares.

(b)   If (a) above applies and a company meets its requirements, the company will be deemed to have remained in compliance with (2) above as to membership and share ownership, and to that extent will not be liable to have its recognition revoked under regulation 9.1(b) of the Recognised Bodies Regulations.

14.07   Information and documentation

(1) A recognised body must supply any information and documentation relating to its composition and structure or to any of its managers, employees,

members or owners, as and when requested to do so by the Solicitors Regulation Authority.

(2) A recognised body must notify the Solicitors Regulation Authority within seven days of any change to:

(a) its name;

(b) its registered office and/or any of its practising addresses;

(c) its managers; or

(d) its members and/or shareowners if it is a company.

(3) A recognised body must notify the Solicitors Regulation Authority within seven days if it is an unlimited company and it is re-registered as limited under the Companies Act 1985.

(4) If a relevant insolvency event within the meaning of paragraph 32(1A) of Schedule 2 to the Administration of Justice Act 1985 occurs in relation to a recognised body its managers must notify the Solicitors Regulation Authority within seven days.

(5) If a recognised body which is an oversea company or a societas Europaea registered outside England, Wales and Scotland is subject to an event in its country of incorporation analogous to a winding-up order or administration order under Part II of the Insolvency Act 1986, a resolution for voluntary winding-up, or the appointment of an administrative receiver, the directors must notify the Solicitors Regulation Authority within seven days.

14.08   Mental Health Act equivalents

In this rule:

(a) references to a person who lacks capacity under Part 1 of the Mental Capacity Act 2005 include a "patient" as defined by section 94 of the Mental Health Act 1983 and a person made the subject of emergency powers under that Act, and equivalents in other Establishment Directive states; and

(b) references to a Court of Protection deputy appointed under section 19 of the Mental Capacity Act 2005 include a Court of Protection receiver appointed under the Mental Health Act 1983, and equivalents in other Establishment Directive states.

Guidance to rule 14 – Recognised bodies

The legal and regulatory framework

1. A recognised body is a partnership, LLP or company recognised by the SRA under section 9 of the Administration of Justice Act 1985 and regulation 2 of the SRA Recognised Bodies Regulations 2009.

2. Rule 12 (Framework of practice) states that solicitors and RELs must not provide services to the public in England and Wales except through a firm which is a recognised body or a recognised sole practitioner (both regulated by the SRA) or through an authorised non-SRA firm, or as permitted under rule 13 (In-house practice, etc.) in respect of law centres, advice centres, etc. Rule 14 governs the composition and structure of a recognised body and the services a recognised body may provide. The rule is largely based on the requirements of section 9A of the Administration of Justice Act 1985.

3. A recognised body, and a "manager" or employee of a recognised body, are subject to the Code and other SRA rules, subject to regulation by the SRA, and subject to disciplinary sanctions of the SRA and the Solicitors Disciplinary Tribunal.

4. In this guidance the term "manager" has a special meaning, as in rule 14 and in the Recognised Bodies Regulations. It means:

    (a)   a partner, or a person held out as a partner, in an unincorporated firm;

    (b)   a member of an LLP; or

    (c)   a director of a company.

    In other words the "manager" as an individual does not necessarily have to perform any particular management function – although the "manager" will be subject to the rules him- or herself, and in many circumstances will also be responsible under the rules and in law for the conduct of the recognised body.

The three fundamental requirements

5. The fundamental requirements which must be fulfilled for recognised body status are:

    (a)   the services requirement,

    (b)   the relevant lawyer requirement,

    (c)   the management and control requirement.

    These are explained in more detail below.

The services requirement

6. Rule 14.01(1) sets out the type of services which a recognised body is permitted to provide – legal services and "man (or woman) of affairs" services as provided by solicitors, services as provided by foreign lawyers, and notarial services (if the firm has a "manager" or employee who is a notary).

7. A recognised body is not prohibited from owning a "separate business" –
    i.e. a business which provides "man (or woman) of affairs" services but not
    as a legal practice – so long as there is compliance with rule 21 (Separate
    businesses).

The relevant lawyer requirement

8. Rule 14.01(2)(a) states that at least one "manager" of a recognised body
    must be:

    (a) a solicitor with a current practising certificate;

    (b) an REL; or

    (c) (in the case of a recognised body which is a partnership or LLP) a
         "legally qualified body" with at least one "manager" who is a solicitor
         with a current practising certificate or an REL.

9. A "legally qualified body" is defined as:

    (a) a recognised body,

    (b) an authorised non-SRA firm, or

    (c) a European corporate practice (as defined in rule 24),

    of which lawyers must make up at least 75% of the ultimate beneficial
    ownership.

The management and control requirement

10. The management and control requirement is set out in rule 14.01(3), and is
    aimed at ensuring that every recognised body is at least 75% owned and
    managed by lawyers.

11. More specifically, the management and control requirement is made up of
    the following six tests, which deal with various markers of management,
    ownership and the holding of shares:

    (a) at least 75% of a recognised body's "managers" must be lawyers or
         "legally qualified bodies";

    (b) lawyers must make up at least 75% of the ultimate beneficial
         ownership of the recognised body;

    (c) lawyers and/or "legally qualified bodies" must exercise or control the
         exercise of at least 75% of the voting rights in the recognised body;

    (d) if the recognised body is a company with shares, lawyers and/or
         "legally qualified bodies" must hold (as registered members of the
         company) at least 75% of the shares;

    (e) every owner of the recognised body must be a lawyer, a "legally qualified body" or an individual non-lawyer who is approved by the SRA under regulation 3 of the Recognised Bodies Regulations; and

(f) every non-lawyer owner of the recognised body must be a "manager" of the body unless:

   (i) the recognised body is a company which is wholly or partly owned by a partnership or LLP which is a "legally qualified body";

   (ii) the non-lawyer owner is a "manager" of the partnership or LLP; and

   (iii) the non-lawyer owner is precluded under the partnership agreement or members' agreement from exercising or authorising any vote in relation to the company.

12. "Lawyers" in the context of the management and control requirement means practising lawyers – solicitors, barristers, notaries, legal executives, licensed conveyancers, patent agents, trade mark agents, law costs draftsmen, European lawyers of Establishment Directive professions, and RFLs.

Some regulatory provisions

13. Recognition is granted on an annual basis, and an application for renewal has to be made by 31 October in each year. There is an annual recognition fee and an annual contribution to the Compensation Fund. Applications for initial recognition, and for renewal of recognition, are made under regulation 2 of the Recognised Bodies Regulations.

14. The "relevant lawyer requirement" basically provides that there must be at least one solicitor or REL "manager". The "management and control requirement" basically provides that at least 75% of the management and ownership must be in the hands of lawyers.

15. In addition, rule 14 provides that the partners in a recognised body which is a partnership, the members of a recognised body which is an LLP, and the members and shareowners of a recognised body which is a company must comprise some combination of the following:

(a) practising lawyers of England and Wales (solicitors, barristers, notaries, legal executives, licensed conveyancers, patent agents, trade mark agents, law costs draftsmen);

(b) practising European lawyers of Establishment Directive professions;

(c) RFLs;

(d) individuals approved by the SRA under regulation 3 of the Recognised

Bodies Regulations as suitable to be a "manager" of a recognised body – such individuals fall into one of three categories:

(i)   non-lawyers;

(ii)   lawyers of foreign legal professions whose members are not eligible to become RFLs;

(iii)   non-practising barristers or non-practising foreign lawyers, whose professional rules or training regulations prevent them from changing status so as to be able to practise through the recognised body as practising lawyers;

an application for SRA approval of an individual as suitable to be a "manager" must be made under regulation 3 of the Recognised Bodies Regulations by the recognised body or prospective recognised body concerned;

(e)   "legally qualified bodies" – recognised bodies, authorised non-SRA firms, or European corporate practices.

16. In relation to the directors of a recognised body which is a company, the "relevant lawyer requirement" has the effect that at least one director must be a solicitor or REL. The "management and control requirement" has the effect that at least 75% of the directors must be lawyers. Rule 14 further provides that the directors must comprise some combination of the following:

(a)   practising lawyers of England and Wales (solicitors, barristers, notaries, legal executives, licensed conveyancers, patent agents, trade mark agents, law costs draftsmen);

(b)   practising European lawyers of Establishment Directive professions;

(c)   RFLs;

(d)   individuals approved by the SRA under regulation 3 of the Recognised Bodies Regulations.

17. A solicitor must have a current practising certificate in order to be a partner, a director, a member or a shareowner in a recognised body. Under section 1A of the Solicitors Act 1974, a solicitor must have a current practising certificate in order to be employed in a recognised body in England and Wales in connection with the provision of any legal services.

18. Every recognised body must have at least one practising address in England and Wales. A recognised body incorporated in England and Wales as an LLP or company must have its registered office in England or in Wales, and must practise from that office. These requirements as to the registered office do not apply to a recognised body incorporated outside England and Wales

– whether it is an LLP incorporated in Scotland, or a company incorporated in Scotland, Northern Ireland or some other Establishment Directive state.

Note that the fact that a firm has been recognised as a recognised body under Scottish law does not exempt it from having to be recognised as a recognised body by the SRA.

19. A recognised body may practise as a firm in its own right (a partnership, LLP or company), or it may wholly or partly own another recognised body, or be wholly or partly owned by another recognised body. A recognised body which is a company or LLP can be a partner together with solicitors, RELs, RFLs and/or other recognised bodies in a partnership which is itself a recognised body; or it can be a member together with solicitors, RELs, RFLs and/or other recognised bodies in an LLP which is itself a recognised body.

20. A recognised body may practise outside England and Wales in addition to practising in England and Wales.

21. If your firm practises overseas through an associated firm which has no office in England and Wales it does not have to be a recognised body – and indeed cannot be a recognised body because a recognised body has to have at least one practising address in England and Wales.

Compliance with rules

22. In addition to these rules, a recognised body must comply with the Solicitors' Indemnity Insurance Rules, the Solicitors' Accounts Rules and (unless authorised by the FSA) with the Solicitors' Financial Services (Scope) Rules and the Solicitors' Financial Services (Conduct of Business) Rules.

(a) Indemnity insurance

23. The Solicitors' Indemnity Insurance Rules require a recognised body to have "qualifying insurance" from a "qualifying insurer" (with some limited scope for exemptions in respect of RELs' participation in recognised bodies). The basic minimum level of cover is £2 million for any one claim. A recognised body with limited liability (i.e. an LLP, a limited company, or a partnership one or more of whose partners is an LLP or a limited company) is required to have minimum cover of £3 million for any one claim. Some recognised bodies which are nominee companies escape the requirement for an extra £1 million cover – see note 28(d) below. A recognised body may also have additional "top-up" cover, from any insurer.

(b) Accountants' reports

24. If a recognised body holds or receives client money, it will in due course have to deliver an accountant's report to the SRA. This obligation also

extends to the "managers" of the recognised body. The names of the current "managers" along with the name of the recognised body must appear on the accountant's report, as well as the name of any employee or "manager" who or which has held or received client money, and any individual employee or "manager" who has operated a client's own account as signatory.

Charging a member's interest in a recognised body – 14.04(11), 14.05(3) and 14.06(3)

25. A partner in a recognised body which is a partnership, or a member of a recognised body which is an LLP, or a member or shareowner of a recognised body which is a company, must not create any charge or other third party interest over his or her interest in the body, except, in the case of a company, that a member may hold a share as nominee for a person who is eligible under the rules to own a share. The purpose is to ensure that control of the recognised body remains solely in the hands of persons who are eligible to be members, and that there is no breach of the management and control condition.

Steps to be taken to deal with certain emergencies

26. Rule 14 contains a number of provisions setting out what must be done if certain events befall a recognised body and its members, directors or shareowners. It is essential to deal with these situations in accordance with the rules:

(a) an unforeseeable event which would put the body in breach of the relevant lawyer requirement – see 14.01(2)(b);

(b) certain specified events (e.g. imprisonment, or incapacity caused by illness) which demonstrate that the last solicitor or REL whose role ensures compliance with the relevant lawyer requirement is no longer suitable to fulfil that role – see 14.01(2)(c);

(c) an unforeseeable event which would put the body in breach of the management and control requirement – see 14.01(3)(f);

(d) certain specified events (e.g. imprisonment, or incapacity caused by illness) which demonstrate that the last lawyer whose role ensures compliance with the management and control requirement is no longer suitable to fulfil that role – see 14.01(3)(g);

(e) a foreseeable event which causes a partnership to be in breach of the relevant lawyer requirement or the management and control requirement – see 14.04(3)(a);

(f) an event in relation to a partnership which results in there being no remaining partner – see 14.04(3)(b);

(g)   a partnership change which results in there being only one remaining solicitor or REL principal who could not reasonably have made prior arrangements – see 14.04(4);

(h)   a partnership split, where the new firm was in a position to make prior arrangements – see 14.04(6) and (7);

(i)   a partnership split, where the new firm could not reasonably have made prior arrangements – see 14.04(7) and (8);

(j)   certain specified events (e.g. imprisonment, or incapacity caused by illness) which demonstrate that a partner is no longer suitable to fulfil that role, and which leave only one partner who is not subject to such an event – see 14.04(10);

(k)   death of a member or shareowner of a company – see 14.06(5)(a) and (b);

(l)   member or shareowner of a company ceases to be eligible to be a member or shareowner – see 14.06(6)(a) and (b);

(m) member or shareowner of a company becomes insolvent but remains eligible to be a member or shareowner – see 14.06(7)(a) and (b);

(n)   Court of Protection deputy appointed in respect of a member or shareowner of a company – see 14.06(8)(a) and (b).

Executor, trustee and nominee companies

27. If you wish to operate an executor, trustee or nominee company in conjunction with your main practice you should bear the following matters in mind:

(a)   An English executor, trustee or nominee company itself provides the executor, trustee or nominee service. If run in conjunction with your practice it is a "business" for the purpose of rule 21 (Separate businesses), whether or not it is dormant for Companies Act purposes and whether or not a charge is made for its services. The company must therefore be a recognised body, or you will breach rule 21 – see 21.02(1)(g) and note 11 of the guidance to rule 21.

(b)   An overseas executor, trustee or nominee company cannot be a recognised body. It can be run in accordance with rule 12 (Framework of practice), as an overseas practice. Alternatively, it can be operated as a "separate business" provided that you comply with rule 21 (Separate businesses) in relation to the company. See also note 12 of the guidance to rule 21.

28. In relation to an English executor, trustee or nominee company, you should also note that:

(a) a recognised body, when holding money or receiving dividends as nominee, holds client money, and it must have its own client account, in its own name;

(b) a single set of accounting records may be used for the company and the main practice and a single accountant's report can be delivered for both, if the relevant accounting periods are the same, and provided the accountant deals with the accounts for each separately;

(c) a wholly owned executor, trustee or nominee company can be covered by the same policy of qualifying insurance as your main practice, but only if the company is named on the policy and certificate of insurance as a separate insured; and

(d) a nominee company may be exempt from the requirement to have an extra £1 million qualifying insurance if it can show that:

   (i) it is a nominee company only;

   (ii) all the directors of the company are partners or members in your main practice;

   (iii) it holds assets only for clients of your main practice;

   (iv) it can act only as agent for your main practice; and

   (v) all fees accrue to the benefit of your main practice.

Companies providing company secretarial services

29. Your firm may own a company whose purpose is to provide company secretarial services to clients of the firm. Such a company may either be operated as a legal practice (and must therefore be a recognised body), or it may be operated as a "separate business" (and must therefore be operated in compliance with rule 21 and may also need to be separately regulated by HMRC under the anti-money laundering legislation).

Service companies

30. A firm may have a wholly owned service company which has no face to the public and provides no services to the public but carries out administrative functions concerned with the running of the firm, such as the employment of staff, the hiring of premises, furniture and equipment and general maintenance. Such a company does not need to be a recognised body and is not a "separate business". The books of the company must be made available if the SRA requires an inspection of accounts. See also notes 14 and 15 of the guidance to rule 21 (Separate businesses).

Rule 15   Overseas practice

Introduction

Rule 15 is specific to overseas practice, which is defined in rule 24 (Interpretation) and means practice from an office outside England and Wales, except in the case of an REL, where it means practice from an office in Scotland or Northern Ireland.

Rule 15 applies the provisions of these rules to your overseas practice. Sometimes rule 15 disapplies one of these rules, or a provision in one of the rules, and in some cases substitutes alternative provisions.

Rule 15 also makes specific provisions in relation to accounts, deposit interest and professional indemnity, because the equivalent domestic rules do not apply to your overseas practice.

The purpose of applying different provisions to overseas practice is to ensure similar protection for clients but by way of rules which are more adaptable to conditions in other jurisdictions.

Rule 15 – Overseas practice

15.01   Core duties (rule 1) application, and conflicts of rules

The core duties

(1)   (a)   Rule 1 (Core duties) applies to your overseas practice.

(b)   In relation to activities outside England and Wales which fall outside the scope of practice as defined by rule 24, whether undertaken as a lawyer or in some other business or private capacity:

(i)   rule 1.06 (Public confidence) applies to you if you are a solicitor, an REL or an RFL;

(ii)   rule 10.01 (Not taking unfair advantage) applies to you if you are a solicitor; and within the UK if you are an REL;

(iii)   rule 15.10(2)(a)(ii) and (iii), (b) and (c) (undertakings given outside the course of practice) apply to you if you are a solicitor, and within the UK if you are an REL;

(iv)   rules 12.03(2) and (3) (practice in another capacity than as an RFL) and 12.03(4)(a) (holding out as a lawyer of England and Wales) apply to you if you are an RFL, and 12.03(5) (wrongfully doing immigration work) applies to your activities in Scotland or Northern Ireland.

General application of these rules to overseas practice

(2) (a) Subject to (3) and (4) below, these rules apply, in relation to practice from an office outside the UK:

    (i) to a solicitor as an individual, whether or not the solicitor's firm or employer is subject to these rules;

    (ii) to a solicitor-controlled recognised body (as defined in rule 24); and

    (iii) to a lawyer of England and Wales other than a solicitor, and to a non-lawyer, in relation to practice as a manager of a solicitor-controlled recognised body,

and notwithstanding the application of the rules to its solicitor managers and solicitor employees, a recognised body which is not a solicitor-controlled recognised body is not itself subject to these rules in relation to practice from such an office.

(b) Subject to (3) and (4) below, these rules apply, in relation to practice from an office in Scotland or Northern Ireland:

    (i) to a solicitor or REL as an individual, whether or not the solicitor's or REL's firm or employer is subject to these rules;

    (ii) to a solicitor-controlled recognised body;

    (iii) to an REL-controlled recognised body (as defined in rule 24);

    (iv) to a lawyer of England and Wales other than a solicitor, to a European lawyer registered with the Bar Standards Board and to a non-lawyer, in relation to practice as a manager of a solicitor-controlled recognised body or an REL-controlled recognised body; and

    (v) a solicitor who was formerly an REL, when practising as a lawyer of an Establishment Directive profession,

and notwithstanding the application of the rules to its solicitor and REL managers and its solicitor and REL employees, a recognised body which is not a solicitor-controlled recognised body or an REL-controlled recognised body is not itself subject to these rules in relation to practice from such an office.

Modification of these rules in relation to overseas practice

(3) If this rule states that a rule or a provision of these rules does not apply to your overseas practice, you may disregard that rule or provision in relation to your overseas practice, but you must comply with any alternative provision which is substituted by this rule.

(4) If compliance with any applicable provision of these rules would result in your breaching local law, you may disregard that provision to the extent necessary to comply with that local law.

15.02 Client relations (rule 2)

(1) Rule 2 (Client relations) does not apply to your overseas practice but you must comply with (2) to (4) below.

15

(2) (a) You must pay to the client any commission received, unless:

   (i) the client, having been told the amount of the commission (or an approximate amount if the precise amount is not known) has agreed that you or your firm may keep the commission; or

   (ii) in all the circumstances it is not reasonable to pay the commission to the client.

   (b) In deciding whether it is reasonable to pay a commission to a client you must have regard to all the circumstances, including the law governing the retainer and the prevailing custom of lawyers in the jurisdiction in which you are practising.

(3) If you are a sole practitioner, a partner in a partnership, or a recognised body to which this rule applies, you must not exclude or attempt to exclude by contract all liability to a client. However, you may limit your liability, provided that such limitation:

   (a) is not below the minimum level of cover you would need in order to comply with 15.26 below;

   (b) is brought to the client's attention; and

   (c) is in writing.

(4) (a) (i) You must not enter into an arrangement to receive a contingency fee for work done in prosecuting or defending any contentious proceedings before a court of England and Wales, a British court martial or an arbitrator where the seat of the arbitration is in England and Wales, except as permitted by statute or the common law.

   (ii) If you enter into a conditional fee agreement with a client in relation to such proceedings, you must explain, both at the outset and, where appropriate, as the matter progresses:

      (A) the circumstances in which the client may be liable for your costs, and whether you will seek payment of these from the client, if entitled to do so; and

      (B) if you intend to seek payment of any or all of your costs from the client, you must advise the client of their right to an assessment of those costs.

   (b) You must not enter into an arrangement to receive a contingency fee for work done in prosecuting or defending any contentious proceedings before a court of an overseas jurisdiction or an arbitrator where the seat of the arbitration is overseas except to the extent that a lawyer of that jurisdiction would be permitted to do so.

15.03   Conflict of interests (rule 3)

Rule 3 (Conflict of interests) applies to your overseas practice, except that you do not have to comply with 3.07 to 3.22 (provisions relating to conveyancing of land) if the land in question is situated outside England and Wales.

15.04   Confidentiality (rule 4)

Rule 4 (Confidentiality and disclosure) applies to your overseas practice.

15.05   Business management (rule 5)

(1)   Rule 5 (Business management in England and Wales) does not apply to your overseas practice but you must comply with (2) to (4) below.

(2)   You must not set up as a solicitor sole practitioner outside England and Wales, or as an REL sole practitioner in Scotland or Northern Ireland, unless you have been entitled to practise as a lawyer for a minimum of 36 months within the last 10 years.

(3)   You must ensure that your firm has at least one manager who has been entitled to practise as a lawyer for a minimum of 36 months within the last 10 years, if you are:

   (a)   a solicitor manager of a firm which is not a recognised body, and solicitors control the firm, either directly as partners, members or owners, or indirectly by their ownership of bodies corporate which are partners, members or owners, or

   (b)   a solicitor or REL manager of a firm which is not a recognised body and which is practising from an office in Scotland or Northern Ireland, and solicitors and/or RELs control the firm, either directly as partners, members or owners, or indirectly by their ownership of bodies corporate which are partners, members or owners.

(4)   If you are:

   (a)   a solicitor sole practitioner practising from an office outside England and Wales, or an REL sole practitioner practising from an office in Scotland or Northern Ireland;

   (b)   a solicitor or REL manager within (3)(a) or (b) above;

   (c)   in relation to an office outside the UK, a solicitor-controlled recognised body or a manager of a solicitor-controlled recognised body who is a lawyer of England and Wales or a non-lawyer; or

   (d)   in relation to an office in Scotland or Northern Ireland, a solicitor, an REL, a solicitor-controlled recognised body or a manager of a solicitor-controlled recognised body who is a lawyer of England and Wales or a non-lawyer, an REL-controlled recognised body or a manager of an REL-controlled recognised body who is a lawyer of England and Wales or a non-lawyer, you must ensure that the firm is managed and supervised with a view to ensuring that its affairs are properly conducted at all times; and that clients' matters receive proper attention, and are supervised so as to ensure that the quality of the work is checked with reasonable regularity by suitably experienced and competent persons within the firm.

15

15.06   Equality and diversity (rule 6)

Rule 6 (Equality and diversity) does not apply to your overseas practice, but rule 1 (Core duties) will always apply.

15.07   Publicity (rule 7)

(1)   Rule 7 (Publicity) applies to your overseas practice, except as set out in (2) and (3) below.

(2)   Rule 7 does not apply to the website, e-mails, text messages or similar electronic communications of any practice you conduct from an office in an EU state other than the UK.

(3)   Rule 7.07 (Letterhead, website and e-mails) does not apply, but:

(a)   if an REL is named on the letterhead (including a fax heading) of an office in Scotland or Northern Ireland, the letterhead must also identify:

(i)   the European jurisdiction(s) – local or national as appropriate – under whose professional title the REL is practising;

(ii)   the REL's professional title(s), expressed in an official language of the European state concerned; and

(iii)   the fact that the REL is registered with the Solicitors Regulation Authority of England and Wales; and

(b)   you must make clear on your firm's letterhead (including a fax heading) that it is the letterhead of a law firm, if you are:

(i)   a solicitor sole practitioner practising from an office outside England and Wales, or an REL sole practitioner practising from an office in Scotland or Northern Ireland; or

(ii)   a solicitor manager of a firm which is practising from an office outside England and Wales, and solicitors control the firm, either directly as partners, members or owners, or indirectly by their ownership of bodies corporate which are partners, members or owners; or

(iii)   a solicitor or REL manager of a firm which is practising from an office in Scotland or Northern Ireland, and solicitors and/or RELs control the firm, either directly as partners, members or owners, or indirectly by their ownership of bodies corporate which are partners, members or owners.

15.08   Fee sharing (rule 8)

Rule 8 (Fee sharing) applies to your overseas practice.

15.09   Referrals of business (rule 9)

(1) Rule 9 (Referrals of business) does not apply to your overseas practice, but you must comply with (2) below.

(2) When you accept referrals of business from other persons and when you refer business to other persons, you must ensure that there is no breach of rule 1 (Core duties) or any other applicable provision of these rules.

15.10   Relations with third parties (rule 10)

(1) Rule 10 (Relations with third parties) applies to your overseas practice except as provided in (2) and (3) below.

(2) Rule 10.05 (Undertakings) does not apply, but:

    (a) you must fulfil an undertaking which you give:

        (i)   in the course of practice;

        (ii) outside the course of practice, but as a "solicitor"; or

        (iii) if you are an REL based at an office in Scotland or Northern Ireland, and you give the undertaking within the UK, outside your practice as an REL, but as a lawyer of an Establishment Directive profession;

    (b) you must fulfil an undertaking within a reasonable time; and

    (c) if you give an undertaking which is dependent upon the happening of a future event, you must notify the recipient immediately if it becomes clear that the event will not occur.

(3) Rule 10.06 (Dealing with more than one prospective buyer in a conveyancing transaction) applies only if the land in question is situated in England and Wales.

15.11   Litigation and advocacy (rule 11)

Rule 11 (Litigation and advocacy) applies to your overseas practice in relation to litigation or advocacy conducted before a court, tribunal or inquiry in England and Wales or a British court martial. Rule 11 does not apply to your overseas practice in relation to litigation or advocacy conducted before a court or tribunal in another jurisdiction, but rule 1 (Core duties) will always apply.

15.12   Framework of practice (rule 12)

Rule 12 (Framework of practice) applies to your overseas practice.

15.13   In-house practice overseas (rule 13)

(1)   Rule 13.04 (Pro bono work) applies to your overseas practice. The other provisions of rule 13 (In-house practice, etc.) do not apply to your overseas practice, but you must comply with (2) below.

15

(2)   (a)   Subject to (b) below, you may act as an in-house lawyer, but only for:

   (i)   your employer;

   (ii)   a company or organisation controlled by your employer or in which your employer has a substantial measure of control;

   (iii)   a company in the same group as your employer;

   (iv)   a company which controls your employer; or

   (v)   an employee (including a director or a company secretary) of a company or organisation under (i) to (iv) above, provided that the matter relates to or arises out of the work of that company or organisation, does not relate to a claim arising as a result of a personal injury to the employee, and no charge is made for your work unless those costs are recoverable from another source.

   (b)   If you are a solicitor registered in another state under the Establishment Directive with the professional body for a local legal profession you may practise in-house to the extent that a member of that legal profession is permitted to do so.

15.14   Recognised bodies (rule 14)

(1)   Rule 14 (Recognised bodies) applies to a recognised body in relation to the recognised body's overseas practice.

(2)   Rule 14 applies to your overseas practice as:

   (a)   a manager of a recognised body, if you are a lawyer of England and Wales or an individual non-lawyer;

   (b)   a member of, or the owner of a share in, a recognised body which is a company, if you are a solicitor or (in relation to practice from an office in Scotland or Northern Ireland) an REL,

   except that 14.02(2)(c), (3) and (4) apply only to the extent that a rule applies to the recognised body, manager or employee by virtue of this rule or rule 23.

(3)   If you are a solicitor or an REL you are not required to comply with rule 14 in order to practise through a firm which has no office in England and Wales, but you must comply with 12.01(2) or 12.02(2).

15.15   Deposit interest

(1)   You must comply with (2) below, if you are:

   (a)   a solicitor sole practitioner practising from an office outside England

and Wales, or an REL sole practitioner practising from an office in Scotland or Northern Ireland;

(b) a solicitor-controlled recognised body or (in relation to practice from an office in Scotland or Northern Ireland) a solicitor-controlled recognised body or an REL-controlled recognised body;

(c) a solicitor manager of a firm which is practising from an office outside the UK, and solicitors control the firm, either directly as partners, members or owners, or indirectly by their ownership of bodies corporate which are partners, members or owners; or

(d) a solicitor or REL manager of a firm which is practising from an office in Scotland or Northern Ireland, and solicitors and/or RELs control the firm, either directly as partners, members or owners, or indirectly by their ownership of bodies corporate which are partners, members or owners.

(2) If interest ought, in fairness, to be earned for the client on client money held under (1) above, you must ensure that:

(a) the client money is dealt with so that proper interest is earned upon it, and that the interest is paid to the client;

(b) the client is paid a sum equivalent to the interest that would have been earned if the client money had earned proper interest; or

(c) any alternative written agreement with the client setting out arrangements regarding the payment of interest on that money is carried out.

(3) In deciding whether interest ought, in fairness, to be earned for a client on client money, you must have regard to all the circumstances, including:

(a) the amount of the money;

(b) the length of time for which you are likely to hold the money; and

(c) the law and prevailing custom of lawyers practising in the jurisdiction in which you are practising.

15.16   European cross-border practice (rule 16)

Rule 16 (European cross-border practice) applies to your overseas practice, to the extent that such practice is European cross-border practice as defined in 16.01(1).

15.17   Insolvency practice (rule 17)

Rule 17 (Insolvency practice) does not apply to your overseas practice except in relation to appointments appertaining to orders made in the courts of England and Wales.

15.18   Property selling (rule 18)

Rule 18 (Property selling) applies to your practice from offices in Scotland or Northern Ireland but not to your practice from offices outside the UK.

15.19   Financial services (rule 19)

(1)   Rule 19 (Financial services) does not apply to your overseas practice except as provided in (2) below.

(2)   Rule 19 applies to regulated activities you conduct:

   (a)   from an office in Scotland or Northern Ireland; or

   (b)   into the UK from an office outside the UK.

15.20   Rights and obligations of practice (rule 20)

Rule 20 (Rights and obligations of practice) applies to your overseas practice.

15.21   Separate businesses (rule 21)

(1)   (a)   Rule 21 (Separate businesses) applies to you if you practise from an office in England and Wales and you have a separate business, wherever the separate business is situated.

   (b)   If you do not practise from an office in England and Wales but you practise from an office outside England and Wales and you have a separate business, rule 21 does not apply but you must comply with (2) below, wherever the separate business is situated.

(2)   In relation to your separate business:

   (a)   you must do nothing in the course of practice, or in the course of making referrals to the business or accepting referrals from the business, which would contravene rule 1 (Core duties);

   (b)   you must not allow the separate business to be held out or described in such a way as to suggest that it is carrying on the practice of a lawyer regulated by the Solicitors Regulation Authority;

   (c)   you must ensure that all paperwork, documents, records or files relating to the separate business and its customers are kept separate from those of any firm or in-house practice, even where a customer of the separate business is also a client of the firm or in-house practice;

   (d)   you must not allow the client account of your firm or in-house practice to be used to hold money for the separate business, or for customers of the separate business in their capacity as such; and

   (e)   you must ensure that if you or your firm refer(s) a client to the separate business, the client is first informed of your interest in the separate business, that the separate business is not regulated by the Solicitors Regulation Authority of England and Wales, and that the statutory protections attaching to clients of a lawyer regulated by the Authority are not available to clients of the separate business.

15.22   Waivers (rule 22)

Rule 22 (Waivers) applies to your overseas practice.

15.23   Application of these rules (rule 23)

Rule 23 (Application of these rules), with the exception of 23.01(3), does not apply to your overseas practice.

15.24   Interpretation (rule 24)

Rule 24 (Interpretation) applies to your overseas practice.

15.25   Commencement and repeals (rule 25)

Rule 25 (Commencement and repeals) applies to your overseas practice.

15.26   Professional indemnity

(1)   You must comply with (2) below in relation to your overseas practice, unless you are practising only in-house in compliance with 15.13.

(2)   (a)   You must ensure that in relation to your overseas practice you are at all times covered by insurance or other indemnity against professional liabilities.

(b)   The extent and amount of the insurance or other indemnity need not exceed the current requirements of the Solicitors' Indemnity Insurance Rules or any other current rules made under section 37 of the Solicitors Act 1974 but must be reasonable having regard to:

(i)   the nature and extent of the risks you incur in your overseas practice;

(ii)   the local conditions in the jurisdiction in which you are practising; and

(iii)   the terms upon which insurance or other indemnity is available.

15.27   Accounts

Practice from an office outside the UK

(1)   You must comply with (3) and (4) below in relation to practice from an office outside the UK if you are:

(a)   a solicitor sole practitioner who has held or received client money;

(b)   a solicitor-controlled recognised body which has held or received client money as a firm;

(c)   a lawyer of England and Wales, or a non-lawyer, who is a manager of a solicitor-controlled recognised body which holds or receives client money;

(d) a solicitor manager of any other firm which is controlled by solicitors, either directly as partners, members or owners, or indirectly by their ownership of bodies corporate which are partners, members or owners, if the firm holds or receives client money;

(e) a solicitor who holds or receives client money as a named trustee;

(f) a lawyer of England and Wales, or a non-lawyer, who is a manager of a solicitor-controlled recognised body and who holds or receives client money as a named trustee.

Practice from an office in Scotland or Northern Ireland

(2) You must comply with (3) and (4) below in relation to practice from an office in Scotland or Northern Ireland if you are:

(a) a solicitor or REL sole practitioner who has held or received client money;

(b) a solicitor-controlled recognised body or an REL-controlled recognised body which has held or received client money as a firm;

(c) a lawyer of England and Wales, an REL, a European lawyer registered with the Bar Standards Board or a non-lawyer, who is a manager of a solicitor-controlled recognised body, or an REL-controlled recognised body, which holds or receives client money;

(d) a solicitor or REL manager of any other firm which is controlled by solicitors and/or RELs, either directly as partners, members or owners, or indirectly by their ownership of bodies corporate which are partners, members or owners, if the firm holds or receives client money;

(e) a solicitor or REL who holds or receives client money as a named trustee;

(f) a lawyer of England and Wales, a European lawyer registered with the Bar Standards Board or a non-lawyer, who is a manager of a solicitor-controlled recognised body or an REL-controlled recognised body and who holds or receives client money as a named trustee.

Dealings with client money

(3) In all dealings with client money, you must ensure that:

(a) it is kept in a client account separate from money which is not client money;

(b) on receipt, it is paid without delay into a client account and kept there, unless the client has expressly or by implication agreed that the money shall be dealt with otherwise or you pay it straight over to a third party in the execution of a trust under which it is held;

(c) it is not paid or withdrawn from a client account except:

(i) on the specific authority of the client;

(ii)   where the payment or withdrawal is properly required:

    (A)   for a payment to or on behalf of the client;

    (B)   for or towards payment of a debt due to the firm from the client or in reimbursement of money expended by the firm on behalf of the client; or

    (C)   for or towards payment of costs due to the firm from the client, provided that a bill of costs or other written intimation of the amount of the costs incurred has been delivered to the client and it has thereby (or otherwise in writing) been made clear to the client that the money held will be applied in payment of the costs due; or

(iii) in proper execution of a trust under which it is held;

(d)   accounts are kept at all times, whether by written, electronic, mechanical or other means, to:

    (i)   record all dealings with client money in any client account;

    (ii) show all client money received, held or paid, distinct from any other money, and separately in respect of each client or trust; and

    (iii) ensure that the firm is able at all times to account, without delay, to each and every client or trust for all money received, held or paid on behalf of that client or trust; and

(e)   all accounts, books, ledgers and records kept in relation to the firm's client account(s) are preserved for at least six years from the date of the last entry therein.

Accountants' reports

(4) (a)   You must deliver an accountant's report in respect of any period during which you or your firm have held or received client money and you were subject to (3) above.

(b)   The accountant's report must be signed by the reporting accountant, who must be an accountant qualified in England and Wales or in the overseas jurisdiction where your office is based, or by such other person as the Solicitors Regulation Authority may think fit. The Authority may for reasonable cause disqualify a person from signing accountants' reports.

(c)   The accountant's report must be based on a sufficient examination of the relevant documents to give the reporting accountant a reasonable indication whether or not you have complied with (3) above during the period covered by the report, and must include the following:

    (i)   your name, practising address(es) and practising style and the name(s) of the firm's managers;

    (ii) the name, address and qualification of the reporting accountant;

15

(iii) an indication of the nature and extent of the examination the reporting accountant has made of the relevant documents;

(iv) a statement of the total amount of money held at banks or similar institutions on behalf of clients and trusts, and of the total liabilities to clients and trusts, on any date selected by the reporting accountant (including the last day), falling within the period under review; and an explanation of any difference between the total amount of money held for clients and trusts and the total liabilities to clients and trusts;

(v) if the reporting accountant is satisfied that (so far as may be ascertained from the examination) you have complied with (3) above during the period covered by the report, except for trivial breaches, or situations where you have been bound by a local rule not to comply, a statement to that effect; and

(vi) if the reporting accountant is not sufficiently satisfied to give a statement under (v) above, details of any matters in respect of which it appears to the reporting accountant that you have not complied with (3) above.

Guidance to rule 15 – Overseas practice

How these rules apply to overseas practice

1. These rules apply, in different ways, to the following in respect of their overseas practice:

   (a) solicitors;

   (b) RELs;

   (c) recognised bodies;

   (d) non-lawyers who are managers of recognised bodies; and

   (e) other lawyers of England and Wales and European lawyers registered with the Bar Standards Board, who are managers of recognised bodies.

2. Because of the lighter touch regulation in respect of overseas practice, the rules regulate, in essence, the practice of individual solicitors and RELs in respect of their overseas practice (outside England and Wales for solicitors, and in Scotland and Northern Ireland for RELs), and the practice of recognised bodies. They also regulate individual non-solicitor lawyer and non-lawyer managers of recognised bodies. In some situations, the rules apply only to certain types of recognised body or solicitors involved in certain types of practice.

3. The situation, in more detail, is as follows:

   (a) A solicitor, as an individual, is subject to these rules in relation to practice from an office outside England and Wales, whether or not the solicitor's firm or employer is subject to the rules.

(b)   An REL, as an individual, is subject to these rules in relation to practice from an office in Scotland or Northern Ireland (but not in relation to practice from an office outside the UK) whether or not the REL's firm or employer is subject to the rules.

(c)   A "solicitor-controlled recognised body" (in which English lawyers form the dominant, or equal largest, group of lawyers – see rule 24) is subject to the rules in relation to practice from an office outside England and Wales;

(d)   An "REL-controlled recognised body" (in which RELs and English lawyers together form the dominant, or equal largest, group of lawyers – see rule 24) is subject to the rules in relation to practice from an office in Scotland or Northern Ireland;

(e)   A lawyer of England and Wales other than a solicitor is subject to the rules in relation to practice as a manager of a "solicitor-controlled recognised body" from an office outside England and Wales;

(f)   A lawyer of England and Wales other than a solicitor is subject to the rules in relation to practice as a manager of an "REL-controlled recognised body" from an office in Scotland or Northern Ireland;

(g)   A European lawyer registered with the Bar Standards Board is subject to the rules in relation to practice as a manager of a "solicitor-controlled recognised body" or an "REL-controlled recognised body" from an office in Scotland or Northern Ireland;

(h)   A non-lawyer is subject to the rules in relation to practice as a manager of a "solicitor-controlled recognised body" from an office outside England and Wales;

(i)   A non-lawyer is subject to the rules in relation to practice as a manager of an "REL-controlled recognised body" from an office in Scotland or Northern Ireland.

4.   A recognised body which is not a "solicitor-controlled recognised body" or an "REL-controlled recognised body" will not itself have to comply with the rules. However, individual solicitors who are managers or employees will still be subject to the rules (and so will individual RELs in Scotland or Northern Ireland).

5.   Non-lawyer employees of a recognised body or a recognised sole practitioner are not subject to the rules in respect of overseas practice.

6.   RFLs are not subject to the rules in respect of overseas practice.

Core duties – 15.01(1)

7. Rule 1 (Core duties) applies to your overseas practice because these duties are fundamental to the legal profession. However, although lawyers' professional cultures are usually similar, legal and professional requirements vary from jurisdiction to jurisdiction, and therefore the specific expectations of clients, local lawyers and the courts will be different. It may be necessary to clarify in advance what rules you are bound by in relation to your dealings with your client, the opposing party and the opposing party's lawyer, and in particular it may be necessary to clarify in advance the rules by which the opposing party's lawyer is bound.

In some jurisdictions all communications between lawyers (written or by word of mouth) are automatically regarded as not to be produced in court and as not to be disclosed to others, even the lawyers' clients. In other jurisdictions such communications must be marked "confidential" before they are to be regarded in this way. On the other hand, in some jurisdictions (as will normally be the case for an English solicitor) the lawyer has to keep the client fully informed of all relevant communications from the lawyer acting for another party, and marking a letter "confidential" is no more than a reminder to the recipient that it is not to be disclosed to anyone but the other lawyer's client. In some jurisdictions, if a lawyer wishes to indicate that a letter is sent in an attempt to settle a dispute, and is not to be produced in court, the lawyer should mark the letter as "without prejudice".

These national differences give rise to many misunderstandings, so you need to be careful in conducting cross-border correspondence. Rule 16.05 lays down specific requirements in relation to cross-border correspondence in Europe.

Conflicts of rules – 15.01(4)

8. A conflict of rules can arise when you are required to comply with two sets of rules, but if you comply with one you will breach the other. This situation can arise when:

    (a) you are practising in another jurisdiction and you are required by local or EU legislation to comply with the rules of the local legal profession – for instance, you are a solicitor registered in another jurisdiction under the Establishment Directive, and there is a conflict between one of the local rules and one of the solicitors' rules; or

    (b) you are practising under dual title, e.g. as a solicitor and as a New York attorney, and a rule of the New York Bar conflicts with one of the solicitors' rules.

9. If a local rule applies, you cannot choose to comply only with that rule, if you can also comply with the solicitors' rule. You must comply with both,

which will mean meeting the stricter standard. However, 15.01(4) addresses the possibility of a conflict of rules by disapplying any provisions of the solicitors' rules to the extent (and no more) that it conflicts with an applicable local rule. In a situation where compliance with both rules might be possible but perhaps create a bizarre result, application can be made to the SRA for a waiver.

10. Rule 15 modifies the provisions of other rules to allow for adaptation to the legal and professional framework of the jurisdiction in which you are practising. Sometimes more general provisions are substituted, in recognition of the fact that legal and market conditions may be very different in other jurisdictions.

11. Where a rule relates closely to the legal or regulatory framework in England and Wales it may be disapplied by rule 15 without a substitute. If a rule applies in part – for example rule 3 (Conflict of interests) – or in full – for example rule 4 (Confidentiality and disclosure), you will need to refer to that rule and its guidance, as well as the provisions in rule 15 and this guidance. Even if rule 15 has completely replaced the provisions of another rule, the guidance on the corresponding rule may help you to understand how you are expected to act.

Client relations – 15.02

12. This provision embodies three general principles.

   (a) You must account to your client for any commission or secret profit, unless your client agrees otherwise in full knowledge of the amount or approximate amount involved. However, the requirement does not apply if, in all the circumstances, it is not reasonable to pay the commission to the client, taking account of the wide differences in conditions outside England and Wales. For example, the general custom, or the custom in legal practice in that jurisdiction might make it reasonable to deal with commissions in a different way.

   (b) You must not attempt to exclude all liability to your client. For more information on limitation of liability, see the guidance to 2.07 where appropriate to your overseas practice.

   (c) You must not enter into an unlawful contingency fee arrangement (see also the guidance to 2.04).

Equality and diversity – 15.06

13. Because rule 6 (Equality and diversity) largely reflects UK statutes its detailed requirements are unsuitable for application outside the jurisdiction. However rule 1 (Core duties) applies to your overseas practice. Rule 1.01 (Justice and the rule of law) requires that "You must uphold the rule of law and the proper administration of justice". This would normally include

15

compliance with the equality and diversity provisions of the jurisdiction(s) in which you practise.

Publicity – 15.07

14. The requirements of rule 7 (Publicity) on publicity apply except as regards the e-mails, websites, etc. of an office in an EU state other than the UK, and the requirements of 7.07 (Letterhead, website and e-mails) which are replaced by 15.07(3) in relation to your overseas practice. When considering your publicity in relation to the guidance to rule 7 you should bear in mind that the law of the jurisdiction in which your overseas office is based will apply rather than the law of England and Wales; and that you may also be directly subject to local rules. You should therefore interpret the guidance to rule 7 in the light of the following:

   (a) Publicity intended for a jurisdiction outside England and Wales must comply with:

      (i) any applicable law or rules regarding lawyers' publicity in the jurisdiction in which your office is based;

      (ii) the applicable provisions of rule 7 and 15.07; and

      (iii) if the publicity is intended for a third jurisdiction, the rules in force in the "target" jurisdiction governing lawyers' publicity.

   (b) Your publicity will not breach rule 7 through being incidentally received in a jurisdiction where it is not permitted (this is important in relation to a website, which can be accessed worldwide).

   (c) Your website must comply with the E-Commerce Directive 2000/31/EC and, if you are established anywhere within the EU, with the relevant implementing legislation and the rules which apply to you by virtue of your establishment in an EU state other than the UK.

Fee sharing – 15.08

15. In general, you must not share your professional fees except with other lawyers or law firms, or with non-lawyer managers or owners within your firm, or with your employee, or with a retired manager, member, owner or predecessor, or the dependants or personal representatives of a deceased manager, member, owner or predecessor. You may, however, share your professional fees with a non-lawyer business for the purpose of facilitating the introduction of capital and/or the provision of services to your firm, though not in relation to European cross-border practice – see rule 8 (Fee sharing) and rule 16 (European cross-border practice) and the attached guidance.

Undertakings – 15.10(2)

16. Rule 15.10(2)(a)(i) (undertakings given in the course of practice) applies to undertakings given by:

    (a) a solicitor, however practising;

    (b) an REL, however practising, practising in Scotland or Northern Ireland;

    (c) a "solicitor-controlled recognised body" practising outside the UK or any of its managers who is a lawyer of England and Wales or a non-lawyer;

    (d) a "solicitor-controlled recognised body" or an "REL-controlled recognised body" practising in Scotland or Northern Ireland or any of its managers who is a lawyer of England and Wales, a European lawyer registered with the Bar Standards Board or a non-lawyer.

    This guidance is derived from rule 15.01(2) and the definition of "practice" in rule 24.

Framework of practice – 15.12

17. An overseas firm – that is, a firm which has no office in England and Wales – may have lawyer principals, directors and owners who are not registered with the SRA but would need to be registered if the firm had an office in England and Wales. An overseas firm may also have non-lawyer managers and/or owners, provided there is majority control by lawyers and no breach of applicable local rules, or rules applying in an Establishment Directive state.

    A recognised body which has non-lawyer managers or owners cannot have an office in an Establishment Directive state other than the UK unless the rules for local lawyers would permit a local lawyer to practise through a business of that composition and structure.

In-house practice overseas – 15.13

18. If you are employed at an office outside England and Wales (or in Scotland or Northern Ireland if you are an REL) 15.13 replaces rule 13 (In-house practice, etc.) with more general requirements. If your employer is structured in a way which would allow a solicitor (or an REL) to be a manager or owner under 12.01(2) and 12.02(2) you will be practising in a firm as defined in rule 24 and will not be practising in-house.

19. Note also that if you are registered with another regulatory body under the Establishment Directive rule 15.13(2)(b) allows you to practise in-house to the extent allowed to the profession governed by that regulatory body. This may be more or less restrictive than the requirements of these rules.

Deposit interest – 15.15

20. In relation to overseas practice, you are not bound by the interest requirements in the Solicitors' Accounts Rules 1998, but by those in 15.15. You must ensure that a client gets proper interest – but this is subject to the proviso that the circumstances must be such that interest ought, in fairness, to be earned for the client. This might not be so if the interest is or would be negligible, or it is customary in that jurisdiction to deal with interest in a different way. It is also open to you to enter into a written agreement with the client regarding the payment of interest.

European cross-border practice – 15.16

21. The requirements of rule 16 (European cross-border practice) are applied in full. European cross-border practice is:

    (a) any professional activity in a CCBE state other than the UK, whether or not you are physically present in that CCBE state; and

    (b) any professional contact with a lawyer of a CCBE state other than the UK.

    "CCBE state" is defined in rule 24 (Interpretation). A list of the CCBE states and the legal professions covered by the CCBE Code appears in note 1 of the guidance to rule 16 (European cross-border practice).

22. For the purpose of rule 16 (European cross-border practice), "professional contacts" and "professional activities" taking place within a firm or in-house practice do not constitute European cross-border practice.

Separate businesses – 15.21

23. Rule 21 (Separate businesses) and 15.21 do not regulate your separate business, but regulate the interface between a firm or an in-house practice and a business which is not regulated by the SRA, wherever the separate business is situated or carries on business. Therefore, if you have a separate business but have no office in England and Wales only 15.21 will apply. However, if you also practise from an office in England and Wales, the more detailed provisions of rule 21 will apply.

24. Rule 15.21 completely replaces the provisions of rule 21 (Separate businesses) if you practise wholly outside England and Wales. It applies a lighter regime than rule 21. The requirements of 15.21 are mainly designed to ensure that:

    (a) your compliance with rule 1 (Core duties) as a person regulated by the SRA is not compromised by your involvement with the separate business;

(b) you keep the separate business truly separate from any firm or in-house practice; and

(c) you ensure that people who obtain services from the separate business know it is not carrying on the practice of a lawyer regulated by the SRA.

Professional indemnity – 15.26

25. In relation to overseas practice, you are not bound by the Solicitors' Indemnity Insurance Rules but by 15.26, which requires that you must be covered by insurance if you are a manager or employee of a firm. The insurance must be reasonable, and it is not "reasonable" insurance to have none at all. The extent and amount of the insurance under 15.26 need not exceed the minimum requirements for practice from an office in England and Wales, but local law may apply more onerous requirements.

Accounts – 15.27

26. In relation to overseas practice, you are not bound by the Solicitors' Accounts Rules 1998 but by 15.27, which imposes similar but more general provisions. If an applicable local rule conflicts with a provision of 15.27, you will still be expected to comply with any other provisions of 15.27 that do not conflict.

27. Although the Solicitors' Accounts Rules 1998 do not apply, they may provide useful information about keeping accounts, the kind of checks an accountant might make, and the preparation of accountants' reports. Also, if your firm has offices in and outside England and Wales, a single accountant's report may be submitted covering your practice from offices both in, and outside, England and Wales – such a report must cover compliance both with the Solicitors' Accounts Rules 1998 and rule 15.27(3) of the Solicitors' Code of Conduct 2007.

28. The accounting requirements and the obligation to deliver an accountant's report in 15.27 are designed to apply to you in relation to money held or received by your firm unless it is primarily the practice of lawyers of other jurisdictions. The fact that they do not apply in certain cases is not intended to allow a lower standard of care in the handling of client money – simply to prevent the Solicitors' Accounts Rules 1998 applying "by the back door" in a disproportionate or inappropriate way.

Rule 16   European cross-border practice

Introduction

The purpose of rule 16 is to apply the provisions of the CCBE Code to European cross-border practice. This is necessary to provide a system of mutual professional understanding for ·professional relations between lawyers of different CCBE states. Although the CCBE Code contains a large number of requirements, rule 16 contains only those requirements which are not replicated elsewhere in these rules.

16

Rule 16 – European cross-border practice

16.01   Definition and application

Definition

(1) (a)   European cross-border practice is:

    (i)   any professional activity in a CCBE state other than the UK, whether or not you are physically present in that CCBE state; and

    (ii)   any professional contact with a lawyer of a CCBE state other than the UK.

(b)   For the purposes of this rule professional contacts and professional activities taking place within a firm or in-house legal department are not European cross-border practice.

Application of this rule

(2) (a)   If you are a solicitor this rule applies to your European cross-border practice from an office in, or outside, England and Wales.

(b)   If you are an REL this rule applies to your European cross-border practice from an office within the UK.

(c)   If you are an RFL and you are a manager or employee of a recognised body or the employee of a recognised sole practitioner, this rule applies to your European cross-border practice from an office in England and Wales.

(d)   This rule applies to a recognised body as follows:

    (i)   A solicitor-controlled recognised body is subject to the rule in relation to its European cross-border practice from any of its offices, wherever situated.

(ii)   An REL-controlled recognised body is subject to the rule in relation to its European cross-border practice from any of its offices in the UK.

(iii) A recognised body which is not within (i) or (ii) is subject to the rule in relation to its European cross-border practice from any of its offices in England and Wales.

(e)   If you are a manager of a recognised body and you are not a solicitor but you are a lawyer of England and Wales or a non-lawyer, this rule applies to you to the extent that the rule applies to the body itself under (d) above.

(f)   If you are a manager of a recognised body and you are registered with the Bar Standards Board under the Establishment Directive, this rule applies to your European cross-border practice from an office of the recognised body in the UK to the extent that the rule applies to the body itself under (d) above.

16.02   Occupations considered incompatible with legal practice

(1) If you act in legal proceedings or proceedings before public authorities in a CCBE state other than the UK, you must, in that state, comply with any rules regarding occupations incompatible with the practice of law, as if you were a lawyer of that state, whether or not you are based at an office in that state.

(2) If you are a solicitor based at an office in a CCBE state other than the UK, you must respect any rules regarding participation in commercial or other activities not connected with the practice of law, as they are applied to lawyers of that state.

16.03   Fee sharing with non-lawyers

(1) You must not share your professional fees with a non-lawyer situated in a CCBE state other than the UK except:

(a)   within a firm which is permitted under rule 12 (Framework of practice); or

(b)   with a retired manager, member, owner or predecessor of the firm, or the dependants or personal representatives of a deceased manager, member, owner or predecessor.

(2) If you are practising from an office in a CCBE state other than the UK, whether or not you are actually present at that office, you must not share your professional fees from that practice with a non-lawyer, except:

(a)   within a firm which is permitted under rule 12 (Framework of practice); or

(b)   with a retired manager, member, owner or predecessor of the firm, or the dependants or personal representatives of a deceased manager, member, owner or predecessor.

16.04   Co-operation between lawyers of different CCBE states

(1)   If you are approached by a lawyer of a CCBE state other than the UK to undertake work which you are not competent to undertake, you must assist that lawyer to obtain the information necessary to find and instruct a lawyer capable of providing the service asked for.

(2)   When co-operating with a lawyer of a CCBE state other than the UK you must take into account the differences which may exist between your respective legal systems and the professional organisations, competencies and obligations of lawyers in your respective states.

16.05   Correspondence between lawyers in different CCBE states

(1)   If you are practising from an office in a CCBE state and you want to send to a lawyer in a different CCBE state (with the exception of the UK) a communication which you wish to remain "confidential" or "without prejudice", you must, before sending the communication, clearly express your intention in order to avoid misunderstanding, and ask if the lawyer is able to accept the communication on that basis. When you send the communication you must express your intention clearly at the head of the communication or in a covering letter.

(2)   If you are the intended recipient of a communication from a lawyer in another CCBE state which is stated to be "confidential" or "without prejudice", but which you are unable to accept on the basis intended by that lawyer, you must inform the sender accordingly without delay. If the communication has already been sent you must return it unread without revealing the contents to others. If you have already read the communication and you are under a professional duty to reveal it to your client you must inform the sender of this immediately.

16.06   Paying referral fees to non-lawyers

You must not pay a fee, commission or any other compensation to a non-lawyer as a consideration for referring a client to you:

(a)   if the non-lawyer is situated in a CCBE state other than the UK; or

(b)   if you are practising from an office in a CCBE state other than the UK, whether or not you are physically present at that office.

16.07   Disputes between lawyers in different member states

(1)   If you consider that a lawyer in a CCBE state other than the UK has acted in breach of a rule of professional conduct you must draw the breach to the other lawyer's attention.

(2)   Before commencing any form of proceedings against the other lawyer, you must inform the Law Society and the other lawyer's bar or law society in order to allow them an opportunity to assist in resolving the matter.

Guidance to rule 16 – European cross-border practice

1. Since 1990 the CCBE Code, interpreted in the light of article 1 of the CCBE
    Code and the CCBE's Explanatory Memorandum, has been binding upon
    solicitors in relation to their European cross-border practice. The current
    version of the CCBE Code applies in relation to all the CCBE states and
    their legal professions, which are as follows.

Albania	avukat
Armenia	pastaban
Austria	Rechtsanwalt
Belgium	avocat/advocaat/Rechtsanwalt
Bulgaria	advokat
Croatia	odvjetnik
Cyprus	dikegóros
Czech Republic	advokát
Denmark	advokat
Estonia	vandeadvokaat
Finland	asianajaja/advokat
FYRO Macedonia	advokat
France	avocat
Georgia	advokati
Germany	Rechtsanwalt
Greece	dikegóros
Hungary	ügyvéd
Iceland	lögmaður
Ireland	solicitor; barrister
Italy	avvocato
Latvia	zvērināts advokāts
Liechtenstein	Rechtsanwalt
Lithuania	advokatas
Luxembourg	avocat/Rechtsanwalt
Malta	avukat; prokuratur legali
Moldova	avocet
Montenegro	advokat
Netherlands	advocaat
Norway	advokat
Poland	adwokat; radca prawny
Portugal	advogado
Romania	avocat
Serbia	advokat
Slovakia	advokát/advokátka

Slovenia	odvetnik/odvetnica
Spain	abogado/advocat/abokatu/avogado
Sweden	advokat
Switzerland	Rechtsanwalt/Anwalt/Fürsprecher/Fürsprech/ avocat/avvocato/advokat
Turkey	avukat
Ukraine	advokat
United Kingdom	solicitor; barrister/advocate

2. If you comply with these rules in relation to your practice generally, and with rule 16 in relation to European cross-border practice, you will also comply with the requirements of the CCBE Code, as interpreted in the light of article 1 of the CCBE Code and the CCBE's Explanatory Memorandum.

Incompatible occupations – 16.02

3. Rule 16.02(1) prohibits you from pursuing any occupation prohibited to local lawyers as incompatible with the practice of law, in another CCBE state in which you act in legal proceedings or proceedings before a public authority. This does not prevent you from pursuing such an occupation in the UK if it is permitted under these rules, or in another CCBE state where it is allowed.

4. Rule 16.02(2) requires you to "respect" the rules regarding incompatible occupations in a CCBE state where you are established. If you are registered under the Establishment Directive any such local rule will apply to you directly. If you are established in a CCBE state, but you are not subject to the Establishment Directive, you may not be subject to the host state rule but rule 16 will apply. "Respect" for a rule is not the same as an obligation to comply with that rule, but the SRA Board would expect you to comply with the spirit of such a rule where it is not unreasonable to do so.

Fee sharing – 16.03

5. Rule 16.03 permits fee sharing in European cross-border practice within a law firm, and between law firms. Fee sharing is permitted, for instance, with an overseas practice which includes non-lawyers, provided a controlling majority of the owners and managers are lawyers.

6. Although 8.02 (Fee sharing with other non-lawyers) allows you to share fees with a non-lawyer "fee sharer" in some circumstances, this is prohibited by 16.03 in respect of European cross-border practice.

7. Interpreting how this prohibition applies to a firm sharing fees with a non-lawyer fee sharer operating in more than one state, and how it applies to a firm practising in more than one state, may be complex. For example:

(a) rule 16.03 would prohibit your firm, wherever it is practising, from sharing fees with a non-lawyer company whose principal place of business is in a CCBE state other than the UK, or with a non-lawyer company's branch establishment in a CCBE state other than the UK; and

(b) if your firm has its main office in the UK and a branch office in another CCBE state, the fees of the branch office cannot be shared with a non-lawyer company wherever situated, so the firm cannot share a percentage of its fees as a whole with a non-lawyer company. However, the firm could share a percentage of the fees of its UK office, and of any office in a state which is not a CCBE state, with a non-lawyer company, provided:

   (i) the non-lawyer company is situated in the UK or in a state which is not a CCBE state; and

   (ii) the requirements of 8.02 are met.

Correspondence between lawyers in different CCBE states – 16.05

8. Rule 16.05 reflects the requirements of article 5.3 of the CCBE Code. Differences between the ways in which client business is conducted in different states can give rise to misunderstandings between lawyers, and this provision is designed to help avoid such misunderstandings. Terms such as "confidential" and "without prejudice" are not of universal application.

   (a) "Confidential"

   In some states all communications between lawyers (written or by word of mouth) are automatically regarded as not to be produced in court and as not to be disclosed to others, even the lawyers' clients. In other states such communications must be marked "confidential" before they are to be regarded in this way.

   On the other hand, in some states, including the UK, the lawyer has to keep the client fully informed of all relevant communications from the lawyer acting for another party, and marking a letter "confidential" is no more than a reminder to the recipient that it is not to be disclosed to anyone but the other lawyer's client.

   (b) "Without prejudice"

   In some states, if a lawyer wishes to indicate that a letter is sent in an attempt to settle a dispute, and is not to be produced in court, the lawyer should mark the letter as "without prejudice".

   These important national differences give rise to many misunderstandings, so you need to be careful in conducting cross-border correspondence.

9. Where 16.05 applies, you must ask in advance whether your communication can be accepted on the basis you intend, and you must express your intention clearly at the head of your communication or in a covering letter.

10. If 16.05 applies and you are informed that a communication is to be sent to you on a basis which you are not able to respect – for example, that it must not be disclosed to your client – you must inform the other lawyer immediately so that the communication is not sent. If it has already been sent you must return it to the sender unread and without revealing its contents or referring to it in any way. It can happen that, as a result of misunderstanding between sender and recipient, the recipient has already read the communication. If this happens to you, you may be under a professional duty to reveal the contents to your client, either under these rules or under rules of an Establishment Directive state in which you are registered. If so you must tell the sender immediately.

Referral fees – 16.06

11. Rule 16.06 permits, in European cross-border practice, the payment of a referral fee or commission to another law firm. It is permitted, for instance, to pay a referral fee to an overseas practice which includes non-lawyers, provided a controlling majority of the owners and managers are lawyers.

12. Rule 9 (Referrals of business), which refers to practice from an office in England and Wales, allows you to have an arrangement with a non-lawyer for the referral of clients, and, subject to disclosure, to pay the introducer. However, such payments are prohibited by 16.06 in respect of European cross-border practice whether from an office in England and Wales or from an overseas office.

13. As with the prohibition on fee sharing with a non-lawyer, there are complexities involved in interpreting how the prohibition applies to a firm practising in more than one state, and to an arrangement with a non-lawyer introducer operating in more than one state. For example:

   (a) if your firm has its main office in the UK and a branch office in another CCBE state, the branch office cannot pay a referral fee to a non-lawyer company wherever situated, but the UK office, and any office in a state which is not a CCBE state, could do so provided that:

      (i)   the non-lawyer company is situated in the UK or in a state which is not a CCBE state; and

      (ii) in respect of payments from an office in England and Wales the requirements of rule 9 are met, or in respect of payments from an overseas office the requirements of 15.09(2) are met; and

   (b) rule 16.06 would prohibit your firm, wherever it is practising, from paying a referral fee to a non-lawyer company whose principal place of business is in a CCBE state other than the UK, or to a non-lawyer company's branch establishment in a CCBE state other than the UK.

Disputes between lawyers in different CCBE states – 16.07

14. If a professional dispute arises between you and a lawyer in a CCBE state other than the UK, it is desirable that the dispute be settled in a friendly way, and this is the purpose of the requirements of 16.07. Under 16.07(2) you will need to contact the Law Society's International Unit.

Rule 17   Insolvency practice

Introduction

If you are a solicitor or an REL, and an insolvency practitioner in a firm, rule 17 applies to you when you accept appointments and act as an appointment holder. Rule 17 should be read in conjunction with the Code of Ethics produced by the Joint Insolvency Committee and adopted by all recognised professional bodies (RPBs) including the Solicitors Regulation Authority. The purpose of the Joint Insolvency Committee's Code of Ethics is to ensure your independence and objectivity when acting as an appointment holder and that you can identify and avoid conflicts of interest. The rule does not apply to your overseas practice except in relation to appointments appertaining to orders made in the courts of England and Wales.

17

Rule 17 – Insolvency practice

17.01

If you are a solicitor or an REL you must, when accepting an appointment or acting as an appointment holder as an insolvency practitioner, comply with the Code of Ethics produced by the Joint Insolvency Committee and adopted by the Solicitors Regulation Authority Board.

Guidance to rule 17 – Insolvency practice

1. You must comply with the requirements of the Insolvency Act 1986 and other relevant legislation in relation to accepting appointments and acting as an appointment holder.

2. You should have regard to the other guidance and best practice promulgated from time to time by the SRA as an RPB on all issues relating to appointment holding, including professional independence.

Rule 18   Property selling

Introduction

This rule sets out requirements for providing property selling services through your firm. Requirements for providing property selling services through a separate business are dealt with under rule 21 (Separate businesses).

The seller is your client, and any property selling work you do is, in addition to this rule, subject to the same law and professional rules binding on you in relation to your other work.

The rule applies to your overseas practice from offices in Scotland or Northern Ireland but not to your overseas practice from offices outside the UK.

18

Rule 18 – Property selling

18.01   Standards of property selling services

(1)   When providing property selling services through your firm, you must:

   (a)   ensure that you, or the relevant staff, are competent to carry out the work;

   (b)   not seek from any prospective buyer a pre-contract deposit in excess of any prescribed limit; and

   (c)   promptly send to your client written accurate details of any offer you have received from a prospective buyer in respect of an interest in the property (other than those of a description which your client has indicated in writing that they do not want to receive).

(2)   If you are the person who is responsible for marketing a residential property you must comply with any Home Information Packs Regulations made under the Housing Act 2004.

(3)   (a)   In 18.01(1) above:

      (i)   "competent" includes meeting any standards of competence set by the Secretary of State under section 22 of the Estate Agents Act 1979; and

      (ii)   "prescribed limit" means any limit prescribed by the Secretary of State under section 19 of the Estate Agents Act 1979.

   (b)   In 18.01(2) "the person who is responsible for marketing a residential property" has the meaning used in sections 151–153 of the Housing Act 2004.

18.02   Statement on the cost

(1) When accepting instructions to act in the sale of a property, you must, at the outset of communication between you and the client, or as soon as is reasonably practicable, and before the client is committed to any liability towards you, give the client a written statement setting out your agreement as to:

   (a)   the identity of the property;

   (b)   the interest to be sold;

   (c)   the price to be sought;

   (d)   the amount of your fee or the method of its calculation;

   (e)   the circumstances in which your fee is to become payable;

   (f)   regarding any payments to be made to others, and charged separately:

      (i)   the amount, or the method by which they will be calculated; and

      (ii)   the circumstances in which they may be incurred; and

   (g)   the incidence of VAT.

(2) You must also, within the written statement:

   (a)   state whether or not you are to have "sole agency" or "sole selling rights". The statement must also include a clear explanation of the intention and effect of those terms, or any similar terms used; and

   (b)   if the statement refers to a "ready, willing and able" buyer (or similar term), include a clear explanation of the term.

18.03   Conflict of interests

(1) In addition to your duties under rule 3 (Conflict of interests), when selling property you must comply with the following requirements.

   (a)   If you or any connected person has, or is seeking to acquire, a beneficial interest in the property or in the proceeds of sale of any interest in the property, you must promptly inform your client in writing.

   (b)   If you act in the sale of property, even if not in the conveyancing, you must not act for the buyer in the negotiations.

   (c)   If a prospective buyer makes an offer for a client's property, you must promptly inform the client in writing if, to your knowledge, you or any connected person has been instructed, or is to be instructed by the buyer to sell an interest in land, and that sale is necessary to enable the buyer to buy from the client or results from that prospective purchase.

   (d)   If you have, or to your knowledge any connected person has, a beneficial interest in a property or in the proceeds of sale of any interest in it, you must promptly inform in writing any person negotiating to acquire or dispose of any interest in that property. You must make this disclosure before entering into any negotiations with a prospective buyer.

(e) You must not discriminate against a prospective buyer because they are unlikely to instruct you to sell an interest in land, which sale is necessary to enable the buyer to buy from your client or results from that prospective purchase.

(f) When acting for a seller, you must restrict communication with the buyer to your property selling function. In particular:

(i) you must communicate about legal matters so far as possible only through the buyer's solicitor; and

(ii) you must not lead the buyer to believe that they are receiving legal advice from you.

18

(g) When acting for a seller, if you arrange for a mortgage to be available on the property in order to facilitate the sale, you may inform prospective buyers of the availability of the mortgage (subject to the buyer's status) but, unless exempted by rule 3 (Conflict of interests) you must also inform prospective buyers in writing:

(i) that you cannot advise or act for the prospective buyer in respect of the mortgage;

(ii) that the mortgage may not be the only one available; and

(iii) that the prospective buyer should consult their own lawyer.

(2) In 18.03(1) above:

(a) "connected person" means:

(i) spouse, former spouse, reputed spouse, brother, sister, uncle, aunt, nephew, niece, direct descendant, parent or other direct ancestor;

(ii) any employee of your firm, and any member of your employee's family;

(iii) any owner or employee of an associated firm defined in rule 24 (Interpretation) or any member of their families;

(iv) any company of which you are a director or employee, or any LLP of which you are a member or employee, or any company in which you, either alone or with any other connected person or persons are entitled to exercise, or control the exercise of, one-third or more of the voting power at any general meeting;

(v) any company of which any of the persons mentioned in (i) to (iii) above is a director or employee, or any LLP of which any of them is a member or employee, or any company in which any of them, either alone or with any other connected person or persons, is entitled to exercise, or control the exercise of, one-third or more of the voting power at any general meeting; and

(vi)   any other "associate" as defined in section 32 of the Estate Agents Act 1979; and

(b)   "you" includes anyone with whom you carry on a joint property selling practice, and owners of an associated firm as defined in rule 24 (Interpretation).

18.04   Waivers

In spite of 22.01(1) (Waivers), the Solicitors Regulation Authority Board shall not have power to waive any of the provisions of this rule.

Guidance to rule 18 – Property selling

General – business structures and property selling

1.   You may sell property through a separate business – see notes 8 and 9 below and rule 21 (Separate businesses) – or as part of the general work of your firm, or through a firm formed especially for that purpose, either alone or with other firms. If you form a property selling firm with solicitors from other firms, it will be a distinct firm for all purposes.

2.   A jointly owned property selling firm may be incorporated as a SEAL (Solicitors' Estate Agency Limited). A SEAL is defined in 3.12. See rule 3 (Conflict of interests) for the position of a SEAL regarding conflicts of interests.

3.   A further alternative for firms wishing to co-operate in selling property is a joint Property Display Centre (PDC), where the principal activity carried on is publicising properties in the sale of which an individual participating firm is instructed. It is also possible for a single firm to establish its own PDC. A PDC:

(a)   is not itself a firm, and is not a separate entity; it is an administrative extension of the practices of the participating firms, and its address should be notified to the Information Directorate of the SRA;

(b)   can have no clients; it may merely carry out certain activities on behalf of the participating firms (only individual participating firms may be instructed in the sale of a property);

(c)   is a place where the principal activity carried on is the display and dissemination of information about properties which the individual participating firms have for sale; and

(d)   cannot carry on any part of your professional practice. In particular no negotiations may be conducted at the PDC; prospective buyers must be referred to the individual participating firm instructed in the sale of the property in question. Instructions to sell a property may only be accepted at offices of participating firms. To avoid problems with rule 3 (Conflict of interests), the participating firms must operate totally independently so far as their professional business, including property selling, is concerned.

4. You and the other participating firms may wish to establish a joint service company to carry out support functions connected with the running of the PDC, e.g. hiring premises and equipment. The service company (as with a service company established by an individual firm of solicitors) cannot carry on any legal practice or have any dealings with the property selling or property buying public.

5. As no part of the professional practice of the participating firms is carried out at the PDC, rule 5 (Business management in England and Wales) does not apply. Nor would rule 5 apply to a PDC established by a single firm. The participating firms, or the single firm, would nevertheless be responsible for the activities of the PDC staff and would have a duty to supervise them.

6. If you sell property you may share your professional fees with an estate agent who is your sub-agent for a sale – see 8.01(g).

7. You may properly provide structural surveys and formal valuations of property through your firm. You must ensure that you, or relevant staff, have the appropriate level of competence.

8. You may provide property selling services through a separate business – see 21.04(1)(c). If so, you must comply with the safeguards in 21.05. Note also that a separate business will not fall within the exemption in section 1 of the Estate Agents Act 1979 (see note 10 below). The effect of this is that your separate business providing property selling services will be subject to all the provisions of the Estate Agents Act 1979.

9. If you are selling a property through a separate business, your firm may do the seller's conveyancing, but may not normally do the buyer's conveyancing unless you comply with 21.05(2)(f), and:

(a) your firm is not doing the seller's conveyancing; or

(b) your firm is allowed to act for both buyer and seller under rule 3 (Conflict of interests).

Your separate business may, however, provide mortgage related services to the buyer even if your firm is doing the seller's conveyancing.

Standards of property selling services – 18.01

10. Section 1(2)(a) of the Estate Agents Act 1979 exempts from that Act "things done in the course of his profession by a practising solicitor or a person employed by him." This exemption is on the basis that certain

standards, set out in the Act, are already required of you under the rules of professional conduct. These standards are contained in rule 18 and in other rules of professional conduct, all of which remain applicable when you are selling property.

11. These standards are:

(a)   a requirement of competence, imposed by 18.01(1)(a);

(b)   a prohibition on making false statements as set out in section 1 of the Property Misdescriptions Act 1991 – "a false or misleading statement about a prescribed matter" (section 1(1)). A prescribed matter is "any matter relating to land which is specified in an order made by the Secretary of State" (section 1(5)). A statement can be made by pictures as well as words. Any false statement will be a breach of 1.02 (Integrity);

(c)   a prohibition on seeking a pre-contract deposit in excess of the prescribed limit, imposed by 18.01(1)(b);

(d)   requirements for the holding of clients' money and the keeping of client accounts, which are imposed on you under the Solicitors' Accounts Rules 1998;

(e)   requirements relating to the provision of information to clients, imposed on you by 18.01(1)(c) and 18.02; this also reflects rule 2 (Client relations);

(f)   requirements relating to conflict of interests. Some of these are imposed on you by 18.03, and some by rule 3 (Conflict of interests). In addition to the general provisions on conflict of interests (3.01 to 3.06), you should also have regard to the provisions specifically on conveyancing, property selling and mortgage related services (3.07 to 3.22). Note that there are also special conflict provisions where you sell property through a separate business – see notes 8 and 9 above and 21.05(2)(f); and

(g)   requirements relating to home information packs resulting from the Housing Act 2004 and the Home Information Pack Regulations (No. 2) 2007 (SI 2007/1667). These are imposed on you by 18.01(2).

Statement on the cost – 18.02

12. If you are acting for a seller in marketing a property, you have a duty to have a home information pack for the property under the Housing Act 2004. The Home Information Pack Regulations (No. 2) 2007 set out the requirements in relation to home information packs.

13. Under the Housing Act, enforcement of the Regulations in respect of non-solicitor estate agents is carried out by the Office of Fair Trading.

Because of the exemption of solicitors' services from the provisions of the Estate Agents Act 1979, enforcement of the requirements of the Regulations in respect of solicitors is carried out by the SRA. Similarly, the redress scheme operated by the Ombudsman for Estate Agents does not apply to solicitors: redress is provided by the Legal Complaints Service.

14. Notes 15 to 18 below set out the detailed information requirements to help you comply with 18.02. These requirements correspond to those in the Estate Agents (Provision of Information) Regulations 1991 (SI 1991/859) and the Schedule to those Regulations.

15. A clear explanation of the intention and effect of the terms sole agency/sole selling rights or similar terms, given to clients will take the following form.

18

"**Sole agency**

You will be liable to pay a fee to us, in addition to any other costs or charges agreed, if unconditional contracts for the sale of the property are exchanged at any time:

• with a buyer introduced by us with whom we had negotiations about the property in the period during which we have sole agency; or

• with a buyer introduced by another agent during the period of our sole agency.

Sole selling rights

You will be liable to pay a fee to us, in addition to any other costs or charges agreed, in each of the following circumstances:

• if unconditional contracts for the sale of the property are exchanged in the period during which we have sole selling rights, even if the buyer was not found by us but by another agent or by any other person, including yourself; or

• if unconditional contracts for the sale of the property are exchanged after the expiry of the period during which we have sole selling rights but to a buyer who was introduced to you during that period or with whom we had negotiations about the property during that period."

16. A clear explanation of the term "ready, willing and able" given to clients will take the following form.

"A buyer is a 'ready, willing and able' buyer if he or she is prepared and is able to exchange unconditional contracts for the purchase of your property. You will be liable to pay a fee to us, in addition to any other costs or charges agreed, if such a buyer is introduced by us in accordance with your instructions and this must be paid even if you subsequently withdraw and unconditional contracts for sale are not exchanged, irrespective of your reasons."

17. If, by reason of the provisions of the statement in which any of the terms referred to above appear, any of the prescribed explanations is in any way misleading, you should alter the content of the explanation so as accurately to describe the liability of the client to pay a fee in accordance with those provisions. Subject to this requirement, you should reproduce the explanations prominently, clearly and legibly without any material alterations or additions. They should be given no less prominence than that given to any other information in the statement apart from the heading, firm names, names of the parties, numbers or lettering subsequently inserted.

18. You may quote or publicise a composite fee for property selling and conveyancing, but should be prepared to quote separate fees if asked. The separate fees may total more than the composite fee.

Conflict of interests – 18.03

19. The requirements of 18.03 are similar to those imposed on estate agents by the Estate Agents (Undesirable Practices) (No.2) Order 1991 (SI 1991/1032).

20. It is important to read the requirements of 18.03 in close conjunction with rule 3 (Conflict of interests).

Waivers – 18.04

21. The exemption from the Estate Agents Act 1979, explained in note 10 above, is on the basis that the standards in rule 18 are complied with in all circumstances. For this reason there is no power to waive rule 18.

Rule 19   Financial services

Introduction

This rule sets out the requirements for ensuring that your independence is preserved when acting in connection with the provision of financial services for clients, both through your firm and through a separate business.

The rule applies to your overseas practice in relation to regulated activities you conduct from an office in Scotland or Northern Ireland and to regulated activities you conduct into the UK from an office outside the UK.

Rule 19 – Financial services

19.01   Independence

(1)   You must not, in connection with any regulated activity:

    (a)   be an appointed representative; or

    (b)   have any arrangement with other persons under which you could be constrained to recommend to clients or effect for them (or refrain from doing so) transactions:

        (i)   in some investments but not others;

        (ii)   with some persons but not others; or

        (iii)   through the agency of some persons but not others; or

    (c)   have any arrangement with other persons under which you could be constrained to introduce or refer clients or other persons with whom you deal to some persons but not others.

(2)   You must not have any active involvement in a separate business which is an appointed representative, unless it is the appointed representative of an independent financial adviser.

(3)   Paragraph (1)(b) and (c) above shall not apply to arrangements in connection with any of the following types of investments:

    (a)   regulated mortgage contracts;

    (b)   general insurance contracts; or

    (c)   pure protection contracts.

(4)   In this rule:

    (a)   "appointed representative" has the meaning given in the Financial Services and Markets Act 2000;

    (b)   "general insurance contract" is any contract of insurance within Part I of

Schedule 1 to the Financial Services and Markets Act 2000 (Regulated Activities) Order 2001 (SI 2001/544);

(c) "investment" means any of the investments specified in Part III of the Financial Services and Markets Act 2000 (Regulated Activities) Order 2001 (SI 2001/544);

(d) "pure protection contract" has the meaning given in rule 8(1) of the Solicitors' Financial Services (Scope) Rules 2001;

(e) "regulated activity" means an activity which is specified in the Financial Services and Markets Act 2000 (Regulated Activities) Order 2001 (SI 2001/544); and

(f) "regulated mortgage contract" has the meaning given by article 61(3) of the Financial Services and Markets Act 2000 (Regulated Activities) Order 2001 (SI 2001/544).

Guidance to rule 19 – Financial services

1. Independence is a core duty (1.03). However rule 19 sets out the exact scope of this duty when carrying on regulated activities.

2. Note that under the Financial Services and Markets Act 2000 the Financial Services Authority (FSA) is the single statutory regulator of financial services business. Under the Financial Services and Markets Act 2000, if you carry on "regulated activities" you will need either to be regulated by the FSA or to rely on the Part XX exemption.

3. The SRA is not therefore able to authorise you to conduct investment business. However, Part XX of the Financial Services and Markets Act 2000 makes special provision for professional firms which do not carry on mainstream investment business but which may carry on regulated activities in the course of other work such as conveyancing, corporate, matrimonial, probate and trust work. Part XX enables firms regulated by the SRA which meet certain conditions to be treated as exempt professional firms and to carry on activities known as exempt regulated activities. These firms will not need to be regulated by the FSA but will be able to carry on exempt regulated activities under the supervision of and regulation by the SRA. This exemption does not apply to an authorised non-SRA firm simply by virtue of that firm having a solicitor as a manager, owner or employee. If you are a solicitor practising in an authorised non-SRA firm, neither you nor the firm will be exempt under Part XX simply because you are a solicitor. However, the firm may benefit from an exemption relating to its own regulator under Part XX.

4. In carrying out the functions of a designated professional body, the SRA is required to make rules governing the carrying on of regulated activities by its members. In accordance with this requirement, the Solicitors' Financial

Services (Scope) Rules 2001 set out the scope of the activities which may be undertaken by firms under the Part XX exemption in the Financial Services and Markets Act 2000. You should refer to these rules and the Solicitors' Financial Services (Conduct of Business) Rules 2001 regarding the carrying on of regulated activities.

5. This rule applies specifically in connection with regulated activities. It prohibits you from being an appointed representative (i.e. a tied agent) or from being actively involved in a separate business which is an appointed representative unless the separate business is the appointed representative of an independent financial adviser.

6. It also prevents you from entering into any restrictive arrangements in connection with regulated activities that could constrain the advice you give to clients or the referrals that you make. However, it would not prevent you from regularly introducing clients to a particular broker, provided that you have not entered into any arrangement which could constrain you to use that broker.

7. The prohibition on entering into restrictive arrangements does not apply to arrangements in connection with:

(a) regulated mortgage contracts;

(b) general insurance contracts, for example after the event insurance; or

(c) pure protection contracts, for example term assurance.

This means that you would not be prevented from having an arrangement under which an introducer stipulates that you might only sell one particular insurance policy – for example, if there is a conditional fee agreement, provided that it is suitable for the client's needs and you have informed the client of the constraint. Although the prohibition in rule 19 does not apply to arrangements in connection with particular types of investments, you must still comply with 1.03 (Independence) and rule 9 (Referrals of business).

Rule 20   Rights and obligations of practice

Introduction

Rule 20 sets out the requirements for certification and provision of information to the Solicitors Regulation Authority, and authorises solicitors, RELs and RFLs to do certain reserved work and immigration work.

Rule 20 – Rights and obligations of practice

20.01   Reserved work and immigration work

Solicitors

(1)   As a solicitor, provided that you comply with 20.02(1) you are authorised by the Solicitors Regulation Authority:

    (a)   to undertake the following reserved work:

        (i)   the exercise of any right of audience which solicitors had immediately before 7 December 1989;

        (ii)   the exercise of any additional right of audience if you have a relevant higher courts advocacy qualification awarded by the SRA or another approved regulator;

        (iii)   the conduct of, and the preparation of documents in, court and immigration tribunal proceedings;

        (iv)   the preparation of instruments and the lodging of documents relating to the transfer or charge of land;

        (v)   the preparation of trust deeds disposing of capital;

        (vi)   the preparation of papers on which to found or oppose a grant of probate or a grant of letters of administration;

        (vii)   the administration of oaths and statutory declarations; and

    (b)   to undertake immigration services not included under (a) above, and to provide immigration advice.

RELs

(2)   As an REL, you are authorised by the Solicitors Regulation Authority:

    (a)   to undertake the following reserved work:

        (i)   the exercise of any right of audience which solicitors had immediately before 7 December 1989;

    (ii)   the exercise of any additional right of audience provided that you have a relevant higher courts advocacy qualification awarded by the SRA or another approved regulator;

    (iii)   the conduct of, and the preparation of documents in, court and immigration tribunal proceedings;

    (iv)   the preparation of instruments and the lodging of documents relating to the transfer or charge of land, provided you are a member of a profession listed under regulation 12 of the European Communities (Lawyer's Practice) Regulations 2000;

    (v)   the preparation of trust deeds disposing of capital;

    (vi)   the preparation of papers on which to found or oppose a grant of probate or a grant of letters of administration, provided you are a member of a profession listed under regulation 13 of the European Communities (Lawyer's Practice) Regulations 2000;

    (vii)   the administration of oaths and statutory declarations;

  (b)   to undertake immigration services not included under (a) above, and to provide immigration advice.

(3)   When as an REL you exercise a right of audience before a court under (2)(a)(i) or (ii), conduct court litigation under (2)(a)(iii) or prepare court documents under (2)(a)(iii) you must act in conjunction with a solicitor or barrister authorised to do that work.

RFLs

(4)   As an RFL working within 12.03(1) you are authorised by the Solicitors Regulation Authority:

  (a)   to undertake the following reserved work:

    (i)   advocacy before immigration tribunals; and

    (ii)   the conduct of, and the preparation of documents in, immigration tribunal proceedings;

  (b)   to undertake immigration services which are not reserved work and are not included under (a) above, and to provide immigration advice.

Recognised bodies

(5) (a)   A recognised body is authorised by the Solicitors Regulation Authority to undertake the following reserved work:

    (i)   advocacy before a court or immigration tribunal provided the manager or employee exercising the right of audience is authorised by the Solicitors Regulation Authority, or otherwise entitled, to do so;

    (ii)   the conduct of proceedings in a court or immigration tribunal;

      (iii)   the preparation of documents in proceedings before a court or immigration tribunal;

      (iv)   the preparation of instruments and the lodging of documents relating to the transfer or charge of land, provided the body has a manager who is an individual authorised to do that work, or a body corporate with a manager who is authorised to do that work;

      (v)   the preparation of trust deeds disposing of capital;

      (vi)   the preparation of papers on which to found or oppose a grant of probate or a grant of letters of administration, provided the body has a manager who is an individual authorised to do that work, or a body corporate with a manager who is authorised to do that work;

      (vii)   the administration of oaths and statutory declarations.

  (b)   A recognised body is authorised to undertake immigration services which are not within (a) above, and to provide immigration advice.

  (c)   A recognised body which has an individual working in the practice who is authorised by the Master of the Faculties to do the work is authorised to provide notarial services within paragraph 7 of Schedule 2 to the Legal Services Act 2007.

20

Recognised sole practitioners

(6) (a)   A recognised sole practitioner who is a solicitor is authorised by the Solicitors Regulation Authority:

      (i)   to provide any reserved work which the solicitor is authorised to provide under (1)(a) above, and any other advocacy service to the extent that an employee of the firm exercising a right of audience is authorised by the Solicitors Regulation Authority, or otherwise entitled, to do so;

      (ii)   to undertake immigration services which are not within (i) above, and provide immigration advice; and

      (iii)   to provide notarial services within paragraph 7 of Schedule 2 to the Legal Services Act 2007, if the sole practitioner or an employee of the firm is authorised by the Master of the Faculties to do the work.

  (b)   A recognised sole practitioner who is an REL is authorised by the Solicitors Regulation Authority:

      (i)   to provide any reserved work which the REL is authorised to provide under (2)(a) above, and any other advocacy service to the extent that an employee of the firm exercising a right of audience is authorised by the Solicitors Regulation Authority, or otherwise entitled, to do so;

> (ii)   to undertake immigration services which are not within (i) above, and provide immigration advice; and
>
> (iii) to provide notarial services within paragraph 7 of Schedule 2 to the Legal Services Act 2007, if the sole practitioner or an employee of the firm is authorised by the Master of the Faculties to do the work.

20.02   Practising certificates

(1) If you are practising as a solicitor you must, whether practising in a firm or in-house:

(a)   have in force a practising certificate issued by the Solicitors Regulation Authority; or

(b)   be exempt under section 88 of the Solicitors Act 1974 from holding a practising certificate.

(2) You will be practising as a solicitor if you are involved in legal practice and:

(a)   your involvement in the firm or the work depends on your being a solicitor;

(b)   you are held out explicitly or implicitly as a practising solicitor;

(c)   you are employed explicitly or implicitly as a solicitor; or

(d)   you are deemed by section 1A of the Solicitors Act 1974 to be acting as a solicitor.

(3) In (2) above "legal practice" includes not only the practice of law but also the provision of other services such as are provided by solicitors.

(4) If you are a solicitor who was formerly an REL, and you are practising from an office in the UK as a lawyer of an Establishment Directive profession, you must have in force a practising certificate issued by the Solicitors Regulation Authority, even if you are not practising as a solicitor.

20.03   Sole practitioners

(1) If you are a solicitor or REL you must not practise as a sole practitioner unless:

(a)   the Solicitors Regulation Authority has first authorised you as a recognised sole practitioner by endorsing your practising certificate or certificate of registration to that effect; or

(b)   your practice falls within (2) below and you are therefore exempt from the obligation to be a recognised sole practitioner.

(2) For the purpose of (1) above and section 1B of the Solicitors Act 1974 you are deemed not to be practising as a sole practitioner if:

(a)   your practice is conducted entirely from an office or offices outside England and Wales;

(b)   your practice consists entirely of work as a temporary or permanent employee and any firm which employs you takes full responsibility for you as an employee; or

(c)   your practice consists entirely of:

   (i)   providing professional services without remuneration for friends, relatives, companies wholly owned by you or your family, or registered charities;

   (ii)   administering oaths and statutory declarations; and/or

   (iii) activities which could constitute practice but are done in the course of discharging the functions of any of the offices or appointments listed in paragraph (b) of the definition of "Private Practice" in rule 3.1 of the Solicitors' Indemnity Insurance Rules.

(3)   (a)   Within 28 days of the death of a recognised sole practitioner, an emergency application may be made for recognition as a recognised sole practitioner by a solicitor or an REL who is:

   (i)   the sole practitioner's executor;

   (ii)   a practice manager appointed by the sole practitioner's personal representatives; or

   (iii) an employee of the firm;

   and if the application is granted, recognition will be deemed to run from the date of death.

   (b)   Recognition in the capacity of personal representative, practice manager or employee will not be renewed for any period after the winding up of the estate or 12 months from the date of death, whichever is the earlier.

20.04   Participation in legal practice

(1)   If you are a solicitor, REL or RFL and you are:

(a)   a manager, member or owner of:

   (i)   a recognised body; or

   (ii)   a body corporate which is a manager of a recognised body; or

(b)   employed in England and Wales in connection with the provision of legal services by:

   (i)   a recognised sole practitioner;

   (ii)   a recognised body; or

   (iii) a body corporate which is a manager of a recognised body;

it must be in your capacity as a solicitor, REL or RFL. This does not prevent you practising also as an individual authorised by an approved regulator other than the Solicitors Regulation Authority or providing services as a member of a non-lawyer profession.

(2)　Subject to (3) below, if you are a solicitor, REL or RFL and you are:

　　(a)　a manager, member or owner of:

　　　　(i)　an authorised non-SRA firm; or

　　　　(ii)　a body corporate which is a manager of an authorised non-SRA firm; or

　　(b)　employed in England and Wales in connection with the provision of legal services by:

　　　　(i)　an authorised non-SRA firm; or

　　　　(ii)　a body corporate which is a manager of an authorised non-SRA firm,

it must be in your capacity as a solicitor, REL or RFL or as an individual authorised by an approved regulator other than the Solicitors Regulation Authority. This does not prevent you practising in both capacities or providing services as a member of a non-lawyer profession in addition to practising as a lawyer.

(3)　If you are a solicitor who is employed by, or is a director of, an authorised non-SRA firm, section 1A of the Solicitors Act 1974 will require you to practise through that firm in the capacity of solicitor, even if also practising in some other capacity.

20.05　Duty to co-operate with the Solicitors Regulation Authority and the Legal Complaints Service

(1)　You must deal with the Solicitors Regulation Authority and the Legal Complaints Service in an open, prompt and co-operative way.

(2)　You must:

　　(a)　provide the Solicitors Regulation Authority with information necessary in order to issue you with a practising certificate, or deal with renewal of registration or renewal of recognition, as appropriate; and

　　(b)　during the period your practising certificate, registration or recognition is in force, notify the Authority of any changes to relevant information about you, or your firm or in-house practice.

(3)　As a solicitor, REL, RFL or recognised body you must act promptly to:

　　(a)　investigate whether any person may have a claim for redress resulting from an act or omission of yours;

　　(b)　provide the Solicitors Regulation Authority with a report on the outcome of such an investigation, identifying persons who may have such a claim;

　　(c)　notify such persons that they may have a right of redress against you, providing them with information as to the nature of the possible claim, about the firm's complaints procedures and about the Legal Complaints Service;

(d)   where you have identified a person who may have a claim for redress, ensure that the matter is dealt with under the firm's complaints procedures as if that person had made a complaint,

if required by the Solicitors Regulation Authority in relation to a matter specified by the Authority.

20.06   Reporting serious misconduct and serious financial difficulty

You must (subject, where necessary, to your client's consent) report to the Solicitors Regulation Authority if:

(a)   you become aware of serious misconduct by a solicitor, an REL, an RFL, a recognised body, a manager of a recognised body, or an employee of a recognised body or recognised sole practitioner;

(b)   you have reason to doubt the integrity of a solicitor, an REL or an RFL, a manager of a recognised body or an employee of a recognised body or recognised sole practitioner; or

(c)   you have reason to believe that a solicitor, an REL, an RFL, a recognised body, a manager of a recognised body, or a firm is in serious financial difficulty which could put the public at risk.

20.07   Obstructing complaints

(1)   You must not try to hinder or prevent a person who wishes to report your conduct to the Solicitors Regulation Authority or the Legal Complaints Service from doing so.

(2)   You must not victimise a person for reporting your conduct to the Solicitors Regulation Authority or the Legal Complaints Service.

(3)   You must not on your own or on your clients' behalf enter into an agreement which would attempt to preclude the Solicitors Regulation Authority or the Legal Complaints Service from investigating any actual or potential allegation of professional misconduct.

(4)   Unless you can properly allege malice, you must not issue defamation proceedings in respect of a complaint to the Solicitors Regulation Authority or the Legal Complaints Service.

20.08   Production of documents, information and explanations

(1)   You must promptly comply with:

(a)   a written notice from the Solicitors Regulation Authority that you must produce for inspection by the appointee of the Solicitors Regulation Authority all documents held by you or held under your control and all information and explanations requested:

(i)   in connection with your practice; or

(ii)   in connection with any trust of which you are, or formerly were, a trustee;

for the purpose of ascertaining whether any person subject to these rules is complying with or has complied with any provision of these or any other rules, codes or mandatory guidance made or issued by the Solicitors Regulation Authority; and

(b)   a notice given by the Solicitors Regulation Authority in accordance with section 44B or 44BA of the Solicitors Act 1974 for the provision of documents, information or explanations.

(2)   You must provide any necessary permissions for information to be given so as to enable the appointee of the Solicitors Regulation Authority to:

(a)   prepare a report on the documents produced under (1) above; and

(b)   seek verification from clients, staff and the banks, building societies or other financial institutions used by you.

(3)   You must comply with all requests from the Solicitors Regulation Authority or its appointee as to:

(a)   the form in which you produce any documents you hold electronically; and

(b)   photocopies of any documents to take away.

(4)   A notice under this rule is deemed to be duly served:

(a)   on the date on which it is delivered to or left at your address;

(b)   on the date on which it is sent electronically to your e-mail or fax address; or

(c)   seven days after it has been sent by post or document exchange to your last notified practising address.

20.09   Dealing with claims

(1)   If you are a sole practitioner or a manager of a firm and you discover an act or omission which could give rise to a claim, you must inform the client.

(2)   If a client makes a claim against you, or notifies an intention to do so, or if you discover an act or omission which could give rise to a claim, you must:

(a)   inform the client that independent advice should be sought (unless the client's loss, if any, is trivial and you promptly remedy that loss);

(b)   consider whether a conflict of interests has arisen, and if so not act further for the client in the matter giving rise to the claim; and

(c)   notify your compulsory professional indemnity insurer under the Solicitors' Indemnity Insurance Rules or 15.26 or, if appropriate, the Solicitors Indemnity Fund Ltd.

20.10   Compliance with conditions

If you are a solicitor, REL, RFL or recognised body you must comply with any condition which the Solicitors Regulation Authority (or previously the Law Society) has imposed on your practising certificate, registration or recognition.

Guidance to rule 20 – Rights and obligations of practice

Scope of rule 20

1.   In summary, rule 20:

(a)   formally authorises solicitors, RELs, RFLs, recognised bodies and recognised sole practitioners to do specific types of reserved work and immigration work;

(b)   requires practising solicitors to have a practising certificate unless they are exempt under section 88 of the Solicitors Act 1974;

(c)   sets out the requirement that a solicitor or REL who wishes to practise as a sole practitioner must be authorised as a recognised sole practitioner;

(d)   requires that a solicitor's, REL's or RFL's participation in a law firm must be as a practising lawyer;

(e)   requires co-operation with regulators in providing information;

(f)   requires reporting of serious misconduct;

(g)   requires fair dealing with clients in relation to claims and complaints;

(h)   requires compliance with conditions imposed by the SRA.

Reserved work and immigration work – 20.01

Solicitors

2.   Provided you hold a practising certificate or are exempt under section 88 of the Solicitors Act, rule 20.01 authorises you to conduct advocacy (but note that for advocacy in the higher courts you will need to have obtained a qualification to exercise a right of audience), litigation, reserved instrument activities, probate activities, immigration work and to administer oaths.

RELs

3. If you are an REL 20.01 authorises you to do the same work as solicitors, but note that:

    (a) you can only exercise higher rights of audience if you have a higher courts advocacy qualification;

    (b) if you are undertaking advocacy or litigation or drawing court documents you must act in conjunction with a solicitor and/or barrister authorised to do that work;

    (c) only an REL from certain jurisdictions can do reserved instrument activities relating to conveyancing or probate:

        (i) under regulation 12 of the European Communities (Lawyer's Practice) Regulations 2000 (SI 2000/1119), only RELs qualified in Cyprus, the Czech Republic, Denmark, Finland, Hungary, Iceland, the Irish Republic, Liechtenstein, Norway, Slovakia and Sweden are entitled to do reserved conveyancing work in England and Wales; and

        (ii) under regulation 13 of those regulations, only RELs qualified in Austria, Cyprus, Denmark, Finland, Germany, Iceland, the Irish Republic, Liechtenstein, Norway, Slovakia and Sweden are entitled to do reserved probate work in England and Wales.

RFLs

4. If you are an RFL you are authorised:

    (a) to do advocacy before immigration tribunals;

    (b) to conduct, and prepare documents in, immigration tribunal proceedings;

    (c) to do all other immigration work which is not reserved work.

    Note that RFLs are not authorised to do immigration work before the courts.

Recognised bodies

5. Recognised bodies are authorised to do the same reserved work as solicitors, but note that a recognised body can only:

    (a) undertake higher court advocacy work if it has a manager or employee entitled to do that work;

    (b) reserved instrument activities relating to conveyancing, or probate activities if it has a manager who is an individual entitled to do that work, or which is a body corporate with a manager who is entitled to do that work;

(c)   notarial work if it has an individual working in the practice who is authorised to do the work.

Recognised sole practitioners

6.   Recognised sole practitioners are authorised to:

(a)   undertake the reserved work the solicitor or REL sole practitioner is authorised to do as an individual;

(b)   exercise advocacy rights additional to those the solicitor or REL sole practitioner is authorised to exercise as an individual if an employee exercising the right is authorised by the SRA or otherwise entitled to do so;

(c)   undertake notarial work if the sole practitioner or an employee is authorised by the Master of Faculties to do the work.

Reserved work

20

7.   Reserved work is work that is defined in Schedule 2 to the Legal Services Act 2007 as a "reserved legal activity". Certain categories of reserved work (rights of audience in chambers, reserved instrument activities and probate activities) can be done by an unqualified person under the supervision of a manager or fellow employee qualified to do that work – see Schedule 3 to the Legal Services Act.

Immigration work

8.   Immigration work (immigration advice and immigration services) is restricted to certain persons under the Immigration and Asylum Act 1999. Immigration services relating to courts or immigration tribunals are reserved work – advocacy, the conduct of cases, and the preparation of papers. The court work is subject to the normal restriction on court work. Immigration Tribunal work can be done by RFLs who are practising as such. Other immigration work is not reserved work, but can only be done by an authorised person such as a solicitor, a barrister, a legal executive, a member of an Establishment Directive profession, or an RFL practising as such, or under the supervision of an authorised person, or under an exemption given by the Office of the Immigration Services Commissioner.

Financial services

9.   The Financial Services and Markets Act 2000 reserves the provision of "regulated activities" to persons authorised by the Financial Services

Authority (FSA). Certain "regulated activities", ancillary to the provision of a professional service, are exempt from regulation by the FSA when carried out by solicitors' or RELs' firms – see the Solicitors' Financial Services (Scope) Rules. Note that the firm must be a recognised body or recognised sole practitioner to rely on this exemption. For the definition of "regulated activity" see 19.01(4).

Practising certificates – 20.02

10. Rule 20.02 includes, in rule form, the requirements of section 1 of the Solicitors Act 1974. The section reads:

"No person shall be qualified to act as a solicitor unless –

(a)   he has been admitted as a solicitor, and

(b)   his name is on the roll, and

(c)   he has in force a certificate issued by the Society in accordance with the provisions of this Part authorising him to practise as a solicitor (in this Act referred to as a 'practising certificate')."

The issuing of practising certificates under Part II of the Act is the responsibility of the SRA.

11. Under section 1A of the Solicitors Act, a solicitor is always deemed to be acting as a solicitor if he or she is employed, in connection with the provision of any legal services, by a solicitor with a practising certificate, any partnership with at least one member who is a solicitor with a practising certificate, a recognised body, or an individual or firm authorised by any approved regulator under the Legal Services Act 2007.

12. If you practise as a solicitor, whether in a firm or in-house, without having a practising certificate, you will commit a criminal offence, as well as a breach of the rules, unless you are entitled to rely on the exemption in section 88 of the Solicitors Act.

13. Section 88 of the Solicitors Act 1974 exempts from the requirement to hold a practising certificate the solicitor to certain public authorities, and a solicitor who is the "clerk" to such a solicitor. The section reads:

"(1)   Nothing in this Act shall prejudice or affect any rights or privileges of the solicitor to the Treasury, any other public department, the Church Commissioners or the Duchy of Cornwall, or require any such officer or any clerk or officer appointed to act for him to be admitted or enrolled or to hold a practising certificate in any case where it would not have been necessary for him to be admitted or enrolled or to hold such a certificate if this Act had not been passed.

(1A) The exemption from the requirement to hold a practising certificate conferred by subsection (1) above shall not apply to solicitors who are Crown Prosecutors.

(2) Sections 31 and 32(1) shall not apply to, and nothing in this Act shall prejudice or affect any rights or privileges which immediately before the commencement of this Act attached to the office of the Solicitor of the City of London."

14. Although section 88 of the Solicitors Act 1974 preserves certain pre-existing rights, privileges and exemptions, it does not say what these are. They are to be found in a number of statutory provisions of some age, each conferring different rights, privileges or exemptions on different persons. Some of the older provisions do not fit easily into modern conditions and it is not possible to provide a full list of exemptions. The view of the SRA Board is as follows.

(a) A solicitor is exempt who holds office as the solicitor (i.e. the principal solicitor) to:

(i)   the Treasury;

(ii) any other public department;

(iii) the Church Commissioners; and

(iv) the Duchy of Cornwall; or

(v)   a solicitor who is a clerk or officer appointed to act for one of the above.

(b) The exemption relates to the capacity and employment of the solicitor. Thus, for instance, a solicitor who holds office as the principal solicitor to a public department, but in a different capacity or employment administers oaths, cannot rely on the section 88 exemption in respect of that other capacity or employment.

(c) There is no definition of "public department" in the Solicitors Act. In the absence of a definition, the SRA Board takes the view that "any other public department" would include any department of central government in the UK, the National Assembly of Wales and any "non-ministerial department", but would not include other agencies or "non-departmental public bodies".

Assistance in determining whether a department or agency is a "non-ministerial department" or a "non-departmental public body" can be found on the Civil Service website – **www.civilservice.gov.uk**.

(d) Section 88(1A) of the Solicitors Act requires a solicitor who is a Crown Prosecutor to hold a practising certificate.

Being held out as a practising solicitor – 20.02(2)(b)

15. Being described on your firm's notepaper or website as a member of the Law Society is an example of being held out "implicitly" as a solicitor.

16. There is a presumption that you are practising as a solicitor if you are held out (explicitly or implicitly) as a solicitor whilst providing lawyer-like services. The same presumption arises if you are described as a lawyer in such a context, if you have no other legal qualification to justify that description. It is possible in some circumstances to rebut the presumption by ensuring that some such words as "non-practising" are used whenever you are held out as a solicitor or lawyer. However, you cannot rebut the presumption if you rely on being a solicitor in the context of legal practice – for example in order:

    (a)   to be a partner in a firm of lawyers;

    (b)   to be employed as a solicitor or lawyer;

    (c)   to do work in England and Wales which is reserved to solicitors;

    (d)   to do work in another jurisdiction which is reserved to lawyers;

    (e)   to be a registered foreign legal consultant in another jurisdiction; or

    (f)   to be a registered lawyer in another European profession under the Establishment Directive.

    Instructing counsel is not restricted to any particular category of person by statute. However, barristers only accept instructions made professionally on behalf of clients from solicitors and limited categories of non-solicitors – see the Bar Standards Board's website for details – **www.barstandardsboard.org.uk**. If you instruct counsel as a solicitor, you will be practising as a solicitor and must have a practising certificate.

17. If you are dually qualified you may be practising as a member of both professions simultaneously, either through a single combined practice, or through two separate practices. In the latter case you would need separate notepaper, etc., to distinguish the two practices.

18. The context of a description can make a real difference as to whether you are held out as a practising solicitor or not. For example:

    (a)   if you are running a web-based or telephone advice service, and describe yourself as a solicitor (without qualifying the description with words such as "non-practising"), you will need a practising certificate; and

    (b)   if your only work is as an academic and writer, and you have written a legal textbook in which you are described as a solicitor or as a lawyer on the title page, you will not need a practising certificate. This is because there is no context of services normally provided by practising solicitors.

Retirement from practice

19. You may continue to need a practising certificate after you retire, depending on how complete your retirement is. If you have closed your firm, but will continue to hold money for clients only while you submit bills of costs and close your practice accounts, you will still be subject to the Solicitors' Accounts Rules 1998. However, if that is all you are doing you will not need a practising certificate, provided that a solicitor with a practising certificate authorises any withdrawals from your client account.

20. If you have retired but continue to do some work, you may need a practising certificate. For example:

(a) you must have a practising certificate if you continue to work in a firm in connection with the provision of legal services. This would include being a consultant or supervising fee earners, even if you only help out on an occasional basis or cover a professional colleague's holiday absences; or

(b) you must have a practising certificate if you continue to undertake any reserved work.

21. If you are completely retired from all legal work you may still need a practising certificate if, for example:

(a) you continue to be held out as a solicitor or lawyer by your former firm; or

(b) your name appears on your firm's notepaper as a "consultant", unless it is made clear on the notepaper that you are not practising.

Sole practitioners – 20.03

22. From 1 July 2009, rule 20.03 prohibits a solicitor or REL from practising as a sole practitioner in England and Wales unless authorised by the SRA as a recognised sole practitioner or exempt under the rule. Existing sole practitioners who qualify for recognition will be "passported" to recognition as of 1 July 2009. If you wish to set up in sole practice on or after that date you will need to apply to the SRA for your practising certificate (in the case of a solicitor) or your certificate of registration (in the case of an REL) to be endorsed to that effect.

23. The rule exempts solicitors and RELs from this requirement whose practice:

(a) is conducted entirely overseas;

(b)   consists entirely of work for firms which employ and take full responsibility for them (e.g. consultants and locums);

(c)   consists entirely of providing free professional services to friends, relatives, wholly owned companies or registered charities, administering oaths and statutory declarations;

(d)   consists entirely of activities done in the course of discharging the functions of certain offices or appointments.

24. The rule allows a period of 28 days from the death of a recognised sole practitioner to make an emergency application for recognition as a recognised sole practitioner by a solicitor or REL who is:

(a)   the sole practitioner's executor;

(b)   a practice manager appointed by the sole practitioner's personal representatives; or

(c)   an employee of the firm.

If the application is granted, recognition is deemed to run from the date of death.

25. Recognition in the capacity of personal representative, practice manager or employee will not be renewed for any period after the winding up of the estate or 12 months from the date of death, whichever is the earlier.

Participation in legal practice – 20.04

26. Rule 20.04 provides that a solicitor, REL or RFL who is a manager, member or owner of a recognised body, or who is employed in England and Wales in connection with the provision of legal services by a recognised body, a recognised sole practitioner or an authorised non-SRA firm must participate as a solicitor, REL or RFL (even if also in some other capacity as well).

Duty to co-operate with the Solicitors Regulation Authority and the Legal Complaints Service – 20.05

27. Rule 20.05 requires you to deal with any communication from the SRA or the Legal Complaints Service properly. This means that you will need to respond promptly and substantively to communications when appropriate – for example, to a letter referring to a complaint made against you or a member of your firm.

28. The duty imposed by 20.05 may be limited by your legal obligations to your clients or others, for example your obligation to protect clients' confidentiality and privilege.

29. You should note that failure to comply with a request for an explanation of any matter in relation to your conduct may result in the imposition of conditions on a recognised body's recognition, a solicitor's practising certificate or an REL's or RFL's registration, or even refusal by the SRA to issue a practising certificate or renew a registration.

30. Rules 1.02 (Integrity) and 1.06 (Public confidence) require you to act with integrity and to refrain from behaviour likely to diminish the trust the public places in you or the profession. You should therefore, unless there is good reason to the contrary, comply with binding orders or requests for information from the Legal Services Ombudsman. Similarly, it may be appropriate, subject to any overriding duties, to assist the Bar Council or other regulatory body when they are investigating the conduct of a member of their profession. If you are an individual authorised by an approved regulator other than the SRA, you must comply with that regulator's requirements.

31. Abusive communications and unreasonable attempts to delay an investigation or enquiry are inconsistent with the co-operation required by 20.05.

32. Rule 20.05(3) requires solicitors, RELs, RFLs and recognised bodies to take prompt action to comply with an SRA requirement in relation to a specified matter:

    (a) to investigate whether anyone may have a claim for redress;

    (b) to provide the SRA with a report identifying those who may have a claim for redress;

    (c) notify those who may have a claim for redress, providing them with relevant information concerning the complaints process;

    (d) deal with the matter under your firm's complaints procedures as if the person with a claim had made a complaint.

Reporting serious misconduct and serious financial difficulty – 20.06

33. The purpose of 20.06 is to protect the public and the integrity of the profession. Often, professional colleagues will be aware of serious misconduct and/or risk arising from a firm's financial problems before any complaint has been made, and if the SRA is notified it can take timely action. The SRA's Fraud and Confidential Intelligence Bureau will consider information of this nature on an anonymous basis if requested.

34. Unless you are required by law to report a matter, 20.06 does not apply to confidential and/or privileged information another lawyer discloses to you:

    (a) as your client or the client of your firm; or

(b) when seeking advice from a confidential helpline, such as the Solicitors' Assistance Scheme or Lawcare.

35. You will not breach 20.06 if you take no action because you know that someone else has already reported a matter of which you are aware.

36. Whether or not "misconduct" can be considered "serious", and whether or not a firm's financial difficulties could put the public at risk, will depend on the circumstances. In general, any conduct involving dishonesty or deception or a serious criminal offence would amount to "serious misconduct". If in your judgement a firm's financial difficulties present a risk to its clients or to others, you should report the matter, and can do so on a confidential basis if you wish.

37. If reporting misconduct which has taken place within your own firm and which may give rise to a claim, you should also consider your obligations to your insurers. See also note 54 of the guidance to rule 3 (Conflict of interests).

38. If making a report about another lawyer or firm would involve disclosing confidential information, you should obtain your client's consent before proceeding.

39. You should exercise care where there may be evidence of money laundering activities (see the Proceeds of Crime Act 2002, other relevant statutes and regulations, and guidance issued by the Law Society and the SRA on this subject).

Obstructing complaints – 20.07

40. No agreement, whether with a client or a third party, can affect the rights of the SRA or the Legal Complaints Service to investigate misconduct or to consider complaints. To attempt to make such an agreement is a breach of 20.07. Examples of situations that would breach 20.07 are:

(a) accepting instructions to act for a client which involve any agreement preventing the SRA or the Legal Complaints Service from investigating your conduct or the conduct of a member of your firm;

(b) improperly demanding, offering or accepting payment in return for not reporting alleged misconduct;

(c) harassing or bringing improper pressure to bear on a complainant or potential complainant; and

(d) issuing proceedings for defamation against a client or former client in relation to material contained in a complaint to the SRA or the Legal Complaints Service, unless you are alleging malice.

41. The following, however, would not breach 20.07:

(a) proper attempts to persuade the client that the client's complaint is unfounded; and

(b) in a case of inadequate professional services, genuine attempts to propose an agreement to compensate the aggrieved client.

Production of documents, information and explanations – 20.08

42. The SRA will only exercise its powers under 20.08 in accordance with the law, in pursuit of a legitimate aim and proportionate to that aim.

43. The SRA may use or disclose any information obtained under 20.08 and the report prepared by its appointee:

(a) in proceedings before the Solicitors Disciplinary Tribunal;

(b) to the police, the Crown Prosecution Service or the Serious Fraud Office for use in investigating the matter and in any subsequent prosecution, if it appears that you or any manager, employee, member or owner of your firm may have committed a serious criminal offence;

(c) to your regulatory body in your home state or states if you are an REL or RFL;

(d) to the regulatory body with which you are registered, if you are a solicitor registered under the Establishment Directive;

(e) to the regulatory body of any manager or employee of your firm; and/or

(f) to the professional body of which the accountant who has signed the firm's accountant's report is a member, or by which the accountant is regulated (and the information and report may also be taken into account by the SRA in relation to a possible disqualification of that person from signing an accountant's report in future).

44. Note that sections 44B and 44BA of the Solicitors Act 1974 give the SRA power to require the production of documents, give information and to provide explanations for the purpose of investigation whether there has been professional misconduct or regulatory non-compliance.

Dealing with claims – 20.09

45. The aim of 20.09 is to ensure that a claim or a potential claim is dealt with fairly and efficiently. In particular, the client should be advised at the earliest possible opportunity of an act or omission which could give rise to a claim. "Claim" has the meaning given in the Solicitors' Indemnity Insurance Rules (Minimum Terms and Conditions).

46. You must consider whether a conflict of interests has arisen between your interests and your client's. It will be rare for there to be no conflict. Where there is, you must refuse to act further in the matter.

47. Under 2.05 firms must operate a complaints handling procedure. Complaints should be dealt with under that procedure, where appropriate, rather than as claims. For example, if your client makes a complaint purely relating to poor service, it would rarely be appropriate to treat that complaint as a claim.

48. In order that a claim can be dealt with efficiently, you should consult the qualifying insurer or ARP Manager in accordance with the policy terms. In some circumstances, you may need to take limited steps to preserve your client's position.

49. There is no general duty for you to keep under review work which has been concluded. However, if you discover an act or omission which could give rise to a claim relating to a former client, you should notify your compulsory professional indemnity insurer (or, if appropriate, SIF) and seek their advice as to what further steps to take.

50. Under the Solicitors' Indemnity Insurance Rules a firm must provide details of its insurer to a person who asserts a claim against the firm. The details are the name and address of the qualifying insurer and the policy number. It is good practice for you also to provide these details to a potential claimant if you discover an act or omission which could give rise to a claim. The SRA may disclose information regarding a firm's qualifying insurer where it considers it appropriate to do so to any person asserting a claim against the firm.

51. You and your insurers should also comply with the terms of the professional negligence pre-action protocol (available from the website of the Ministry of Justice).

52. The aim of the protocol is to establish a framework in which there is an early exchange of information between the parties so that a claim can be fully investigated and, if possible, resolved without the need for litigation. This includes:

   (a)   ensuring that the parties are on an equal footing;

   (b)   saving expense;

   (c)   dealing with the dispute in ways which are proportionate:

      (i)   to the amount of money involved;

      (ii)   to the importance of the case;

      (iii)   to the complexity of the issues; and

      (iv)   to the financial position of each party; and

(d)   ensuring that the claim is dealt with expeditiously and fairly.

53. The court can make an order for costs against a party for failure to comply with the protocol. While normally it would be a matter for the insurer to ensure that the protocol is complied with, you should be aware of it when asked to provide information to the insurer, and in the occasional circumstances where an insurer may agree to you handling the claim.

Compliance with conditions – 20.10

54. The SRA has powers to impose conditions on your practising certificate, registration as an RFL or REL, on your recognition as a recognised body, or on the practising certificate or registration of a recognised sole practitioner. You must comply with any condition.

In-house solicitors

55. If you are an in-house solicitor, you do not have to hold a practising certificate unless:

(a)   you are held out or employed explicitly as a solicitor, or held out or employed implicitly as a solicitor by using a description or title such as "lawyer" or "counsel";

20

(b)   you do reserved work (other than at the direction and under the supervision of a fellow employee as provided in the Solicitors Act 1974 or under Schedule 3 to the Legal Services Act 2007);

(c)   you rely on your qualification as a solicitor in order to instruct counsel;

(d)   you fulfil the role of a "person qualified to supervise" in the limited circumstances set out in 5.02(1)(c) (law centres), (d)(i) (legal aid) or (d)(ii) (litigation or advocacy for members of the public); or

(e)   you authorise the withdrawal of money from a client account, under rule 23(1)(a) of the Solicitors' Accounts Rules 1998.

56. Solicitors employed by authorised non-SRA firms (such as a firm of licensed conveyancers or patent agents) are not treated as in-house solicitors for the purposes of the rules. They can do work, within the scope of the firm's authorisation, for clients of the firm as well as for the firm itself. They can also do a wider range of work for the firm itself, related bodies, work colleagues or pro bono. See 12.01(1)(d).

Rule 21   Separate businesses

Introduction

A "separate business" is a business which is not a recognised body, a recognised sole practitioner, an authorised non-SRA firm or a firm within 12.01(2)(a)–(d) or 12.02(2)(a)–(d) but which offers a service or services that could properly be offered by a recognised body. Rule 21 regulates the interface between the practice of a solicitor and the operation of a solicitor's separate business:

- to ensure that members of the public are not confused or misled into believing that a business carried on by a solicitor, REL or RFL is regulated by the Solicitors Regulation Authority or another approved regulator when it is not;

- to ensure that the protections afforded to the clients of practising lawyers are in place in relation to certain mainstream legal services; and

- to prevent a solicitor severing part of a case or matter in such a way that the client loses statutory protections.

The rule as it applies to your overseas practice is modified by 15.21.

Rule 21 – Separate businesses

21.01   General

(1) If you are practising from an office in England and Wales as a solicitor, REL, RFL or recognised body, or if you are a manager or employee of a recognised body, or an employee of a recognised sole practitioner, you must comply with the provisions of this rule in relation to:

   (a) services which may not be provided through a separate business;

   (b) services which may be provided through a separate business or (subject to these rules) through a firm or in-house practice; and

   (c) services which fall outside the scope of a solicitor's practice but which may be provided in conjunction with a firm or in-house practice.

(2) This rule applies to your involvement in any separate business whether the separate business is in England and Wales or outside the jurisdiction.

(3) For the avoidance of doubt, in this rule "practising" includes practising as an in-house solicitor or an in-house REL.

21.02   Services which may not be provided through a separate business

(1)   Subject to (2) below, you must not provide any of the following services through a separate business:

(a)   the conduct of any matter which could come before a court, tribunal or inquiry, whether or not proceedings are started;

(b)   advocacy before a court, tribunal or inquiry;

(c)   instructing counsel in any part of the UK;

(d)   immigration advice or immigration services;

(e)   any activity in relation to conveyancing, applications for probate or letters of administration, or drawing trust deeds or court documents, which is reserved to solicitors and others under the Solicitors Act 1974;

(f)   drafting wills;

(g)   acting as nominee, trustee or executor in England and Wales;

(h)   legal advice not included above; or

(i)   drafting legal documents not included above.

Exceptions

(2)   The provisions of (1) above do not apply to prohibit you from providing services through a separate business:

(a)   which carries on your practice as a lawyer of another jurisdiction;

(b)   which carries on your business as a parliamentary agent;

(c)   which is a wholly owned nominee company operated as a subsidiary but necessary part of the work of a separate business providing financial services; or

(d)   which provides legal advice and/or drafts legal documents within (1)(h) and/or (i) above, as a subsidiary but necessary part of some other service which is one of the main services of the separate business.

However, you must comply with the requirements of 21.05 in relation to any such separate business.

21.03   Services which may be provided in conjunction with a firm or in-house practice

(1)   The following services extend beyond, or fall outside, the scope of a solicitor's practice but you may provide such services in conjunction with a firm or in-house practice:

(a)   educational and training activities; and

(b) authorship, journalism and publishing.

(2) Such services are not provided through a separate business for the purpose of this rule.

21.04 Services which may be provided (subject to these rules) either through a firm or in-house practice, or through a separate business

(1) You may provide the following services either (subject to these rules) through a firm or in-house practice, or through a separate business:

(a) alternative dispute resolution;

(b) financial services (except those that cannot form part of a solicitor's practice);

(c) estate agency;

(d) management consultancy;

(e) company secretarial services;

(f) acting as a parliamentary agent;

(g) practising as a lawyer of another jurisdiction;

(h) acting as a bailiff;

(i) acting as nominee, trustee or executor outside England and Wales; or

(j) providing any other business, advisory or agency service which could be provided (subject to these rules) through a firm or in-house practice but is not included in 21.02.

(2) If you provide any service listed in (1) above through a separate business you must comply with 21.05.

21.05 Safeguards in relation to a separate business

(1) If you provide services through a separate business you must do nothing in the course of practice, or in the course of making referrals to the business or accepting referrals from the business, which would breach rule 1 (Core duties).

(2) You must ensure that the following safeguards are in place in relation to a separate business which offers or provides any of the services listed in 21.04(1):

(a) the separate business must not be held out or described in such a way as to suggest that the separate business is carrying on a practice regulated by the Solicitors Regulation Authority or another approved regulator, or that any lawyer connected with your firm is providing services through the separate business as a practising lawyer regulated by the Solicitors Regulation Authority or another approved regulator;

(b) all paperwork, documents, records or files relating to the separate business and its customers must be kept separate from those of any firm or in-house practice, even where a customer of the separate business is also a client of the firm or in-house practice;

(c) the client account or other account used to hold money for the clients of any firm or in-house practice must not be used to hold money for the separate business, or for customers of the separate business in their capacity as such;

(d) if the separate business shares premises, office accommodation or reception staff with any firm or in-house practice:

    (i) the areas used by the firm or in-house practice must be clearly differentiated from the areas used by the separate business; and

    (ii) all customers of the separate business must be informed that it is not regulated by the Solicitors Regulation Authority and that the statutory protections attaching to clients of a lawyer regulated by the Authority are not available to them as customers of that business;

(e) if you or your firm refer a client to the separate business, the client must first be informed of your interest in the separate business, that the separate business is not regulated by the Solicitors Regulation Authority, and that the statutory protections attaching to clients of a lawyer regulated by the Authority are not available to them as customers of the separate business; and

(f) if the separate business is an estate agency, then without prejudice to the provisions of these rules regarding conflicts of interests, neither you nor any firm through which you practise may act in the conveyance for the buyer of any property sold through the estate agency unless:

    (i) the firm shares ownership of the estate agency with at least one other business in which neither you nor the firm have any financial interest;

    (ii) neither you nor anyone else in the firm is dealing with or has dealt with the sale of the seller's property for the separate business; and

    (iii) the buyer has given written consent to you or the firm acting, after your financial interest in the sale going through has been explained to the buyer.

Guidance to rule 21 – Separate businesses

1. A separate business is a business which is not a firm (recognised body, recognised sole practitioner, authorised non-SRA firm or overseas law firm) or an in-house practice but which offers a service or services that could properly be offered by a firm or in-house practice – for instance, title checks, searches, etc. for the provision of Home Information Packs.

2. Providing a service through a separate business means having any active involvement in a separate business which provides that service – see the definitions of "separate business" and "providing a service through a separate business" in rule 24 (Interpretation). You are not providing services through a separate business solely by virtue of being a non-executive director of, or having an insignificant shareholding in, a company which provides, for example, financial services.

3. In England and Wales there is no legal impediment to a non-lawyer giving legal advice, drafting wills or administering estates, or running a business which provides such services. However, the client of a firm or an in-house practice has the protections afforded by these rules, the SRA's regulatory powers, the Compensation Fund and (if a recognised body or recognised sole practitioner provides the service) indemnity insurance under the SRA's compulsory indemnity scheme. The customers of a business which is not a firm or an in-house practice will not have the same protections.

4. Rule 21 applies to you if you are a solicitor, REL or RFL practising from an office in England and Wales, or a recognised body, a manager of a recognised body, or an employee of a recognised body or recognised sole practitioner, practising in England and Wales. The rule does two things:

    (a) it prohibits you from "hiving off" the kind of services a member of the public would expect you to provide as a lawyer regulated by the SRA or another approved regulator (i.e. core legal services) to a business which is not so regulated; and

    (b) it requires you to institute safeguards in relation to other services which you are allowed to "hive off" (the kind of services a member of the public would not necessarily expect to be provided only by a lawyer regulated by the SRA but which are "solicitor-like" services).

    The above applies even if the separate business is overseas.

21

5. The purposes of the rule are:

    (a) to ensure that members of the public are not confused or misled into believing that a business is regulated by the SRA or another approved regulator when it is not;

    (b) to ensure that the protections afforded to the clients of a practising lawyer or firm are in place in relation to core legal services; and

    (c) to prevent a practising lawyer or firm severing part of a case or matter in such a way that the client loses statutory protections.

6. If you are practising wholly outside England and Wales, the provisions of this rule do not apply to you but you must comply with 15.21(2) in relation to your involvement in any separate business.

7.   If you are an in-house solicitor, and you have a separate business in addition to your in-house practice you must comply with rule 21 or, if you are employed outside England and Wales, with 15.21(2).

Business as a professional not regulated by the SRA – 21.02(2)(a) and (b)

8.   Although you may not in general provide core legal services through a separate business, you may have a separate business as a parliamentary agent, or as a lawyer of another jurisdiction. Such a business may undertake some of the activities listed in 21.02(1), and 21.02(2) states that you are not prohibited from having such a business. The safeguards for a separate business as set out in 21.05 are intended to make it clear that the business is governed by a different legal and regulatory regime from that governing services provided by solicitors.

9.   Note that a solicitor who was formerly an REL, when practising in the UK as a lawyer of an Establishment Directive profession, is subject to the rules of professional conduct and the SRA's regulatory procedures as if he or she were practising as a solicitor, and such a practice would not therefore be regarded as a separate business – see 15.01(2)(b)(v), 20.02(4) and 23.01(1)(e), and regulation 36 of the Establishment Directive Regulations.

Legal advice as a necessary and subsidiary part of another service

10. The prohibitions on providing legal advice and drafting legal documents through separate businesses do not apply when the advice or drafting is a necessary but subsidiary part of another service which you are allowed to provide through a separate business. An example would be a management consultancy business giving ancillary advice on obligations under the Data Protection Act 1998.

Executor, trustee and nominee companies

11. You are not allowed to provide executor, trustee or nominee services in England and Wales through a separate business. An executor, trustee or nominee company operated in conjunction with the practice of a firm must be a recognised body, because:

     (a) a company has a separate legal identity, so if a firm owns a company, and the company provides a service to the firm's clients, it is the company and not the firm that provides the service; and

     (b) a company providing a service for clients of a firm will constitute a "business" for the purpose of rule 21, even if the company is dormant for Companies Acts purposes, and even if no charge is made to clients for its services.

12. You are allowed to have a separate business which provides executor, trustee and nominee services outside England and Wales. If you do, you

must put in place the safeguards required. You can, on the other hand, run an executor, trustee or nominee company which provides services only outside England and Wales as an overseas corporate firm within rule 12 (Framework of practice).

Companies providing company secretarial services

13. Your firm may own a company whose purpose is to provide company secretarial services to clients of the firm. Such a company may either be operated as a legal practice (and must therefore be a recognised body), or it may be operated as a "separate business" (and must therefore be operated in compliance with rule 21 and may also need to be separately regulated by HMRC under the anti-money laundering legislation).

Service companies

14. A service company operated for the purpose of providing services only to carry out administrative functions concerned with the running of the firm which wholly owns it, such as the employment of staff, the hiring of premises, furniture and equipment and general maintenance, is not a separate business, and does not require to be a recognised body because it is not regarded as practising.

15. A company incorporated by an individual solicitor to provide that solicitor's services to a firm or in-house practice is not a separate business. If the circumstances of the individual and the company fulfil the requirements of paragraph (c)(iii) of the definition of an "employee" in rule 24, such a company will not be regarded as practising and so will not be required to become a recognised body.

21

Marketing and description of a separate business

16. Under 21.05(2)(a) your separate business must not be held out or described in such a way as to suggest that the separate business is carrying on a practice regulated by the SRA or another approved regulator, or that any lawyer connected with your firm is providing services through the separate business as a practising lawyer regulated by the SRA or another approved regulator. Unlike the more specific safeguards in 21.05(2)(b) to (f), this prohibition has a wide application and amounts to an absolute requirement to take all necessary steps to ensure that customers and third parties dealing with the separate business are not misled. However, it is not intended to prohibit you from running a separate business in association with your firm or mentioning your firm, or the fact that you are a lawyer, in connection with your separate business. The provision will have the following implications:

   (a) You could not properly carry on your separate business under the same name as your firm, because that would create too strong a suggestion that the business, like the firm, is regulated by the SRA or other approved regulator. On the other hand, 21.05(2)(a) does not prohibit you from running your separate business in association with your firm, or using a similar or related name or "brand". However, in order to comply with 21.05(2)(a) you would need to differentiate properly the separate business from your firm and make it clear on the face of any notepaper or other publicity of the separate business using a similar or related name that the services of the separate business are not the services of practising lawyers.

(b) You could not properly market your separate business to potential customers on the basis that it is owned and run by practising solicitors and/or RELs, because that would create too strong a suggestion that the services of the separate business are provided by practising lawyers regulated by the SRA or other approved regulator. On the other hand, 21.05(2)(a) does not prohibit you from marketing your separate business on the basis that it is run and owned by persons who are qualified as lawyers – provided you make it clear that no lawyer involved in the separate business is practising as such through the separate business.

(c) Rule 21.05(2)(a) does not prohibit the use of the word "solicitor", "lawyer" or "attorney" in connection with your separate business. However, it would be a breach of 21.05(2)(a) if such a reference suggested that lawyers regulated by the SRA or other approved regulator practise through the separate business – so any such reference must be appropriately qualified so as to make it clear that the services of the separate business are not the services of practising lawyers. If the reference is in a letterhead or other publicity that statement should be in the same document.

Financial services

17. Examples of financial services which cannot form part of a solicitor's practice (and which will not be covered by qualifying insurance under the Solicitors' Indemnity Insurance Rules) include banking, stockbroking and insurance underwriting.

Rule 22   Waivers

22.01

(1) In any particular case or cases the Solicitors Regulation Authority Board shall have power to waive in writing the provisions of these rules for a particular purpose or purposes expressed in such waiver, to place conditions on and to revoke such waiver.

(2) In spite of (1) above, the Solicitors Regulation Authority Board shall not have power to waive any of the provisions of the following rules:

  (a)   rule 1 (Core duties);

  (b)   rules 3.01 to 3.05 (conflict of interests, excluding provisions relating to alternative dispute resolution, conveyancing and property selling);

  (c)   rule 4 (Confidentiality and disclosure);

  (d)   rule 6 (Equality and diversity);

  (e)   rules 15.01, 15.03, 15.04, 15.18, 15.22, 15.23 and 15.24 (overseas practice provisions which apply provisions that cannot be waived for practice in England and Wales);

  (f)   rule 18 (Property selling);

  (g)   rule 22 (Waivers);

  (h)   rule 23 (Application of these rules); and

  (i)   rule 24 (Interpretation).

Guidance to rule 22 – Waivers

1. If you apply for a waiver, you will need to show that your circumstances are exceptional in order for it to be granted. Advice may be obtained from the Professional Ethics Guidance Team. We would normally expect an application in respect of an individual working in the practice of a recognised body to be made by the recognised body itself.

2. The list in 22.01(2) should not be taken as an indication that any other rule may be waived in any circumstances. A waiver cannot be granted where to do so would run counter to the overall purpose of the rule. For example, it is difficult to foresee circumstances in which many of the provisions of rule 2 (Client relations) would be waived.

3. The SRA Board has confirmed that every existing waiver of the Solicitors' Practice Rules 1990, the Solicitors' Overseas Practice Rules 1990 or the Solicitors' Incorporated Practice Rules 2004 would be extended as a like waiver of the Solicitors' Code of Conduct 2007 for a period of two years

22

from 1 July 2007, or until the date of expiry specified in the waiver if earlier. Every such waiver will expire at the end of the two-year extension period, or earlier if an earlier date of expiry is specified in the waiver. Any firms still holding over on such waivers should consider whether they need to apply for a new waiver and, if so, should contact the Professional Ethics Guidance Team to apply forthwith.

Rule 23   Application of these rules

23.01

These rules apply to you (and "you" must be construed accordingly) in the following circumstances.

Application in relation to practice from an office in England and Wales

(1)   Subject to (2) below, rules 1 to 14 and 16 to 25 of these rules apply to your practice from an office in England and Wales if you are:

    (a)   a solicitor or REL (including a recognised sole practitioner);

    (b)   a recognised body;

    (c)   an RFL who is:

        (i)   the employee of a recognised sole practitioner;

        (ii)   a manager, employee, member or owner of a recognised body;

        (iii)   a manager, member or owner of a body corporate which is a manager, member or owner of a recognised body; or

        (iv)   practising through or employed by an authorised non-SRA firm;

    (d)   any other person who is a manager or employee of a recognised body or the employee of a recognised sole practitioner; or

    (e)   a solicitor who was formerly an REL, when practising as a lawyer of an Establishment Directive profession.

(2)   (a)   Only this rule and rules 1, 12, 20, 21 and 24 apply to you if you are a solicitor, REL or RFL practising through or employed by an authorised non-SRA firm when doing work of a sort authorised by the firm's approved regulator.

    (b)   "Practising through" an authorised non-SRA firm includes:

        (i)   being a partner if the firm is a partnership;

        (ii)   being a member if the firm is an LLP; and

        (iii)   being a director or having an ownership interest if the body is a company,

    even if you undertake no work for your firm's clients.

Application in relation to practice from an office outside England and Wales

(3)   These rules apply to your practice from an office outside England and Wales to the extent specified in rule 15.

23.02

In relation to activities in England and Wales which fall outside the scope of practice as defined by rule 24, whether undertaken as a lawyer or in some other business or private capacity:

(a) rule 1.06 (Public confidence) applies to you if you are a solicitor, an REL or an RFL;

(b) rule 10.01 (Not taking unfair advantage) applies to you if you are a solicitor or REL;

(c) rules 10.05(1)(c) and (d), (2) and (3), (undertakings given outside the course of practice) apply to you if you are a solicitor or REL; and

(d) rules 12.03(2) to (5) (practice in another capacity than as an RFL, holding out as a lawyer of England and Wales, and wrongfully doing reserved or immigration work) apply to you if you are an RFL.

23.03

In relation to acting for seller and buyer "you" must be interpreted in accordance with 3.07(1), and in relation to acting for lender and borrower "you" must be interpreted in accordance with 3.16(1).

Guidance to rule 23 – Application of these rules

1. Rule 23 applies all these rules, except rule 15, to your practice from an office in England and Wales if you are a solicitor, an REL, a recognised body, or any other person who is a manager or employee of a recognised body or an employee of a recognised sole practitioner. The application of the rules to RFLs is dealt with in note 4.

2. These rules are also applied to your practice from an office outside England and Wales but only to the extent specified in rule 15. The key to the application of a rule is, therefore, whether a matter relates to practice from an office in England and Wales, or to practice from an office outside England and Wales. This does not mean that different rules apply at different times during a cross-jurisdictional transaction. For example, if a client gives instructions for a transaction to your London office, then that transaction will fall into the category of practice from an office in England and Wales.

3. These rules (as from 31 March 2009) now apply to employees of recognised bodies and recognised sole practitioners. Such employees, as well as managers of recognised bodies, are subject to new powers given to the SRA to impose a rebuke or a fine of up to £2,000 for a breach of these rules. Some rules, by virtue of their wording or their subject matter, will have no or limited application to employees. For example 5.01(1)

(Supervision and management responsibilities) is applicable only to managers and to firms. Rule 4.01 (Duty of confidentiality) is a prime example of a rule which will apply to all employees, breach of which would make an employee individually culpable – without prejudice to any culpability on the part of the firm. The rules do not apply to non-solicitor employees employed outside England and Wales (except for REL employees employed elsewhere in the UK).

4. The rules apply to an RFL who is a manager or employee of a recognised body or an employee of a recognised sole practitioner, in relation to practice from an office in England and Wales. An RFL who is a manager or employee of an authorised non-SRA firm is subject to the rules in the way set out in note 5. An RFL is not subject to any of the rules in relation to any other form of practice, or outside practice, or in relation to practice from an office outside England and Wales, except as set out in note 6.

5. If you are a solicitor, an REL or an RFL practising as a manager or employee of an authorised non-SRA firm, when doing work of a sort authorised by the firm's approved regulator, rule 1 will apply to you but most of the remainder of these rules, as well as the Accounts Rules, are disapplied – for details see 23.01(2)(a). You will, however, be subject to the rules of the authorised non-SRA firm's regulator and any serious breach of those rules could also be a breach of rule 1. If you do work of a sort which is outside the scope of the firm's authorisation you will be subject to these rules, and to the Accounts Rules, in full. These rules would allow you to do such work for the firm itself, or for related bodies or work colleagues, or pro bono – see also 13.01(2).

6. Certain rules also apply in relation to other forms of practice, and outside practice:

    (a) Under 1.06 (Public confidence), if you are a solicitor, REL or RFL you must not behave in a way that is likely to diminish the trust the public places in you or the legal profession. Rule 1.06 applies to your conduct both in your practice as a solicitor, REL or RFL and outside it, and in England and Wales or anywhere else in the world.

    (b) Under 10.01 (Not taking unfair advantage), if you are a solicitor (anywhere in the world) or an REL (in the UK) you must not, whether in the course of practice or outside it, take unfair advantage of your position.

    (c) Under 10.05(1)(c) and (d), (2) and (3), and 15.10(2)(a)(ii) and (iii), (b) and (c) you must fulfil an undertaking even if it is given outside the course of your practice as a solicitor or as an REL, if you give the undertaking as a solicitor or as a lawyer of another Establishment Directive state, and this applies to a solicitor anywhere in the world and to an REL anywhere in the UK.

23

(d) Under 12.03(2) and (3), if you are an RFL you must not be held out as
     an RFL, or as regulated by or registered with the Law Society or the
     SRA, except in the context of practice as a manager or employee of a
     recognised body or as an employee of a recognised sole practitioner.
     Under 12.03(4)(a) you are prohibited from being held out as a
     solicitor or barrister (or as any other category of lawyer of England
     and Wales unless you have that qualification). All these provisions
     apply outside England and Wales as well as in England and Wales.
     Under 12.03(4)(b)–(d) you must not do reserved work in England and
     Wales – whether or not you are practising as an RFL – unless you have
     a separate qualification which allows you to do that work. Under
     12.03(5), if you are not practising as an RFL you must not do any
     immigration work anywhere in the UK unless you are authorised to do
     so in your own right, or working under the supervision of someone
     (not a solicitor, REL or RFL) who is so authorised.

Rule 24   Interpretation

24.01

In these rules, unless the context otherwise requires, all references to legislation include existing and future amendments to that legislation and:

"approved regulator" means a body listed in paragraph 1 of Schedule 4 to the Legal Services Act 2007 (whether or not that paragraph has been brought into force), or designated as an approved regulator by an order under paragraph 17 of that Schedule, and reference to the Solicitors Regulation Authority as an approved regulator means the Solicitors Regulation Authority carrying out regulatory functions assigned to the Law Society as an approved regulator;

"arrangement" in relation to financial services, fee sharing and the introduction of clients, means any express or tacit agreement between you and another person, whether contractually binding or not;

"associated companies" means two companies which are subsidiary companies of the same holding company;

"associated firms" means two or more partnerships with at least one partner in common; two or more companies without shares with at least one member in common; two or more LLPs with at least one member in common; two or more companies with shares with at least one owner in common, or any combination of these;

"authorised non-SRA firm" means a sole practitioner, partnership, LLP or company authorised to practise by another approved regulator and not by the Solicitors Regulation Authority;

"body corporate" means:

    (a)   a company;

    (b)   an LLP; or

    (c)   a partnership which is a legal person in its own right;

"CCBE" means the Council of the Bars and Law Societies of Europe;

"CCBE Code" means the CCBE's Code of Conduct for European Lawyers;

"CCBE state" means any state whose legal profession is a full member, an associate member or an observer member of the CCBE;

"charity" has the same meaning as in section 96(1) of the Charities Act 1993;

"claim for redress" in rule 20.05(3), has the same meaning as in section 158 of the Legal Services Act 2007;

"client account" in rule 15 (Overseas practice), means an account at a bank or similar institution, subject to supervision by a public authority, which is used only for the purpose of holding client money and/or trust money, and the title or designation of which indicates that the funds in the account belong to the client or clients of a solicitor or REL or are held subject to a trust;

(for the definition of "client account" in relation to practice from an office in England and Wales, see the Solicitors' Accounts Rules 1998);

"client money" in rule 15 (Overseas practice), means money you receive or hold for or on behalf of a client or trust;

(for the definition of "client money" in relation to practice from an office in England and Wales, see the Solicitors' Accounts Rules 1998);

"company" in rule 14 (Recognised bodies), means a company registered under Part I of the Companies Act 1985, an oversea company incorporated in an Establishment Directive state and registered under section 690A or 691 of the Companies Act 1985, or a societas Europaea;

"contentious proceedings" is to be construed in accordance with the definition of "contentious business" in section 87 of the Solicitors Act 1974;

"contingency fee" except in 9.01(4) to (6), means any sum (whether fixed, or calculated either as a percentage of the proceeds or otherwise) payable only in the event of success;

"court" in rule 11 (Litigation and advocacy) means any court, tribunal or enquiry of England and Wales, or a British court martial, or any court of another jurisdiction;

"director" means a director of a company, and includes the director of a recognised body which is a company; and in relation to a societas Europaea includes:

(a)   in a two-tier system, a member of the management organ and a member of the supervisory organ; and

(b)   in a one-tier system, a member of the administrative organ;

"documents" in rule 20 (Rights and obligations of practice) includes documents, whether written or electronic, relating to the solicitor's client and office accounts;

"eligible to be a member or shareowner" in rule 14 (Recognised bodies), mean a person who falls within one of the following categories:

(a)   a solicitor with a practising certificate;

(b)   a registered European lawyer;

(c)   a registered foreign lawyer;

(d)   a lawyer of an Establishment Directive profession (including the UK);

(e)   a lawyer of England and Wales;

(f)   an individual approved under regulation 3 of the Recognised Bodies Regulations as suitable to be a manager of a recognised body;

(g) a legally qualified body,

and "ineligible" must be construed accordingly;

"employee" except in rule 6 (Equality and diversity) includes an individual who is:

(a) employed as a director of a company;

(b) engaged under a contract of service (for example, as an assistant solicitor) by a firm or its wholly owned service company; or

(c) engaged under a contract for services (for example, as a consultant or a locum), made between a firm or organisation and:

(i) that individual;

(ii) an employment agency; or

(iii) a company which is not held out to the public as providing legal services and is wholly owned and directed by that individual,

under which the firm or organisation has exclusive control over the individual's time for all or part of the individual's working week; or in relation to which the firm or organisation has designated the individual as a fee earner in accordance with arrangements between the firm or organisation and the Legal Services Commission pursuant to the Access to Justice Act 1999;

and "employer" and "employment" must be construed accordingly;

"Establishment Directive" means the Establishment of Lawyers Directive 98/5/EC;

"Establishment Directive profession" means any profession listed in Article 1.2(a) of the Establishment Directive, including a solicitor, barrister or advocate of the UK;

"Establishment Directive Regulations" means the European Communities (Lawyer's Practice) Regulations 2000 (SI 2000/1119);

"Establishment Directive state" means a state to which the Establishment of Lawyers Directive 98/5/EC applies – currently all the states of the EU plus Iceland, Liechtenstein, Norway and Switzerland;

"EU" means the European Union;

"European corporate practice" means a lawyers' practice which is a body incorporated in an Establishment Directive state, or a partnership with separate legal identity formed under the law of an Establishment Directive state:

24

(a) which has an office in an Establishment Directive state but does not have an office in England and Wales;

(b) whose ultimate beneficial owners include at least one individual who is not a lawyer of England and Wales but is, and is entitled to practise as, a lawyer of an Establishment Directive profession;

    (c)   whose managers include at least one such individual, or at least one body corporate whose managers include at least one such individual;

    (d)   75% of whose ultimate beneficial ownership is in the hands of individuals who are, and are entitled to practise as, lawyers of Establishment Directive professions, lawyers of England and Wales, and/or RFLs; and

    (e)   75% of whose managers comprise such individuals, and/or bodies corporate 75% of whose managers comprise such individuals;

"European cross-border practice" has the meaning assigned by 16.01(1);

"exempt European lawyer" means a member of an Establishment Directive profession:

    (a)   registered with the Bar Standards Board; or

    (b)   based entirely at an office or offices outside England and Wales,

who is not a lawyer of England and Wales (whether entitled to practise as such or not);

"firm" means any business through which a solicitor or REL carries on practice other than in-house practice;

"foreign lawyer" means a person who is not a solicitor or barrister of England and Wales, but who is a member, and entitled to practise as such, of a legal profession regulated within a jurisdiction outside England and Wales;

"holding company" has the meaning assigned by the Companies Act 1985;

"immigration tribunal" means:

    (a)   the asylum support adjudicators;

    (b)   the Asylum and Immigration Tribunal; and

    (c)   a tribunal hearing an appeal from (a) or (b);

"in-house practice" means a solicitor's practice within 12.01(1)(e) or 12.01(2)(e), or an REL's practice within 12.02(1)(e) or 12.02(2)(e);

"lawyer" means a member of one of the following professions, entitled to practise as such:

    (a)   the profession of solicitor, barrister or advocate of the UK;

    (b)   a profession whose members are authorised to practise by an approved regulator other than the Solicitors Regulation Authority;

    (c)   an Establishment Directive profession other than a UK profession;

    (d)   a legal profession which has been approved by the Solicitors Regulation Authority for the purpose of recognised bodies in England and Wales; or

    (e)   any other regulated legal profession which is recognised as such by the Solicitors Regulation Authority;

"lawyer of England and Wales" means a solicitor with a current practising certificate or an individual who is authorised to practise in England and Wales by an approved regulator other than the Solicitors Regulation Authority, but excludes a member of an Establishment Directive profession registered with the Bar Standards Board under the Establishment Directive;

"legal profession" means a profession whose members are lawyers as defined in this rule;

"legally qualified body" for the purposes of these rules and for the purposes of section 9A(6)(h) and (6C) of the Administration of Justice Act 1985 means a body which would meet the services requirement in 14.01(1) and is:

(a)   a recognised body;

(b)   an authorised non-SRA firm of which individuals who are, and are entitled to practise as, lawyers of England and Wales, lawyers of Establishment Directive professions or RFLs make up at least 75% of the ultimate beneficial ownership; or

(c)   a European corporate practice;

"LLP" means a limited liability partnership formed by being incorporated under the Limited Liability Partnerships Act 2000;

"manager" means:

(a)   a partner in a partnership;

(b)   a member of an LLP; or

(c)   a director of a company;

"member" in relation to a recognised body, means:

(a)   a person who has agreed to be a member of a company and whose name is entered in the company's register of members; or

(b)   a member of an LLP;

"non-lawyer" means:

(a)   an individual who is not a lawyer practising as such; or

(b)   a body corporate or partnership which is not:

(i)   a recognised body;

(ii)   an authorised non-SRA firm; or

(iii) a business, carrying on the practice of lawyers from an office or offices outside England and Wales, in which a controlling majority of the owners and managers are lawyers;

"notary public" means a duly certificated notary authorised to practise by the Master of Faculties;

"officer" in relation to a company, means a director or the company secretary;

24

"overseas" means in or of a jurisdiction other than England and Wales;

"overseas practice" means:

(a)   the practice from an office outside England and Wales of:

    (i)   a solicitor;

    (ii)   a recognised body;

    (iii) a manager of a recognised body who is a lawyer of England and Wales;

(b)   the activities of an individual non-lawyer as a manager of a recognised body practising from an office outside England and Wales;

(c)   the activities of a body corporate as a manager of a recognised body practising from an office outside England and Wales; and

(d)   the practice of an REL from an office in Scotland or Northern Ireland;

"owner" in relation to a body, means a person with any ownership interest in the body;

"partner" means a person who is or is held out as a partner in an unincorporated firm;

"partnership" means an unincorporated partnership, and includes any unincorporated firm in which persons are or are held out as partners, but does not include an LLP;

"person" includes an individual and a body corporate;

"person qualified to direct reserved work" means an individual who is qualified under statute to do the relevant reserved work and who is:

(a)   a fellow-manager; or

(b)   the employer, a manager of the firm or a fellow-employee, if the person doing the work is not a manager;

"practice" means:

(a)   the activities of a solicitor, in that capacity;

(b)   (i)   the activities of an REL in the capacity of lawyer of an Establishment Directive profession, from an office or offices within the UK;

    (ii)   the activities of a member of an Establishment Directive profession registered with the Bar Standards Board under the Establishment Directive, in that capacity, from an office or offices in the UK;

(c)   the activities of an RFL from an office or offices in England and Wales as:

    (i)   the employee of a recognised sole practitioner;

    (ii)   a manager, employee, member or owner of a recognised body or of an authorised non-SRA firm;

(iii) a manager, member or owner of a body corporate which is a manager, member or owner of a recognised body or of an authorised non-SRA firm;

(d) the activities of a recognised body;

(e) the activities of an individual non-lawyer:

(i) as a manager of a recognised body; or

(ii) employed in England and Wales by a recognised body or recognised sole practitioner;

(f) the activities of a body corporate as a manager of a recognised body;

(g) the activities of a lawyer of England and Wales, in that capacity; and

(h) the activities of an authorised non-SRA firm,

and "practise" and "practising" should be construed accordingly;

"practice from an office" includes practice carried on:

(a) from an office at which you are based; or

(b) from an office of a firm in which you are the sole principal, or a manager, or in which you have an ownership interest, even if you are not based there,

and "practising from an office in England and Wales", etc. should be construed accordingly;

"practice through a body" includes having an ownership interest in a body and being a director if the body is a company, even if you yourself undertake no work for the body's clients, and "practising through an authorised non-SRA firm" should be construed accordingly;

"principal" means a sole practitioner or a partner in a partnership;

"providing a service through a separate business" means having any active involvement in a separate business which provides that service, and includes:

(a) any substantial ownership in the business;

(b) any direct control over the business, and any indirect control through another person such as a spouse; and

(c) any active participation in the business or the provision of its services to customers;

(being a non-executive director or providing services under rule 13 (In-house practice, etc.) or 15.13 (In-house practice overseas) does not, on its own, constitute active involvement);

"publicity" includes all promotional material and activity, including the name or description of your firm, stationery, advertisements, brochures, websites, directory entries, media appearances, promotional press releases, and direct approaches to potential clients and other persons, whether conducted in

24

person, in writing, or in electronic form, but does not include press releases prepared on behalf of a client;

"Recognised Bodies Regulations" means the SRA Recognised Bodies Regulations 2009;

"recognised body" means a partnership, company or LLP for the time being recognised by the Solicitors Regulation Authority under section 9 of the Administration of Justice Act 1985 and the Recognised Bodies Regulations;

"recognised sole practitioner" means a solicitor or REL authorised by the Solicitors Regulation Authority under section 1B of the Solicitors Act 1974 to practise as a sole practitioner;

"register of European lawyers" means the register of European lawyers maintained by the Solicitors Regulation Authority under regulation 15 of the Establishment Directive Regulations;

"register of foreign lawyers" means the register of foreign lawyers maintained by the Solicitors Regulation Authority under the Courts and Legal Services Act 1990;

"REL (registered European lawyer)" means an individual registered with the Solicitors Regulation Authority under regulation 17 of the Establishment Directive Regulations;

"REL-controlled recognised body" means a recognised body in which RELs, or RELs together with lawyers of England and Wales and/or European lawyers registered with the Bar Standards Board, constitute the national group of lawyers with the largest (or equal largest) share of control of the recognised body either as individual managers or by their share in the control of bodies which are managers, and for this purpose RELs and European lawyers registered with the Bar Standards Board belong to the national group of England and Wales;

"reserved work" means the following activities:

(a)   advocacy before a court or immigration tribunal;

(b)   the conduct of proceedings in a court or immigration tribunal;

(c)   the preparation of documents in proceedings before a court or immigration tribunal;

(d)   the preparation of instruments and the lodging of documents relating to the transfer or charge of land, and the preparation of trust deeds disposing of capital, within paragraph 5 of Schedule 2 to the Legal Services Act 2007, and the preparation of any other instrument coming within sub-paragraph (1)(c) of that paragraph;

(e)   the preparation of papers on which to found or oppose a grant of probate or a grant of letters of administration;

(f)   the administration of oaths and statutory declarations;

(g) notarial activities within paragraph 7 of Schedule 2 to the Legal Services Act 2007;

"RFL (registered foreign lawyer)" means an individual registered with the Solicitors Regulation Authority under section 89 of the Courts and Legal Services Act 1990;

"separate business" means a business which is not a recognised body, a recognised sole practitioner, an authorised non-SRA firm or a firm within 12.01(2)(a)–(d) or 12.02(2)(a)–(d) but which offers a service or services that could properly be offered by a recognised body;

"shareowner" means:

(a) a member of a recognised body which is a company with a share capital, who owns a share in the body; or

(b) a person who is not a member of a company with a share capital, but owns a share in the body, which is held by a member as nominee;

"societas Europaea" means a European public limited liability company within the meaning of article 1 of Council Regulation 2157/2001/EC;

"sole practitioner" means a solicitor or REL practising as a sole principal, and does not include a solicitor or REL practising in-house;

"solicitor-controlled recognised body" means a recognised body in which lawyers of England and Wales constitute the national group of lawyers with the largest (or equal largest) share of control of the recognised body either as individual managers or by their share in the control of bodies which are managers;

"subsidiary company" has the meaning assigned by the Companies Act 1985;

"UK" means United Kingdom;

"ultimate beneficial owners" in relation to a body means all those individuals who together beneficially own the body, whether:

(a) directly, as partners in a partnership, members of an LLP or shareholders in a company, or

(b) indirectly:

(i) as beneficial owners of shares held by nominees or trustees, or

(ii) by way of an ownership interest in one or more intermediate bodies corporate, or

(iii) by way of some combination of (i) and (ii) above;

and "ultimate beneficial ownership" should be construed accordingly;

"undertaking" in 10.05 and 15.10, means a statement made by you or your firm to someone who reasonably relies upon it, that you or your firm will do something or cause something to be done, or refrain from doing something.

24

The undertaking can be given orally or in writing and need not include the words "undertake" or "undertaking".

"voting rights" in a body includes the right to vote in a partners', members', directors' or shareholders' meeting or otherwise in relation to the body, and "control the exercise of voting rights" shall be interpreted as including de facto as well as legal control over such rights.

Rule 25   Commencement and repeals

25.01

(1)   These rules, together with the Solicitors' Recognised Bodies Regulations 2007, shall come into force on 1 July 2007.

(2)   The following provisions are repealed by these rules:

    (a)   the Solicitors' Practice Rules 1990;

    (b)   the Solicitors' Publicity Code 2001;

    (c)   the Solicitors' Introduction and Referral Code 1990;

    (d)   the Employed Solicitors Code 1990;

    (e)   the Solicitors' Separate Business Code 1994;

    (f)   the Solicitors' Costs Information and Client Care Code 1999;

    (g)   the Law Society's Code for Advocacy;

    (h)   the Solicitors' Anti-Discrimination Rules 2004;

    (i)   the Solicitors' Overseas Practice Rules 1990; and

    (j)   the Solicitors' Incorporated Practice Rules 2004.

(3)   These rules also replace the conduct obligations imposed by virtue of *The Guide to the Professional Conduct of Solicitors* (1999) and Guide Online.

(4)   For the avoidance of doubt, the following will remain in force after the coming into force of these rules:

    (a)   the Solicitors' Accounts Rules;

    (b)   the Solicitors' Indemnity Insurance Rules;

    (c)   the Solicitors' Indemnity (Enactment) Rules;

    (d)   the Solicitors' Financial Services (Scope) Rules;

    (e)   the Solicitors' Financial Services (Conduct of Business) Rules;

    (f)   the Solicitors' Compensation Fund Rules; and

    (g)   the Solicitors' Compensation Fund (Foreign Lawyers' Contributions) Rules.

(5)   As of 31 March 2009:

    (a)   the Solicitors' Recognised Bodies Regulations 2007 are replaced by the SRA Recognised Bodies Regulations 2009, and

    (b)   the Solicitors' Compensation Fund (Foreign Lawyers' Contributions) Rules are repealed.

(6)   Until 1 July 2009:

25

    (a)   there is no requirement for a solicitor or REL practising in England and Wales as a sole practitioner to be a recognised sole practitioner; and

    (b)   rules which apply to a recognised sole practitioner are to be interpreted as applying to a solicitor or REL practising in England and Wales as a sole practitioner.

(7)   The provisions of rule 7.07(1) requiring

    (a)   a partnership to have on its website and e-mails the words "regulated by the Solicitors Regulation Authority", and to have on its letterhead, fax heading, website and e-mails the name under which the partnership is recognised and the number allocated to it by the Authority, shall not apply until 1 October 2009;

    (b)   an LLP or company to have on its website and e-mails the words "regulated by the Solicitors Regulation Authority" shall not apply until 1 October 2009;

    (c)   a sole practice to have on its website and e-mails the words "regulated by the Solicitors Regulation Authority", and to have on its letterhead, fax heading, website and e-mails the name under which the sole practice is recognised and the number allocated to it by the Authority, shall not apply until 1 January 2010.

Guidance to rule 25 – Commencement and repeals

1.   See note 3 of the guidance to rule 22 (Waivers) regarding commencement of the Solicitors' Code of Conduct 2007 and waivers of repealed rules.

SRA Recognised Bodies Regulations 2009

Rules dated 31 March 2009 and commencing 31 March 2009, made by the Solicitors Regulation Authority Board under sections 79 and 80 of the Solicitors Act 1974 and sections 9 and 9A of the Administration of Justice Act 1985, with the concurrence of the Master of the Rolls and the Lord Chancellor under paragraph 16 of Schedule 22 to the Legal Services Act 2007, making provision as to:

- the procedures for, and the circumstances in which, bodies may be recognised by the SRA as suitable to undertake the provision of legal services, the duration of recognition and the circumstances in which recognition will expire or may be revoked;

- the procedures for, and the circumstances in which, individuals who are not legally qualified may be approved by the SRA as suitable to be managers of recognised bodies, and the circumstances in which such approval may be withdrawn;

- the form and manner of applications relating to the recognition of a body, the approval of an individual, and other applications under rules applying to recognised bodies, their managers and employees, and the fees to accompany such applications;

- the circumstances in which a body's recognition may be made subject to a condition;

- appeals relating to recognition of a body, conditions on recognition, or approval of an individual;

- the names used by recognised bodies; and

- the register of recognised bodies.

PART 1 – APPLICATIONS, CONDITIONS AND APPEALS

Regulation 1 – Form, timing and fees for applications

1.1 Applications under these regulations, or under any other rule which applies to a recognised body, its manager or employee, must comprise:

    (a) the prescribed form, correctly completed;

    (b) the fee or fees for the application, as determined from time to time by the SRA Board;

    (c) if the application is for recognition or for renewal of recognition, any prescribed contribution to the Solicitors' Compensation Fund;

(d)   such additional information, documents and references as may be specified by the SRA; and

(e)   any additional information and documentation which the SRA may reasonably require.

It is not necessary to submit all documents, information and payments simultaneously, but an application will only have been made once the SRA has received all of the documentation, information and payments comprising that application.

1.2   An application for renewal of recognition must be sent to the SRA so as to arrive on or before the renewal date.

1.3   A recognised body must notify the SRA on or before the renewal date if it does not intend to apply for renewal of recognition.

Regulation 2 – Initial recognition and renewal of recognition

2.1   The SRA may grant an application for initial recognition or renewal of recognition, if it is satisfied that the applicant body is a partnership, LLP or company which meets the conditions in (a) to (d) below:

(a)   the body complies with rule 14 of the Solicitors' Code of Conduct in relation to:

    (i)   its formation as a body corporate or partnership;

    (ii)   its composition and structure, including any necessary approval of a participant under Regulation 3; and

    (iii)   its practising address (and if appropriate, its registered office) in England and Wales;

(b)   the body complies with the Solicitors' Indemnity Insurance Rules;

(c)   the body complies with (or has a waiver of) rule 5.02 of the Solicitors' Code of Conduct; and

(d)   if the body is a partnership, it has adopted a name under which it is to be registered, and which complies with rule 7 of the Solicitors' Code of Conduct.

2.2   The SRA may refuse an application for initial recognition if:

(a)   the SRA is not satisfied that a manager or a person with an interest in the body is a suitable person to be engaged in the management or ownership of a recognised body, taking into account that person's history, character, conduct or associations;

(b)   the SRA is not satisfied that the body's managers or owners are suitable, as a group, to operate or control a business providing regulated legal services; or

(c)   for any other reason the SRA reasonably considers that it would be against the public interest to grant recognition.

2.3　In reaching a decision under 2.2 the SRA may take into account:

(a)　any event listed in regulation 3.1 of the SRA Practising Regulations applying to a manager of the applicant body;

(b)　any other conduct on the part of a manager of the applicant body which calls into question his or her honesty, integrity or respect for law;

(c)　failure or refusal to disclose, or attempts to conceal, any matter within (a) or (b) above in relation to the application;

(d)　that the SRA is not satisfied that the managers of the applicant body, taken together, have sufficient skills and knowledge to run and manage a business which provides regulated legal services,

and any other facts which the SRA reasonably considers should be taken into account.

2.4　An application for initial recognition of a body which will not comply with 2.1(c) will be treated as including an application for a waiver of rule 5.02 of the Solicitors' Code of Conduct.

2.5　If, when considering an application for renewal of recognition, the SRA:

(a)　is not satisfied that the body's managers, taken together, are suitable to run and manage a business providing regulated legal services; or

(b)　considers that for any other reason it would not be in the public interest to renew the body's recognition, the SRA may defer renewal of recognition pending a decision whether the body's recognition should be revoked under regulation 9.

2.6　A grant of initial recognition takes effect from the date of the decision unless otherwise stated.

2.7　(a)　When granting an application for recognition or for renewal of recognition the SRA may impose a condition in accordance with regulation 4.

(b)　The granting of recognition free of conditions under regulation 2 does not prevent the SRA subsequently imposing a condition under regulation 4.

Regulation 3 – Approval of an individual as suitable to be a manager

3.1　An individual who is not a lawyer of England and Wales, an REL, an RFL or an exempt European lawyer must be approved by the SRA under this regulation in order to be:

(a)　a manager or owner of a recognised body; or

(b)　a manager of a body corporate which is a manager of a recognised body.

3.2   The following are not eligible for approval under this regulation:

(a)   a member (practising or non-practising) of any profession coming within the meaning of lawyer of England and Wales (including a solicitor);

(b)   an REL;

(c)   an RFL;

(d)   an exempt European lawyer; and

(e)   a member (practising or non-practising) of any profession eligible for approval by the SRA under paragraph 2(2) of Schedule 14 to the Courts and Legal Services Act 1990;

except that an individual who is not a solicitor or a practising member of any profession of lawyers, but is a non-practising barrister or a non-practising member of another profession of lawyers, and who is prevented by his or her professional rules or training regulations from changing status so as to able to practise through the recognised body as a practising lawyer, may apply for approval under this regulation.

3.3   The SRA has a discretion to reject an application under regulation 3 if it is not satisfied that the individual concerned is suitable to be involved in the provision of legal services, and to exercise influence over the conduct of the recognised body concerned because:

(a)   the applicant, the individual concerned or any recognised body or authorised non-SRA firm in which that individual has previously been a manager or employee, has been:

(i)   reprimanded, made the subject of disciplinary sanction or ordered to pay costs by the Solicitors Disciplinary Tribunal, or struck off or suspended by the Court;

(ii)   rebuked or fined by the SRA under section 44D of the Solicitors Act 1974 or paragraph 14B of Schedule 2 to the Administration of Justice Act 1985;

(iii)   intervened in by the SRA (or previously by the Law Society);

(iv)   notified in writing by the SRA (or previously by the Law Society) that it does not regard as satisfactory an explanation given at the SRA's (or the Society's) request; or

(v)   made the subject of disciplinary sanction by, or refused registration with or authorisation by, another approved regulator, professional or regulatory tribunal, or regulatory authority, whether in England and Wales or elsewhere,

in respect of a matter involving the individual concerned;

(b)   the individual concerned:

(i)   has been committed to prison in civil or criminal proceedings;

(ii)   has been disqualified from being a company director;

(iii) has been removed from the office of charity trustee or trustee for a charity by an order within the terms of section 72(1)(d) of the Charities Act 1993;

(iv) is an undischarged bankrupt;

(v) has been adjudged bankrupt and discharged;

(vi) has entered into an individual voluntary arrangement or a partnership voluntary arrangement under the Insolvency Act 1986;

(vii) has been a manager of a recognised body which has entered into a voluntary arrangement under the Insolvency Act 1986;

(viii) has been a director of a company or a member of an LLP which has been the subject of a winding up order, an administration order or administrative receivership; or has entered into a voluntary arrangement under the Insolvency Act 1986; or has been otherwise wound up or put into administration in circumstances of insolvency;

(ix) lacks capacity (within the meaning of the Mental Capacity Act 2005) and powers under sections 15 to 20 or section 48 of that Act are exercisable in relation to that individual;

(x) is the subject of outstanding judgments involving the payment of money;

(xi) is currently charged with an indictable offence, or has been convicted of an indictable offence or any offence under the Solicitors Act 1974, the Financial Services and Markets Act 2000, the Immigration and Asylum Act 1999 or the Compensation Act 2006;

(xii) has been the subject of an order under section 43 of the Solicitors Act 1974;

(xiii) has been the subject of an equivalent circumstance in another jurisdiction to those listed in (i) to (xi); or

(xiv) has been involved in other conduct which calls into question his or her honesty, integrity or respect for law;

(c) the applicant or the individual concerned fails to disclose, refuses to disclose or seeks to conceal any matter within (a) or (b) above in relation to the application.

3.4 (a) The application for approval must be made by the recognised body or prospective recognised body concerned and may be made:

(i) when applying for initial recognition; or

(ii) at any time after recognition has been granted.

(b) It is for the applicant body to demonstrate that the individual concerned meets the criteria for approval.

(c) The applicant body must:

    (i) co-operate, and secure the co-operation of the individual concerned, to assist the SRA to obtain all information and documentation the SRA requires in order to determine the application;

    (ii) obtain all other information and documentation in relation to that individual which the prescribed form requires the body to obtain and keep; and

    (iii) keep all information and documentation under (ii) above for a period of not less than 6 years after the individual concerned has ceased to be a manager of the body.

(d) The individual concerned must confirm in writing on the face of the application that the information supplied about him or her is correct and complete.

3.5 (a) Approval takes effect from the date of the decision unless otherwise stated.

(b) The SRA's decision to approve or refuse approval must be notified in writing to the applicant body and, separately, to the individual concerned.

(c) If the applicant body is a recognised body it must not allow the individual concerned to become a manager until it has received written notice that the individual has been approved.

(d) Approval continues until:

    (i) it is withdrawn; or

    (ii) two years have elapsed during which the individual has not been a manager of a recognised body.

3.6 The SRA may at any time require the production of information or documentation from:

(a) an approved individual;

(b) a recognised body in which an approved individual is a manager; or

(c) the body which originally obtained approval for that individual and holds information and documentation under 3.4(c)(iii) above;

in order to satisfy the SRA that the individual met the criteria for approval or continues to meet the criteria for approval.

3.7 (a) The SRA may decide to withdraw approval if it is not satisfied that an approved individual met the criteria for approval or continues to meet the criteria for approval or if information or documentation is not promptly supplied in response to a request made under regulation 3.6.

(b) Subject to (c) below, withdrawal of approval takes effect on expiry of the notice period under regulation 6.2(b) or on such later date as may be stated in the notice.

(c)   If an appeal is made before the withdrawal of approval takes effect, the withdrawal of approval is suspended pending determination or discontinuance of the appeal, unless in the opinion of the SRA the proceedings on that appeal have been unduly protracted by the appellant or are unlikely to be successful.

3.8   Where withdrawal of approval relates to a director of a company, the SRA may set separate dates for that individual ceasing to be a director and disposing of his or her shares.

Regulation 4 – Conditions on recognition

4.1   The SRA may impose one or more conditions on a recognised body's recognition:

(a)   when granting initial recognition;

(b)   when granting renewal of recognition;

(c)   when granting approval of an individual under regulation 3;

(d)   when deciding to withdraw approval of an individual under regulation 3; or

(e)   at any other time.

4.2   The purposes for which the SRA may impose a condition are set out in (a) to (g) below.

(a)   The SRA considers that:

(i)   the condition would limit, restrict, halt or prevent an activity or activities on the part of the body, or of a manager or employee of the body, which is putting or is likely to put at risk the interests of clients, third parties or the public, and

(ii)   it is in the public interest to impose the condition.

(b)   The SRA considers that:

(i)   the condition would limit the activities of a manager or employee of the body who is considered unsuitable to undertake a particular activity, either at all or save as specified in the condition, and

(ii)   it is in the public interest to impose the condition.

(c)   The SRA considers that:

(i)   the condition would limit, halt or prevent a risk to clients, third parties or the public arising from a business agreement or association which the body has or is likely to enter into, or a business practice which the body has or is likely to adopt, and

(ii)   it is in the public interest to impose the condition.

(d) A relevant insolvency event within the meaning of paragraph 32(1A) of Schedule 2 to the Administration of Justice Act 1985 has occurred in relation to a recognised body, and:

  (i) the event has not triggered expiry of recognition under regulation 10, and

  (ii) the SRA considers that it is in the public interest to impose the condition.

(e) The SRA considers that imposing the condition will, in the public interest, facilitate closer monitoring by the SRA of compliance with rules and regulations on the part of the body.

(f) The SRA considers that imposing the condition will, in the public interest, require the body concerned to take specified steps conducive to the carrying on of efficient practice by that body.

(g) The SRA considers, in any other case concerning a body which is currently recognised, that it would be in the public interest to impose the condition.

4.3 A condition imposed under this regulation takes effect from the date on which the condition is imposed unless a later date is specified in the condition.

Regulation 5 – Temporary emergency recognition following a partnership split

5.1 If a partnership split brings into being a new partnership which is not a recognised body:

  (a) the SRA must be notified within 7 days; and

  (b) temporary emergency recognition may be granted, subject to 5.2 to 5.4 below, so as to enable the partners in the new partnership to practise through the new partnership for a limited period without breach of the law.

5.2 An application for temporary emergency recognition may be made by telephone, provided that details given by telephone are confirmed in writing the same day; and must be made (or confirmed) on the prescribed form at the earliest possible opportunity, and accompanied by all information and documentation the SRA may reasonably require.

5.3 The SRA may grant an application for temporary emergency recognition if the following conditions are met.

  (a) The SRA must be satisfied that the partners could not reasonably have commenced an application for recognition in advance of the change.

  (b) The partnership must otherwise comply with rule 14 of the Solicitors' Code of Conduct in relation to its composition and structure and its practising address in England and Wales.

(c)   The partnership must comply with the Solicitors' Indemnity Insurance Rules, and must have adopted a name under which it is to be registered and which complies with rule 7 of the Solicitors' Code of Conduct.

5.4   Temporary emergency recognition:

(a)   may be granted initially for 28 days;

(b)   may be extended in response to a reasonable request by the applicant;

(c)   must be extended (subject to (g) below) pending determination of a substantive application for initial recognition commenced during the currency of a temporary emergency recognition;

(d)   may be granted or extended subject to such conditions as the SRA thinks fit, in circumstances falling within regulation 4;

(e)   is to be treated as initial recognition for the purpose of these regulations;

(f)   if granted, cannot prejudice the discretion of the SRA to refuse a substantive application for recognition of the body under regulation 2 (which is also, for the purpose of these regulations, to be treated as initial recognition); and

(g)   in exceptional circumstances, and for reasonable cause, may be revoked at any time.

Regulation 6 – Notification of decisions by the SRA

6.1   (a)   The SRA must notify its reasons in writing when it:

(i)   refuses an application;

(ii)   grants an application subject to a condition; or

(iii)   refuses a permission required under a condition on a body's recognition.

(b)   The reasons must be given to the applicant body and to the individual concerned, when refusing approval of an individual under regulation 3.

6.2   The SRA must give 28 days written notice, with reasons:

(a)   to the recognised body concerned, when the SRA decides to impose a condition on the body's recognition, or revoke the body's recognition;

(b)   to the body and the individual concerned, when the SRA decides to withdraw an approval granted under regulation 3.

6.3   The SRA may shorten or dispense with the 28 day period under 6.2 in imposing a condition if it is satisfied on reasonable grounds that it is in the public interest to do so.

Regulation 7 – Appeals

7.1　Before exercising its right of appeal to the High Court:

(a)　under paragraph 2(1)(a) of Schedule 2 to the Administration of Justice Act 1985, against refusal of initial recognition;

(b)　under paragraph 2(1)(b) or (c) of that Schedule, against the imposition of a condition; or

(c)　under paragraph 2(2) of that Schedule, against refusal by the SRA to approve a step which, under a condition on the body's recognition, requires such prior approval,

a body may invoke the SRA's own appeals procedure.

7.2　A body may appeal to the High Court against the SRA's decision to revoke the body's recognition, but must first invoke the SRA's own appeals procedure.

7.3　A body, and/or the individual concerned, may appeal to the High Court against the SRA's decision:

(a)　not to approve the individual under regulation 3; or

(b)　to withdraw its approval of the individual under regulation 3, but must first invoke the SRA's own appeals procedure.

7.4　(a)　An application for initial recognition under regulation 2 is deemed, for the purpose of any appeal under 7.1(a) above, to be refused on the 90th day after the SRA has received the application and all additional information and documentation required, and duly notified to the applicant on that day, if by the end of that day the SRA has not notified the applicant body of its decision.

(b)　An application for approval of an individual under regulation 3 is deemed, for the purpose of any appeal under 7.3(a) above, to be refused on the 90th day after the SRA has received the application and all additional information and documentation required, and duly notified to the applicant on that day, if by the end of that day the SRA has not notified the applicant body, and the individual concerned, of its decision.

7.5　(a)　Appeals under the SRA's own appeals procedure must be made within 28 days of receipt of the SRA's reasons for refusal, or within 28 days of deemed refusal under 7.4 above.

(b)　An appeal to the High Court must be made:

(i)　within 28 days of notification of the relevant decision; or

(ii)　within 28 days of notification of refusal of an appeal under the SRA's own appeals procedure, whichever is the later.

7.6　An appeal under the SRA's own appeals procedure under 7.3(a) above shall be treated as an application for the purpose of these regulations.

PART 2 – DURATION OF RECOGNITION, RENEWAL DATE, REVOCATION AND EXPIRY

Regulation 8 – Duration of recognition and renewal date

8.1   Except where transitional provisions in 8.5 to 8.7 apply, recognition is renewable yearly and the renewal date is 31 October in each successive year.

8.2   Recognition continues in force unless it is revoked, or unless it expires under regulation 10 or is suspended by the High Court.

8.3   Renewal of recognition commences on the day following the renewal date.

Passporting

8.4   (a)   All partnerships carrying on the practice of solicitors and/or RELs on 31 March 2009 will be recognised as recognised bodies on 31 March 2009 provided that:

(i)   the composition and structure of the partnership complies with rule 14 of the Solicitors' Code of Conduct; and

(ii)   the partnership is practising from an office in England and Wales.

(b)   The first renewal date for partnerships recognised under this provision is 31 October 2009.

Transitional provisions

8.5   If a body's recognition commenced on or before 1 November 2006, recognition lasts for three years and the renewal date is that stated on the certificate of recognition.

8.6   If a body's recognition commenced after 1 November 2006 but before 31 March 2009:

(a)   recognition lasts until 31 October 2009 and the renewal date is not that stated on the certificate of recognition but 31 October 2009; and

(b)   when applying for renewal of recognition the body will be given credit for fees and contributions already paid in respect of the cancelled period of recognition after 31 October 2009.

8.7   If a body's recognition commenced on or after 31 March 2009 but before 1 November 2009, the renewal date will be 31 October 2009.

Regulation 9 – Revocation of recognition

9.1   The SRA may revoke a body's recognition, if:

(a)   recognition was granted as a result of error or fraud;

(b)   the body would not be eligible to be recognised if it were at that time applying for initial recognition;

    (c)   the renewal date has passed and the SRA has not received an application for renewal of recognition and all required fees, information and documentation;

    (d)   the body has a temporary emergency recognition but has not within the initial 28 day period or any extension of that period commenced a substantive application for recognition;

    (e)   the body has ceased to practise;

    (f)   an approved regulator other than the SRA has authorised the body;

    (g)   the SRA has decided under regulation 2.5 not to renew the body's recognition; or

    (h)   a relevant insolvency event within the meaning of paragraph 32(1A) of Schedule 2 to the Administration of Justice Act 1985 has occurred in relation to the recognised body which has not triggered expiry of recognition under regulation 10,

and the SRA is satisfied that revocation would not present a risk to clients, to the protection of client money or to any investigative process.

9.2 (a)   Subject to (b) below, revocation takes effect on expiry of the notice period under regulation 6.2(a) or on such later date as may be stated in the notice.

    (b)   If an appeal is made before the revocation takes effect, the revocation is suspended pending determination or discontinuance of the appeal, unless in the opinion of the SRA the proceedings on that appeal have been unduly protracted by the appellant or are unlikely to be successful.

Regulation 10 – Expiry of recognition

Subject to 14.04(2) of the Solicitors' Code of Conduct, a body's recognition will automatically expire if the body is wound up or for any other reason ceases to exist.

PART 3 – NAME, THE REGISTER AND CERTIFICATE OF RECOGNITION

Regulation 11 – Name of a recognised body

11.1   A body corporate will be recognised under its corporate name.

11.2   A partnership must elect to have a name under which it is to be recognised.

Regulation 12 – The register of recognised bodies

12.1   The SRA must keep a register of recognised bodies, which may be kept in electronic form.

12.2 The register of recognised bodies must contain, for each recognised body:

(a) the name and number under which the body is recognised;

(b) any other practising styles used by the body;

(c) the recognised body's registered office and registered number, if it is an LLP or company;

(d) the recognised body's principal practising address in England and Wales;

(e) all the recognised body's other practising addresses;

(f) whether the recognised body is a partnership, an LLP or a company; and

(g) if the recognised body is a company, whether it is:

    (i) a company limited by shares;

    (ii) a company limited by guarantee;

    (iii) an unlimited company;

    (iv) an oversea company registered in England and Wales;

    (v) an oversea company registered in Scotland; or

    (vi) a societas Europaea;

(h) a list of the body's managers, and in respect of each manager, whether that manager is:

    (i) a lawyer of England and Wales, and if so the nature of his or her qualification;

    (ii) an REL, and if so his or her professional title and jurisdiction of qualification;

    (iii) an exempt European lawyer registered with the Bar Standards Board, and if so his or her professional title and jurisdiction of qualification;

    (iv) an exempt European lawyer based entirely at an office or offices outside England and Wales, and if so his or her professional title and jurisdiction of qualification;

    (v) an RFL, and if so his or her professional title and jurisdiction of qualification;

    (vi) an individual approved under regulation 3;

    (vii) a company, and if so whether it is a recognised body, a European corporate practice or an authorised non-SRA firm;

    (viii) an LLP, and if so whether it is a recognised body, a European corporate practice or an authorised non-SRA firm; and

    (ix) a partnership with separate legal personality, and if so whether it is a recognised body, a European corporate practice or an authorised non-SRA firm;

(i)   any condition to which the body's recognition is subject; and

(j)   any other reasonable information, necessary for carrying out the SRA's statutory objectives, from time to time prescribed by the SRA.

12.3 (a) Entries in the register must be available for inspection by any member of the public, except that the SRA may withhold an address in exceptional circumstances where the SRA considers that to do so would be in the public interest.

      (b) The date on which, and the circumstances in which, a recognised body's recognition expired or was revoked must be made available to a member of the public on request.

Regulation 13 – Certificates of recognition

13.1   When a body is granted initial recognition or its recognition is renewed, the SRA must issue a certificate of recognition.

13.2   Each certificate of recognition must state, in respect of the recognised body:

(a)   the name and number under which the body is recognised;

(b)   its registered office, if it is an LLP or company;

(c)   its principal practising address in England and Wales;

(d)   whether it is a partnership, an LLP or a company; and if it is a company, whether it is:

      (i)   a company limited by shares;

      (ii)   a company limited by guarantee;

      (iii) an unlimited company;

      (iv) an oversea company registered in England and Wales;

      (v)   an oversea company registered in Scotland;

      (vi) a societas Europaea; or

      (vii) an LLP;

(e)   the date from which recognition is granted or renewed;

(f)   the next renewal date; and

(g)   any condition to which the body's recognition is subject.

PART 4 – INTERPRETATION, WAIVERS RECONSIDERATION AND NOTIFYING THIRD PARTIES

Regulation 14 – Interpretation

In these regulations:

(a) commencing an application means submitting a completed application form, together with the prescribed fee and any Compensation Fund contribution required;

(b) all terms are to be interpreted in accordance with rule 24 of the Solicitors' Code of Conduct;

(c) "prescribed form" means a form prescribed from time to time by the SRA;

(d) "prescribed fee" means the fee prescribed from time to time by the SRA;

(e) "Solicitors' Code of Conduct" means the Solicitors' Code of Conduct 2007; and

(f) "SRA Practising Regulations" means the SRA Practising Regulations 2009.

Regulation 15 – Waivers

In any particular case or cases the SRA shall have power to waive in writing the provisions of these regulations for a particular purpose or purposes expressed in such waiver, and to revoke such waiver.

Regulation 16 – Reconsideration

16.1 The SRA may reconsider or rescind a decision made under these regulations when it appears that the decision maker:

(a) was not provided with material evidence that was available to the SRA;

(b) was materially misled;

(c) failed to take proper account of material facts or evidence;

(d) took into account immaterial facts or evidence;

(e) made a material error of law;

(f) made a decision which was otherwise irrational or procedurally unfair;

(g) made a decision which was otherwise ultra vires; or

(h) failed to give sufficient reasons.

16.2 (a) A decision may be reconsidered under 16.1 only on the initiative of the SRA and if a person duly authorised by the SRA gives a direction to that effect.

(b) That person may also give directions:

(i) for further investigations to be undertaken;

(ii) for further information or explanation to be obtained; and

(iii)   for the reconsideration to be undertaken by the original decision maker or by a different decision maker or panel.

Regulation 17 – Notifying third parties of decisions

The SRA may, if it considers it in the public interest to do so, notify any or all of the following persons of a decision made under these regulations:

(a)   a recognised body or authorised non-SRA firm of which the body or individual concerned is a manager or has an ownership interest;

(b)   a recognised sole practitioner, recognised body or authorised non-SRA firm of which the individual concerned is an employee;

(c)   any approved regulator;

(d)   the Legal Services Board;

(e)   the Legal Complaints Service or the Office for Legal Complaints;

(f)   the regulatory body for any profession of which the individual concerned is a member or which regulates the body concerned;

(g)   any law enforcement agency.

Regulation 18 – Commencement and repeal

These regulations come into force on 31 March 2009 and repeal the Solicitors' Recognised Bodies Regulations 2007.

Index

Rules and guidance are both indexed.
References to whole rules take the form "**rule 1**".
References to sections within a rule take the form "**1.01**" or "**2.01**(1)(a)".
References to guidance notes to the rules take the form "*guid.* 2 [1, 3, 5–6]".

SOLICITORS' CODE OF CONDUCT 2007 (JUNE 2009)